Norms and the Study of Language in Social Life

Language and Social Life

Editors
David Britain
Crispin Thurlow

Volume 24

Norms and the Study of Language in Social Life

Edited by
Janus Mortensen
Kamilla Kraft

DE GRUYTER
MOUTON

ISBN 978-1-5015-2204-8
e-ISBN (PDF) 978-1-5015-1188-2
e-ISBN (EPUB) 978-1-5015-1189-9
ISSN 2364-4303

Library of Congress Control Number: 2021950675

Bibliographic information published by the Deutsche Nationalbibliothek
The Deutsche Nationalbibliothek lists this publication in the Deutsche Nationalbibliografie;
detailed bibliographic data are available on the Internet at http://dnb.dnb.de.

Chapter "Multilingual creativity and emerging norms in interaction: Towards a methodology for micro-diachronic analysis" © Marie-Luise Pitzl

© 2023 Walter de Gruyter GmbH, Berlin/Boston
This volume is text- and page-identical with the hardback published in 2022.
Cover image: Tim Perdue/Moment Open/Getty Images
Typesetting: Integra Software Services Pvt. Ltd.
Printing and binding: CPI books GmbH, Leck

www.degruyter.com

Preface and acknowledgements

The present book is the result of a Colloquium organized as part of Sociolinguistic Symposium 22 in Auckland in June 2018 (*Norms in sociolinguistics – revisiting familiar ground and exploring new frontiers*), and a two-day follow-up Round Table held at the University of Copenhagen in March 2019 (*Norms and the Study of Language in Social Life*). At both events, scholars were invited to debate theoretical and methodological questions related to the notion of norms on the basis of original research.

The resulting book (which also features an epilogue that was commissioned at a later stage) contributes to current understandings of norms as a theoretical construct and empirical object of research in sociolinguistics and related fields, based on research from a range of geographical contexts, including Austria, Denmark, Finland, New Zealand, Norway and the UK, providing a multifaceted view of norms as a central but under-theorised notion in the study of language in social life. The contributors approach the common topic of the book from a range of complementary disciplinary perspectives, including sociolinguistics, linguistic anthropology, ethnomethodology, socio-cognitive linguistics, and pragmatics.

The round table in Copenhagen, hosted by the TMC project (www.tmc.ku.dk), was based on pre-circulated chapter drafts in which all participants were asked to address the following questions in relation to their own research contexts:

- What are "norms"? How are norms conceptualized in your work, and which frameworks do you draw upon?
- How can norms be studied? What sort of data is needed, what sort of methods?
- Why are norms (not) important as a theoretical construct in sociolinguistics? How does the notion of norm relate to other concepts in the literature, inter alia *ideology* and *practice*?
- What can be achieved by studying norms? What are the implications for sociolinguistics as a discipline? What (if any) are the implications beyond academia?

While the final versions of the chapters included here do not offer neat list-like answers to these questions, they all offer perspectives on the questions which we believe will be of interest to a wide range of readers who take an interest in the topic of norms in language and social life.

Following the meeting in Copenhagen, discussions concerning norms have continued amongst the editors and authors in multiple ways, and we would like to thank all contributors for the time and energy they have devoted to the project, not only by working tirelessly on their own chapters, but also by reviewing other chapters in the volume. Similarly, we would like to thank the participants at the

Colloquium and the Round Table for supporting the project and engaging in stimulating discussions, either by presenting work of their own or, in the case of Jürgen Jaspers and Katherine Kappa, by serving as invited discussants. We are also grateful to the members of the TMC project advisory board, Nikolas Coupland, Hartmut Haberland, Anne Holmen, Martha Sif Karrebæk, Elizabeth Lanza, Meredith Marra, and Celia Roberts, for the help and guidance they have offered at several important junctures along the way.

Our work on the book has been financially supported by The Danish Council for Independent Research | Humanities through grant no. 6107-00351, *Transient Multilingual Communities and the Formation of Social and Linguistic Norms* (2016–2019), and this support is gratefully acknowledged. We would also like to thank the series editors and Natalie Fecher and Kirstin Börgen at De Gruyter for their patience and unfaltering support, as well as the Centre for Internationalisation and Parallel Language Use at the University of Copenhagen for hosting the TMC project and the Round Table in 2018.

JM and KK
Copenhagen
May 2021

Contents

Preface and acknowledgements —— V

Janus Mortensen and Kamilla Kraft
1 Introduction: 'Behind a veil, unseen yet present' – on norms in sociolinguistics and social life —— 1

Peter Harder
2 Attitudes, norms and emergent communities —— 21

Spencer Hazel and Dorte Lønsmann
3 Norms, accountability and socialisation in a refugee language classroom —— 43

Irina Piippo
4 Norms in the making – exploring the norms of the teaching register *selkosuomi* in immigrant integration training classrooms in Finland —— 69

Kamilla Kraft and Janus Mortensen
5 Norms and stereotypes: Studying the emergence and sedimentation of social meaning —— 97

Marie-Luise Pitzl
6 Multilingual creativity and emerging norms in interaction: Towards a methodology for micro-diachronic analysis —— 125

Anne Fabricius
7 What's in a sociolinguistic norm? The case of change in prevocalic /r/ in Received Pronunciation —— 157

Meredith Marra, Janet Holmes and Bernadette Vine
8 What we share: The impact of norms on successful interaction —— 185

Nikolas Coupland
9 Normativity, language and Covid-19 —— 211

Index —— 233

Janus Mortensen and Kamilla Kraft
1 Introduction: 'Behind a veil, unseen yet present' – on norms in sociolinguistics and social life

There is no shortage of sources that stipulate the dos and don'ts of social life. Yet, to be a socially competent member of a community, individuals need to be sensitive to social norms beyond what is available as explicitly formulated rules for appropriate behavior. Norms are indispensable and ubiquitous in social interaction, but often exist "behind a veil, unseen yet present" to use a suggestive image from *Britannicus* by the French dramatist, Jean Racine (1670, act 1, scene 1).[1] Dominant thinkers in sociology, with Durkheim (1893) as the perhaps most prominent example, attribute great importance to social norms, treating them as constitutive elements of human societies. In a similar vein, the philosopher Bicchieri (2006) has proposed, using another evocative metaphor, that social norms may be seen as "the grammar of society". So, even though they may often be hidden from view, social norms are arguably fundamental, not only in our everyday lives, but also in the way human sociality has been theorized.

Because of their everyday and theoretical importance, the need to theorize norms and the processes that create and sustain them continues to be a central but challenging task for the social sciences (Hechter & Opp 2001; Xenitidou & Edmonds 2014; Hechter 2018). The chapters in this book explore the notion of

---

[1] The words, *derrière un voile, invisible et présente*, are spoken by Aggrapine, Nero's mother, as she describes (with bitter regret) the influence, now lost, she used to exert over her son, the emperor, and the Roman Senate. English translations vary, of course, in their rendition of the French original. The translation included here is taken from https://en.wikiquote.org/wiki/Jean_Racine (May 2021). In Geoffrey Alan Argent's translation (Racine 2014), the full passage reads: "Those days are past when Nero would report / The heartfelt wishes of his doting court, / When, my hand guiding the affairs of state, / The senate, at my call, would congregate. / Then, veiled but present, I would play my role: / That august body's all-controlling soul."

Acknowledgements: Work on this Introduction has been supported by The Danish Council for Independent Research | Humanities through grant no. 6107-00351, *Transient Multilingual Communities and the Formation of Social and Linguistic Norms* (2016–2019), www.tmc.ku.dk. We would like to thank our collaborators on the TMC project, Dorte Lønsmann, Katherine Kappa, Spencer Hazel, for many inspiring discussions about norms over the years and Nikolas Coupland for his insightful comments on an earlier version of the present text. All remaining shortcomings remain our responsibility.

norms from a range of different perspectives, but they all focus specifically on norms related to language and language use, drawing on or engaging with theoretical and methodological approaches which may be broadly categorized as sociolinguistic. The importance of norms is easily discernible in the sociolinguistic canon (as we will discuss below), but there is no abundance of work within the field focusing *specifically* on the notion of norms (as opposed to work devoted to the related notion of language ideology). Norms are often treated as conceptual primes – convenient building blocks, ready-made for sociolinguistic theorizing – rather than theoretical constructs in need of reflexive attention as part of the sociolinguistic endeavor (cf. Blommaert 2006: 520). The overall aim of this book is therefore to explore and advance current understandings of norms as a theoretical construct and empirical object of research in sociolinguistics.

In this Introduction we set the scene for the ensuing chapters by providing an overview of the way the notion of norms has been used in sociolinguistics, and how it is approached in the present book. As we will explain, this involves challenging the idea of norms as unchanging and uniform abstract entities. Norms are messy, continuously reconstructed, and often contested in social interaction. We argue that the use of language in social life is a prime site for the study of the (re)production of social norms *in general* (and not just linguistic norms) and should therefore be of interest not only to sociolinguists, but also social scientists more generally. Norms may often exist behind a veil, but by exploring how individuals and groups enact – or resist – norms through language use and how they reflexively orient to emerging and sedimented norms through language as part of social interaction, we may catch a glimpse of the processes that continuously help create, sustain, and transform norms as the foundation of human sociality.

1 Norms in the sociolinguistic tradition

As indicated above, the notion of norms has a long history in sociolinguistics. Norms have been of interest not only in the variationist tradition but also in interactional sociolinguistics and the ethnography of speaking, just as norms can be said to be of central concern in the neighboring fields of ethnomethodology, conversation analysis and linguistic anthropology. Labov famously defined the speech community as "participation in a set of shared norms" (1972: 120–121), while Gumperz noted that "the speech varieties employed within a speech community form a system because they are related to *a shared set of social norms*" (1968: 381 our emphasis). Hymes similarly emphasized the importance of norms by devoting the letter 'N' in his SPEAKING mnemonic to a dual focus on "norms of interaction" and "norms of interpretation" (1972: 63). In other words, the notion of norms has for a long time been enlisted within sociolinguistics as a central component in theorizing language at the level of the speech community (language as system), as well as situated language use in specific speech events (language as use). However, as Cameron (1990: 86) pointed out more than 30 years ago, mainly with reference to variationist sociolinguistics, it is often unclear where norms "come from" and how they "get into" individual speakers. To add to that, we might also say that it often remains implicit what (sociolinguistic) norms actually *are* and how they should be theorized, which means that "norms" frequently refer to quite different things. In the following, we offer an overview of some of the central ways the notion of norms has been employed in sociolinguistics and unpack the assumptions they rely on.

Norms related to language and language use are social norms par excellence, but not all social norms are explicitly or directly linguistic, in the sense of having to do with language or language use. The notion of a "linguistic norm" is commonly used to refer to perceived regularities at different levels of linguistic description, including grammar, pronunciation, vocabulary and pragmatics (Thomas & Wareing 1999: 192). When used in this way, norms are generally *descriptive*, though they invariably contain an element of idealization and will therefore never be entirely accurate representations of the phenomena they describe. Linguistic norms may also be used *pre-* or *proscriptively* to stipulate what is considered acceptable/desirable or unacceptable/undesirable in a particular context (cf. Bowerman 2006). When used descriptively, linguistic norms provide an account of what may be considered "normal" in the use of a particular language, capturing "an externally observable pattern of behavior" (Agha 2007: 126). When used pre- or proscriptively, they are cultural phenomena that constitute rules which are subject to policing by some sort of authority, whether official or informal. The linguistic dos and don'ts of social life.

Sociolinguists have often been at pains to counter pre- and proscriptive norms, especially when such norms have been associated with hegemonic conceptions of so-called "standard" vs. "non-standard" varieties (with "standard" varieties invariably in the dominant position). At the same time, sociolinguists have traditionally also been concerned with the enterprise of identifying norms empirically and describing them, though not always in the same way and with the same goals in mind. Two broad orientations can be identified, one associated with the study of language variation and change, the other with more ethnographically oriented approaches to the study of language as part of social life.

In the variationist tradition, scholars have been interested in examining how linguistic norms in a speech community enter into structured variation, observable in the systematic correlation between linguistic structure and social structure. Studies of this kind tend to generate descriptive norms in which the apparent heterogeneity of language use is shown to be structured through co-variation with external social categories such as class, gender, and age. Norms are identified in the aggregate, as they reveal themselves as patterns *of* and *in* language use, and as regularities in the way speakers evaluate language. The variationist approach affords a central place to the concept of norms in the theorization of language variation and change, but, as we mentioned above, the notion of norms it relies on has been criticized for being rather abstract and too reliant on heavy-handed models of societal structure and social categories, inherited from classic functionalist-structuralist social theory.

Ethnographic and interactional lines of sociolinguistic enquiry tend to take more qualitative, context-sensitive approaches to the study of norms. In these traditions, norms are generally seen as sociocultural constructs that guide language use and contribute to meaning making as part of social interaction (cf. Hymes' notion of "norms of interaction" and "norms of interpretation" mentioned above). This perspective entails that the study of norms does not only relate to language-as-system, but encompasses what can be broadly referred to as "norms of verbal conduct" (irrespective of the specific language used, cf. Hymes 1989: 446), including interactional norms such as "avoidance of explicit and direct affront" (Keenan 1989), and the norm-based meanings associated with language choice in particular settings, cf. Blom and Gumperz's (1972) distinction between "metaphorical" and "situational" code-switching. As with the variationist tradition, the approach to norms exemplified by ethnographic and interactional approaches is descriptive (rather than prescriptive), focused on identifying and understanding externally observable patterns of behavior, but the *kinds* of norm under scrutiny are different, offering a complementary view of what constitutes a sociolinguistic norm to the one found in variationist approaches.

The social meaning of sociolinguistic norms – and what it means to follow or break with established norms – is layered, and disentangling these layers is not uncomplicated (cf. Ochs 1992, Kiesling 2005). In interactional sociolinguistics, the insight that the meaning of a particular type of discursive behavior depends on norms of interpretation, and that these norms are often specific to particular sociocultural groups, has given rise to a critical view of the role of norms. In his work on discourse strategies, Gumperz (1982: 131) illustrated how even very subtle linguistic cues can be context-creating, and hence meaning-making. Gumperz's work, particularly his notion of contextualization cues, also illustrated that it requires access to the relevant norms to "decode" context as well as meaning, and not having access to the interpretive framework can have severe (negative) consequences for speakers. As a poignant example of this, Roberts and

Campbell (2005) show how a group of non-UK born job candidates were disadvantaged compared to their UK-born counterparts because they were unacquainted with the local interactional norms for job interviews and therefore unable to deploy the "right" (i.e. the *expected*) kind of "bureaucratically processable" (Iedema 1999) talk that would match the interviewers' norms of interpretation. The candidates ended up being deemed unqualified for the job, and were thus penalized for their inability to perform according to the norms – or what Bourdieu (1991) calls "the rules of the cultural game".

Comparing the traditions briefly reviewed here, it becomes clear that the notion of norms does quite a lot of work – and a number of different jobs – in the sociolinguistic tradition. While normative heterogeneity has to some extent been downplayed in classic variationist approaches (because there is a focus on the shared norms that underpin linguistic variation), the exploration of heterogeneity often takes center stage in interactional sociolinguistics, particularly in studies of intercultural communication. The latter perspective often leads to a critical approach to the study of norms, in which norms are seen as multiple, often in conflict, and invariably related to issues of power. This critical view is not limited to an abstract relationship between notions of "standard" vs. "vernacular" language varieties which might apply at a generalized societal level; it also applies at the level of specific, contextualized instances of social interaction, for instance job interviews. Thus, norms are relevant at multiple levels of description, from the most general and abstract level of describing the norms of the speech community to the norms of specific encounters. At the same time, norms have received quite mixed reviews within the field: In line with the classic view from sociology, norms are generally seen to constitute the "glue" that holds (speech) communities together, but at the same time they are also – on occasion, and from certain perspectives – framed as potential problems for social coherence, complicit in the discursive construction of asymmetrical social relationships.

The contributions in this book draw on different traditions within sociolinguistics, including variationist and interactional sociolinguistics, and some authors also draw inspiration from neighboring fields such as linguistic anthropology, sociology, ethnomethodology, and philosophy. Several authors adopt critical perspectives on norms, but many also emphasize the indispensability of norms, stressing the fundamental role they play in establishing human sociality. The individual chapters are reviewed in Section 3 below. However, before we offer this preview, the next section will provide an introduction to some of the key themes and questions related to norms which are brought up throughout the book. This also allows us to touch upon more recent developments in the way norms have been conceptualized within sociolinguistics broadly conceived.

2 Perspectives on norms in this book

As already mentioned, it is an overarching argument of this book that the study of language in social life is one of the central ways in which social norms may be studied empirically, and sociolinguistics – glossed as "the study of social worlds through language" (Coupland & Jaworski 2009) – is therefore well-positioned to contribute to the general understanding of norms in the social sciences. Approaching norms empirically through the study of language-in-use offers a particular vantage point which allows analysts to explore the emergence and sedimentation of norms well beyond language norms/linguistic norms related to e.g. grammar or pronunciation (cf. Bartsch 1987; Mäkilähde, Leppänen & Itkonen 2019). In taking on this task, the chapters in this book draw on a number of overarching theoretical notions, which we will review in the following. The notions are central to the discussion of norms that runs throughout the book, but it is important to emphasize that contributors can and do take different positions with regards to many of the issues raised.

2.1 Norms and reflexivity

One of the great appeals of working with the notion of norms as a theoretical notion is that social norms can be posited as constructs that mediate between different levels of social and societal organization.[2] Piippo (2012, and Chapter 4, this volume) suggests that we can think of norms as "reflexive models of meaningful, expected and appropriate conduct" which help guide social interaction, including language use, in contexts where they apply. Defined in this way, norms provide us with a particularly interesting perspective on the tug of war between agency and social structure in the organization of social life: Norms can be seen as "individual" and "social" at the same time, and this dual status is made possible by reflexivity, defined as an "activity in which the subject deliberates upon how some item [. . .] pertains or relates to itself" (Archer 2003: 26).

Contributors to the present book vary in their assessment of the extent to which norms are "negotiable", highlighting the fact that "reflexive" should not be taken to imply that norms are something that members of a community can necessarily opt out of at a whim, or easily change. Social norms are sedimented

---

[2] Norms arguably share this feature with the related notion of language ideology, but there is not complete overlap between the two notions (as discussed in several chapters in the book, see e.g contributions by Piippo and Fabricius).

products of social action and cannot be undone by any one individual. Yet, as reflexive models, they can be held up for scrutiny, individually as well as collectively. The level of reflexivity involved when engaging with norms may not be the same for all norms at all times: As we have suggested, norms often exist behind a veil, unseen. Yet, the fact that we are aware of norms and that they have the *potential* to be made objects of reflexive deliberation, called onto the stage, as it were, is an important part of understanding the function of norms in social life.

The view of norms as "reflexive models" relates to several existing proposals in the literature. Thus, drawing on ethnomethodology, Hazel and Lønsmann (Chapter 3, this volume), suggest that a social norm can be compared to what Garfinkel (1967) calls a "scheme of interpretation" which relies on certain "background expectancies". Such expectancies are reflexive and therefore, we would argue, to some extent malleable. In a similar vein, speaking from a more clearly sociolinguistic view, Blommaert has defined sociolinguistic norms as "patterns of metapragmatic valuation that develop over time in the form of 'enregisterment,' the development of specific forms of language use that carry socially recognizable values and that invite and require continuous interactional re-enactment" (2006: 520). Here, reflexivity is arguably also implied, assuming that the "metapragmatic valuation" involved in the emergence of a register (in the sense of Agha 2003) relies on reflexive awareness of the language use of self and other. For a way of speaking to be recognized as a such, i.e., as a style, requires a certain level of individual reflexivity, just as it requires "continuous *interactional* re-enactment" (our emphasis).

2.2 Norms as processes and products

Several chapters in this book explore norms empirically, investigating and highlighting their situationally contingent nature. This approach goes some way towards answering Cameron's (1990) critical questions mentioned above (where do norms "come from" and how do they "get into" speakers?) by suggesting that norms may be theorized as local constructs in-the-making, rather than global, pre-given templates for social behavior. From this perspective, norms emerge in interaction, and rather than asking how they "get into" speakers, the question can be reframed to be a matter of how speakers *orient to* and *enact norms* in interaction, sustaining or challenging them in the process. In this vein, Coupland (this volume) suggests that it may be useful to talk about *normatization* as a process, rather than simply seeing norms as products. Focusing on the processual aspect of norms can be said to mirror concerns in the social sciences more broadly with the dynamics of social processes and social change (e.g. Dahms & Hazelrigg 2010; Green 2016) and, indeed, norms (e.g. Fine 2001). However, as Blommaert has pointed out, "detailed attention to interaction has never really been part of the sociological mainstream" (2018: 18), and this is one of the reasons why we argue that the chapters in this book – due to their empirical approach to the study of norms and normatization as part of social interaction – have something valuable to bring to the study of norms in social life.

Although there is much to be gained from studying norms as processes embedded in social interaction, the notion of norms as reflexive models discussed above entails that norms cannot be reduced entirely to the processes that sustain them. Once established, norms tend to have a certain durability. To take an example, it might be suggested that the notion of indexicality, as it has come to be theorized in sociolinguistics with inspiration from linguistic anthropology (e.g. Silverstein 2003; Agha 2007), implies or presupposes a notion of norms as the "stuff" that mediates between discursive practice and the meanings ascribed to different ways of speaking. Norms of interaction and interpretation do not merely account for what is normal (what speakers do), but also capture what is socially normative (what speakers mutually expect themselves and others to do), and what it "means" to follow or deviate from a particular norm. This means that sociolinguistic norms are indexical, in the sense that they take part in establishing socio-culturally contingent links between ways of speaking and social meaning (Coupland 2007; Eckert 2008; cf. Campbell-Kibler 2007). The links that exist between a linguistic form or a particular discursive practice and its meaning(s) must to some extent be conventional, extending beyond the immediate encounter – at least if the linguistic form or discursive practice is to be used meaningfully for the purposes of communication.

This example can be used to highlight why it is necessary to maintain a notion of norms as "products" which are to some extent capable of travelling in time and space, as partly individual, partly social, reflexive models. However, the focus on process brings out that it does not have to be a matter of *either/or*. Norms may and do travel, but they do not necessarily stay the same in the process. Thus, in the case of norms and indexicality, it may be useful to think of "indexical fields" not as fixed normative products, but as historically and spatially contingent instantiations of processes of "indexicalisation" (Jaffe 2016). It may be tempting – and in some cases useful as an analytical strategy – to reify indexical meanings and the norms they rely on, but this should not blind us to the processes through which indexical meanings are continuously (re)created in and sustained through discourse and social interaction (see also Hynninen & Solin 2018).

2.3 Transient communities and the study of norms

Considering the interplay between process and product in the theorization of norms also leads to a consideration of how norms are established in situations where participants cannot be expected to have the same shared background expectancies from the outset. Several chapters in this book explore this question empirically by studying relatively ephemeral social settings or "transient communities" (cf. Lønsmann, Hazel & Haberland 2017; Mortensen 2017) where participants have different linguistic and sociocultural backgrounds. What is interesting about such social settings is that norms of interaction and other norms of social conduct cannot be assumed to be in place a priori. Hence, participants will need to do "extra" work to establish the normative order of their interaction. This sort of normative work is not *sui generis* or in any substantial way different from processes in other contexts, but in the absence of shared normative ground, the processes tend to be "amplified" and hence more amenable to observation, description, and theorization.

The study of transient social settings, populated by individuals with different sociocultural backgrounds can thus be approached as a "laboratory" for the study of how normative processes unfold. Several chapters in this book suggest that in the absence of a pre-existing shared normative framework, individuals will often fill this normative void with locally established practices (discursive and otherwise) that gradually become normative. That norms play a crucial role in establishing and maintaining human sociality has been known since Durkheim: even though they may not always be immediately observable, norms are the seams that hold the social fabric of society together (cf. Durkheim 1893). What the chapters in this book offer are empirically founded accounts of how this unfolds in practice; how norms emerge over time in particular settings, in an interplay between local practices and wider contextual conditions and constraints. Several chapters in the book take up this methodological challenge and provide innovative suggestions for how linguistic as well as social norms more generally may be studied (see e.g. chapters by Fabricius; Pitzl; Kraft & Mortensen; Marra, Holmes & Vine).

Although norms may thus be said to have an "enabling role" (cf. Harder, this volume) in the creation of human sociality in transient communities, several authors in this book also offer critical perspectives on the role of norms in social life, including transient settings. Social norms are part of social reality and may not easily be changed (cf. the chapter by Harder, this volume), but one of the clear gains of studying norms and conceptualizing them in more theoretically coherent ways is that they are lifted out of their normal status of relative obscurity and made available for critical discussion and reflection. This may have an impact on the way social and linguistic norms are approached not only amongst sociolinguists and likeminded scholars, but also practitioners in classrooms, at construction sites, in service encounters and in the media – which are some of the cases covered by the contributions in this book.

3 The contributions in this book

In addition to the present Introduction, the book consists of seven main chapters and an epilogue which are all introduced in the following. Our ambition is not to provide exhaustive summaries of the contributions but to highlight what we see as some of the central themes emerging throughout the book, while also drawing attention to some of the central conceptual and methodological differences the authors bring to the table. As it will be clear from this preview, the book does not present a unified statement on the topics of norms. In fact, we believe it would be quite impossible –counterproductive, even – to strive for a "neat" account of the phenomenon at hand. As we have discussed above, norms are messy and multilayered, and to understand them and their role in social life, a variety of theoretical perspectives and methodological approaches is needed. For this reason, we have also asked all chapter authors to be quite explicit about how they define norms, and what traditions they draw upon in their work.[3]

In his opening chapter, *Attitudes, norms, and emergent communities* (Chapter 2), Peter Harder offers a conceptual discussion of social norms (including linguistic norms), introducing a distinction between *evaluative* norms and *operational* norms. Evaluative norms are concerned with attitudes and opinions, for instance in relation to notions such as "the standard language" and the social prestige that commonly accrues to standard language speakers. Because they are opinion-based, evaluative norms are subject to negotiation and may undergo change following discussion, while this is not true for operational norms. Drawing on Searle (1995), Harder sees operational norms as constitutive of social reality. They exist collectively as *doxa* and become internalized in the individual as *habitus* through adaptation to the social environment (cf. Bourdieu 1977). Operational norms are thus individual and social at the same time, and they cannot be escaped or done away with by any one individual. Operational norms can and do change, but Harder argues that this takes place at a different time scale and necessarily involves *collective*, not individual, normative reorientation. Engaging in a discus-

---

[3] Similarly, we have not wanted to impose a single norm when it comes to transcription conventions, so chapters that feature transcripts include a transcription key specific to each chapter.

sion with the empirical studies reported in some of the later chapters in the book (Hazel & Lønsmann; Kraft & Mortensen; Fabricius), Harder also offers a useful discussion of the role norms can be said to play in emergent communities. In such settings, where operational norms are not in place *a priori*, a shared *orientation* towards norms is nevertheless crucial in establishing a sense of community and social order. When a normative steady state is not the starting point for social interaction, it will present itself as a target for the participants.

Harder's argument moves at a society-wide scale, taking communities that are already "going concerns" as his prototypical examples. In their chapter on *Norms, accountability and socialisation in a refugee language classroom* (Chapter 3), Spencer Hazel and Dorte Lønsmann adopt a different perspective, focusing on the emergent normative order in a language classroom for recent adult refugees to Denmark. Taking their cue from ethnomethodology and Garfinkel (1967) in particular, Hazel and Lønsmann approach norms as "schemes of interpretation" and "taken-for-granted expectancies" that individuals orient to when evaluating social behavior. Individuals are morally accountable towards these norms, which makes norms a central part of "the moral order" (Garfinkel 1964). This in turn means that breaching a norm is a socially and morally accountable act which requires an excuse. From this theoretical starting point, Hazel and Lønsmann set out to explore a recurring verbal routine in the classroom which concerns excuses for being late. This discursive practice, captured on video as part of ethnographic fieldwork and subsequently transcribed for analysis, works as a way for the participants, teachers, and students alike, to establish a social norm in the classroom for punctuality, along with norms for the appropriate way of producing an excuse if the norm is violated. The routine has a socializing function in the local setting, but Hazel and Lønsmann go further and argue that the routine also has implications beyond the classroom: The Danish language classes are part of a mandatory programme for refugees, introducing them not only to the Danish language but also "Danish workplace culture". Hazel and Lønsmann show how the norm of punctuality becomes the centerpiece of a "scaling project" (Carr & Lempert 2016) in this connection, as the importance of being on time for class is explicitly linked to a putative norm for punctuality on the labor market.

While Hazel and Lønsmann would probably agree that norms have what Harder calls an "enabling" function, they are keen to stress that norms may also have a *differentiating* function, which may be less unequivocally benign. Through the verbal routines, the teachers are established as the arbiters of "the right" norms in operation in the classroom and, by extension, the Danish labor market. At the same time, by being treated as someone who needs instruction in these norms, the refugee participants are being positioned as outsiders. Through their analyses, Hazel and Lønsmann are thus able to show how processes of social inclusion and exclusion, as well as self- and other-positioning, are grounded in specific local discursive practices, and how these practices rely on norms as a constitutive element of the moral order, at multiple levels of social organization.

In Chapter 4, *Norms in the making*, Irina Piippo offers another study of an educational setting, exploring the norms of *selkosuomi* ("easy to understand Finnish"), a teaching register used at an immigrant integration training program in Finland. This research setting constitutes a highly diverse linguistic environment both in terms of languages spoken, degrees of literacy amongst the participants and the scripts they are familiar with. Based on her own earlier work on norms (Piippo 2012) and work at the intersection of sociolinguistics and linguistic anthropology, Piippo defines norms as socially shared reflexive models of meaningful, expected and appropriate conduct (cf. our discussion above in section 2). While Hazel and Lønsmann identify local norms based on the analysis of cases where specific norms are violated and participants subsequently provide accounts for such breaches, Piippo relies on metapragmatic talk when she establishes the case for *selkosuomi*'s status as a register (in the sense of Agha 2007) and the norms that shape it. In addition, she provides a detailed analysis of *selkosuomi* in use, showing how the register is not merely constituted by the use of "simplified" vocabulary and syntax, but in fact involves a range of multimodal resources, including body movements, drawings and other non-verbal semiotic means. Piippo stresses that norms should be seen as processes rather than products, and that they must be studied in their local contexts. Norms are not abstract notions that float around in society, dissociated from social action. On the contrary, norms are empirical phenomena that emerge in particular social contexts, and they should be explored in these settings, through the study of metapragmatic processes. Piippo does not suggest, however, that norms only exist in the local here and now. By showing how the local register of *selkosuomi* relates to and draws on the institutionalized national form of the register, Piippo is able to bring out the scale-transcending or multilayered nature of norms. From this perspective, norms are "local" and "trans-local" at the same time, existing in specific settings in the manner of locally produced adapted imprints of a more general script. In this conceptualization, rather than existing behind a veil, norms may more appropriately be seen as constituting the fabric of social life.

The chapters by Hazel and Lønsmann and Piippo share a focus on classroom settings. By virtue of its socializing function and often asymmetrical setup in terms of power between teachers and students, the classroom may be said to constitute a particularly interesting context in which to observe normativity and "normatization" in action. Yet, the classroom is obviously not unique in this respect. Thus, in Chapter 5, *Norms and stereotypes: Studying the emergence and sedimentation of social meaning*, we (Kraft & Mortensen) explore how members of a management team on a construction site in Norway use and assign value to national stereotypes as part of their interactions. The stereotypes in question concern "Norwegians" and "Swedes" and the relationship between the idealized groups which these labels refer to. By drawing on ethnographic observations and analyses of video recordings of naturally occurring interaction on the site over a period of six months, we explore how the members of the management team gradually imbue stereotypes based on national categories with meaning and establish discursive norms for their use within the group. We argue that the participants draw on and reproduce an interactional norm of "othering" through the use of national stereotypes which comes to function as a resource for negotiating interpersonal relationships in the group, while also allowing the group members to position themselves *vis-à-vis* outsiders. The norms we observe in the data are scale-transcending. In deploying stereotypes as part of their interaction, the members of the management team rely on culturally familiar ideas about "Swedes" and "Norwegians" in existence beyond the scale of the specific group. However, the meanings that develop around the stereotypes, and the norms for how they can (and cannot) be used in interaction are tied to the specific context of the group, including the individual histories of particular members and their shared history as a team.

In Chapter 6, *Multilingual creativity and emerging norms in interaction: Towards a methodology for micro-diachronic analysis*, Marie-Luise Pitzl explores the emergence of norms for language use in what she calls a transient international group (TIG). More specifically, she tracks how norms for the use of multiple languages develop amongst a group of international students during an informal gathering at a pub in Vienna, a speech event included in the Vienna-Oxford International Corpus of English (VOICE). Taking her starting point in the notion of creativity, Pitzl argues that linguistic creativity presupposes and at the same time transcends established language norms. So, in a setting where English has been established as a shared lingua franca, the use of features associated with languages other than English may be seen as a norm-transcending activity and hence a creative form of language use. For Pitzl, a relevant question then becomes when a particular linguistic practice, first seen as divergent and hence "creative", potentially becomes established as a norm in its own right, as other speakers begin to adopt the same or similar practices. Utilizing the coding in VOICE, which includes tags for when languages other than English are used in the interaction, Pitzl shows how norms for language choice can be tracked through the interaction using what she calls a "micro-diachronic" approach. Such an approach, Pitzl argues, allows researchers to move beyond analyses of single instances of interactional sequences (or collections of such instances) and take a broader, longitudinal view on how norms in a TIG become established over time.

In Chapter 7, *What's in a sociolinguistic norm?*, Anne Fabricius works at a very different time scale and at a very different level of linguistic description than Pitzl, tracking change in the norms concerning the production and perception of trilled and tapped prevocalic /r/ in Received Pronunciation in Britain from the 1950s till today. However, despite the differences in time scale and analytical focus, there is considerable overlap between the two chapters, as they both focus on the relationship between variation and change in language. Fabricius positions her contribution explicitly within variationist sociolinguistics and opens with a review of how the notion of norms has been theorized within this strand of sociolinguistics, historically as well as more recently, as the field has increasingly incorporated insights originating in linguistic anthropology. From this vantage point, she argues that sociolinguistic norms are to be found in "the sedimentation of linguistic production and sociolinguistically-directed perception," highlighting how norms relate not only to what speakers *do*, as evidenced in statistically verifiable patterns of speech production, but also how variable speech generates meaning in particular contexts, and how meanings change over time.

Drawing on a corpus of speech data from fourteen RP speakers born between 1880 and 1920, Fabricius shows how the use of tapped and trilled prevocalic /r/ has been declining during the 20th century (cf. Fabricius 2017), amounting to a change in production norms. This is interesting in and of itself, but Fabricius goes further, exploring how the meaning of prevocalic /r/ as a "construct resource" (cf. Fabricius & Mortensen 2013) has changed over time, i.e. how the norms of perception related to this particular feature have undergone change. She does this by complementing the quantitative study of change in production norms with a qualitative case study of a widely discussed Conservative Party Conference address delivered by Geoffrey Cox, Attorney-General of the UK, in July 2018, and its uptake in popular discourse. The speech stood out because of the stentorian and archaic style of delivery adopted by Cox. As Fabricius shows, this style was in part brought off by Cox styling his prevocalic /r/'s in a manner reminiscent of days of old, harking back to a norm which had in effect gone out of fashion before he was born. For some media commentators, Cox's style was successful in evoking an image of "the good old days" (and thus constituted a good match for his pro-Brexit stance), while others evaluated his attempt at retrograde linguistic creativity negatively. This ambiguity shows how change in "production norms" and "perception norms" do not necessarily develop in lockstep, suggesting that a research agenda interested in sociolinguistic change (as opposed to linguistic change) will need to be able to account for both.

In Chapter 8, *What we share: The impact of norms on successful interaction*, Meredith Marra, Janet Holmes, and Bernadette Vine can also be said to be interested in production and perception norms (though they do not use these terms), comparing naturally occurring interaction in close-knit workplace teams to fleeting "frontstage" encounters between customers/visitors and service providers in coffee shops and museums in New Zealand. Marra, Holmes and Vine gloss norms broadly as "shared understandings upon which we draw when negotiating meaning," arguing that norms should be studied empirically as they materialize in discursive practices (aligning with stances represented in chapters by Piippo, Hazel & Lønsmann, and Kraft & Mortensen). Marra et al. argue that norms are abstract entities that cannot be observed empirically, yet shared discursive practices can be taken as "evidence that norms are at play". In established communities of practice, such as workplace teams, which are characterized by a shared repertoire of meaning-making resources (cf. Wenger 1998), norms-as-practices are commonly in evidence. In service encounters, which are often one-off and characterized by transience, this is a different matter. Here participants have not had an opportunity to develop a shared repertoire over time; in fact, they may often, particularly in encounters that involve participants from different (socio-) cultural backgrounds, have quite *different* normative expectations towards the activities they are engaged in. In their data, collected by means of a "mystery shopper method" which helped generate recordings of naturally occurring interaction with little to no attention paid to the act of recording on the part of the service provider, Marra et al. find evidence that sociocultural constraints on the negotiation of meaning *are* in place, on occasion resulting in miscommunication. At the same time, drawing on Scollon's "nexus of practice" model (Scollon 2001), they also suggest that even though each service encounter is one-off and potentially based on different normative expectancies on the part of the participants, there might be "a hint" of an underlying and culturally more widespread shared orientation towards – and understanding of – the components that constitute a service encounter and similar interactional routines.

In the final chapter, *Normativity, language and Covid-19*, Nikolas Coupland uses the requirement for people in the UK to wear face coverings, introduced as a response to the Covid-19 pandemic in July 2020, as his starting point for a general discussion of the notion of normativity. As part of this endeavor, he introduces a number of conceptual distinctions which can be used to unpack the multi-layered nature of social norms. Norms, says Coupland, can be described in terms of the *normative field* they take in their scope, including their specific *focus*, e.g. face coverings, and their *distribution* in social and geographical space. The idea introduced here is that norms can be scoped in different ways, applying to what we have referred to above as different scales. At the same time, a norm can be explored in terms of its *authorship* (who/what is the authority behind the norm?) and the logic or *rationale* on which it is based. *Normative valency* refers to whether a norm is *prescriptive* or *proscriptive*, and to its *intensity*, i.e. relative strength. Norms can also be examined in terms of the response they are met with, what Coupland calls the *field of compliance*. From this perspective, it becomes interesting to explore *styles* of uptake or resistance, for instance how the requirement to wear face coverings can be reappropriated as a fashion opportunity, but also how discourses on protection of the elderly as an exposed group can turn into age discrimination.

In the second part of his chapter, Coupland uses the distinctions introduced in the first part to provide a retrospective commentary on what he sees as some of the key contributions in the preceding chapters. He emphasizes that several chapters present case studies "of social contexts, and normative fields, where norms are not only complex and potentially multiple but [in the terms used above, eds.] imperfectly scoped and amenable to new forms of rationalisation." He further notes that "many of the case studies address key moments of normativity, when shared normative assumptions are lacking and needing to be assembled or reassembled (re-scoped, in terms of focus and distribution) in order to cope with uncertain and/or changing demands." This brings us back to the point made in Harder's chapter about the "enabling" nature of social norms, and what we propose could be seen as their fundamental role in establishing human sociality. In this way, the empirical case studies in the book have not merely illustrated the ubiquity of norms in social interaction, they have in fact highlighted the omnipresence of the process of *norm-making*, what Coupland calls "normatization", as a key driver of human sociality at multiple scales.

4 Normative futures

By relating the general topic of this book to recent and ongoing events following the Covid-19 pandemic and discussing how the pandemic might be understood as a radical context for language-salient normative change in the UK, Coupland's epilogue illustrates how relevant and timely the notion of norms is for contemporary sociolinguistics. Social norms are obviously not a new invention, and the normative processes that we experience at present are not in any substantial way *unique* compared to the processes that have characterized earlier historical periods. Nevertheless, we would like to end this Introduction by suggesting that the need for exploring and theorizing norms in social life is made particularly relevant as a result of the quite explicit concern with (sociolinguistic) norms currently observable in many spheres of public life.

The advent of online participatory media, such as Facebook, Twitter and YouTube (sometimes erroneously referred to as "social" media), has generated not only new forms of "public" discourse, but also a running metalinguistic commentary on the norms which should – or should not – guide that form of conversation. This means that the norms for what it is *possible* and *permissible* to say "in public" are contested. The banning of the former president of the United States from all major participatory media platforms in 2021 is a particularly spectacular example of this, but the general debate which that event relates to is a much more common one: We seem to witness a surge of discussions related to the appropriate use of language, not only in online contexts, but also offline.

Similarly, political disagreements about everything from immigration to lock-down restraints, debates about the societal role and responsibility of news media (fake news), debates related to "identity politics" and many other such discussions are fraught with implicit or explicit discussions about (sociolinguistic) norms. The discussions include questions of how the world and the people and objects within it can be appropriately named, but also how individuals can (and cannot) interact with each other. Again, none of these issues are new as such, but we may be witnessing a situation of increased attention to norms and potential polarization where differences are resolving into opposing and equally intolerant normative regimes, which makes consensus and even intellectual disagreement difficult.

The chapters included in this book do not address these issues in any specific manner, but we believe they serve as a useful illustration of how the study of norms in language and social life provides us with an important starting point for exploring normative processes and their role in creating human sociality.

References

Agha, Asif. 2003. The social life of cultural value. *Language & Communication*. 23 (3). 231–273.
Agha, Asif. 2007. *Language and social relations*. Cambridge: Cambridge University Press.
Archer, Margaret S. 2003. *Structure, agency and the internal conversation*. Cambridge: Cambridge University Press.
Racine, Jean. 2014. *The complete plays of Jean Racine. Volume 5: Britannicus*. (Trans.) Geoffrey Alan Argent. Pennsylvania: The Pennsylvania State University Press.
Bartsch, Renate. 1987. *Norms of language*. London: Longman.
Blom, Jan-Petter & John J. Gumperz. 1972. Social meaning in linguistic structures: Code switching in Northern Norway. In John J. Gumperz & Dell Hymes (eds.), *Directions in sociolinguistics*, 407–434. New York: Holt, Rinehart and Winston.
Blommaert, Jan. 2006. Language ideology. In Keith Brown (ed.), *Encyclopedia of language & linguistics* (2nd edn.), 510–522. Oxford: Elsevier.
Blommaert, Jan. 2018. *Durkheim and the Internet: On sociolinguistics and the sociological imagination*. London: Bloomsbury.

Bourdieu, Pierre. 1977. *Outline of a theory of practice*. (Trans.) Richard Nice. Cambridge: Cambridge University Press.
Bourdieu, Pierre. 1991. *Language & symbolic power*. (Trans.) John Brookshire Thompson. Cambridge: Harvard University Press.
Bowerman, Sean. 2006. Norms and correctness. In Keith Brown (ed.), *Encyclopedia of language & linguistics* (2nd edn.), 701–703. Oxford: Elsevier.
Cameron, Deborah. 1990. Demythologizing sociolinguistics: Why language does not reflect society. In John Joseph & Talbot Taylor (eds.), *Ideologies of language*, 79–93. London: Routledge.
Campbell-Kibler, Kathryn. 2007. Accent, (ING), and the social logic of listener perceptions. *American Speech*. 82 (1). 32–64.
Carr, E. Summerson & Michael Lempert. 2016. Introduction: Pragmatics of scale. In E. Summerson Carr & Michael Lempert (eds.), *Scale: Discourse and dimensions of social life*, 1–21. Oakland: University of California Press.
Coupland, Nikolas. 2007. *Style: Language variation and identity*. Cambridge: Cambridge University Press.
Coupland, Nikolas & Adam Jaworski. 2009. Social worlds through language. In Nikolas Coupland & Adam Jaworski (eds.), *The new sociolinguistics reader*, 1–21. Basingstoke: Palgrave Macmillan.
Dahms, Harry F. & Lawrence Hazelrigg (eds.). 2010. *Theorizing the dynamics of social processes*. Bingley: Emerald.
Durkheim, Émile. 1893. *De la division du travail social*. Paris: Quadrige/Presses Universitaires de France.
Eckert, Penelope. 2008. Variation and the indexical field. *Journal of Sociolinguistics* 12 (4). 453–476.
Fabricius, Anne. 2017. Twentieth-century Received Pronunciation: Prevocalic /r/. In Raymond Hickey (ed.), *Listening to the past: Audio records of accents of English*, 39–65. Cambridge: Cambridge University Press.
Fabricius, Anne H. & Janus Mortensen. 2013. Language ideology and the notion of "construct resource": a case study of modern RP. In Tore Kristiansen & Stefan Grondelaars (eds.), *Language (de)standardisation in Late Modern Europe: Experimental studies*, 375–402. Oslo: Novus Forlag.
Fine, Gary Alan. 2001. Enacting norms: Mushrooming and the culture of expectations and explanations. In Michael Hechter & Karl-Dieter Opp (eds.), *Social Norms*, 139–164. New York: Russel Sage Foundation.
Garfinkel, Harold. 1964. Studies of the routine grounds of everyday activities. *Social Problems*. 11 (3). 225–250.
Garfinkel, Harold. 1967. *Studies in ethnomethodology*. Englewood Cliffs: Prentice-Hall.
Green, Duncan. 2016. *How change happens*. Oxford: Oxford University Press.
Gumperz, John J. 1968. The speech community. In David Sills (ed.), *International encyclopedia of the social sciences*, vol. 9, 381–386. New York: Macmillan.
Gumperz, John J. 1982. *Discourse strategies*. Cambridge: Cambridge University Press.
Hechter, Michael. 2018. Norms in the evolution of social order. *Social Research*. 85 (1). 23–51.
Hechter, Michael & Karl-Dieter Opp (eds.). 2001. *Social norms*. New York: Russell Sage Foundation.

Hymes, Dell. 1972. Models of the interaction of language and social life. In John J. Gumperz & Dell Hymes (eds.), *Directions in sociolinguistics*, 35–71. New York: Holt, Rinehart and Winston.

Hymes, Dell. 1989. Ways of speaking. In Joel Sherzer & Richard Bauman (eds.), *Explorations in the ethnography of speaking* (2nd edn.), 433–452. Cambridge: Cambridge University Press.

Hynninen, Niina & Anna Solin. 2018. Language norms in ELF. In Jennifer Jenkins, Will Baker & Martin Dewey (eds.), *The Routledge handbook of English as a lingua franca*, 267–278. Abingdon: Routledge.

Iedema, Rick. 1999. Formalizing organizational meaning. *Discourse & Society*. 10 (1). 49–65.

Jaffe, Alexandra. 2016. Indexicality, stance and fields in sociolinguistics. In Nikolas Coupland (ed.), *Sociolinguistics: Theoretical debates*, 86–112. Cambridge: Cambridge University Press.

Keenan, Elinor. 1989. Norm-makers, norm-breakers: Uses of speech by men and women in a Malagasy community. In Joel Sherzer & Richard Bauman (eds.), *Explorations in the Ethnography of Speaking* (2nd edn), 125–143. Cambridge: Cambridge University Press.

Labov, William. 1972. *Sociolinguistic patterns*. Philadelphia: University of Pennsylvania Press.

Lønsmann, Dorte, Spencer Hazel & Hartmut Haberland. 2017. Introduction to special issue on transience: Emerging norms of language use. *Journal of Linguistic Anthropology* 27 (3). 264–270.

Mäkilähde, Aleksi, Ville Leppänen & Esa Itkonen. 2019. *Normativity in language and linguistics*. Amsterdam: John Benjamins Publishing Company.

Mortensen, Janus. 2017. Transient multilingual communities as a field of investigation: Challenges and opportunities. *Journal of Linguistic Anthropology*. 27 (3). 271–288.

Piippo, Irina. 2012. *Viewing norms dialogically: An action-oriented approach to sociolinguistic metatheory*. Helsinki: University of Helsinki PhD Dissertation.

Roberts, Celia & Sarah Campbell. 2005. Fitting stories into boxes: Rhetorical and textual constraints on candidates' performances in British job interviews. *Journal of Applied Linguistics*. 2 (1). 45–73.

Scollon, Ron. 2001. *Mediated discourse: The nexus of practice*. London: Routledge.

Searle, John R. 1995. *The construction of social reality*. New York: Free Press.

Silverstein, Michael. 2003. Indexical order and the dialectics of sociolinguistic life. *Language & Communication*. 23 (3–4). 193–229.

Thomas, Linda & Shân Wareing. 1999. *Language, society and power: An introduction*. London: Routledge.

Wenger, Etienne. 1998. *Communities of practice: Learning, meaning, and identity*. Cambridge: Cambridge University Press.

Xenitidou, Maria & Bruce Edmonds (eds.). 2014. *The complexity of social norms*. New York: Springer.

Peter Harder
2 Attitudes, norms and emergent communities

1 Introduction

The aim of this chapter is to throw light on some under-appreciated aspects of the role of norms in relation to linguistic practices. By norms I understand – in accordance with common usage – something like expectations according to which certain behaviours are appropriate. The main point in the following turns on a distinction between two different norm-related aspects of social practices, "evaluative" and "operational" normativity.

The term *norm* has a well-established purely descriptive role in linguistics, including sociolinguistics. Nevertheless, I think it is fair to say that the term, and especially the adjectival form *normative*, carries some predominantly negative overtones. Among the reasons one can mention the following: There is a well-entrenched distinction between normative and descriptive linguistics, where the normative approach is pre-scientific as opposed to descriptive linguistics which deals with language as it is in reality. In addition, the normative approach is associated with what Milroy and Milroy (1991) termed "the complaint tradition": the perennial lamentation about the decay of standards. Further, norms associated with hegemonic power are familiar as a source of oppression, especially in educational contexts. In such cases, norms are understood as the source of unfounded negative evaluation of particular forms of language.

This, however, reflects only one aspect of the nature of norms. The other side is less generally recognized, although it has been part of the picture since Durkheim, one of the founders of sociology: Norms are the stuff of which culture and society consist (cf. Itkonen 2008).

It should be emphasized that these two sides are parts of the same complex picture. In exercising a critical stance towards the manifestations of evaluative normativity indicated above, it is therefore necessary to consider their relations with norms viewed as building blocks of social reality. A descriptive approach to norms must provide a comprehensive account, which is at the same time unified (relating all manifestations of normativity to fundamental features) and differentiated (recognizing the heterogeneity of the phenomena that have been classified as norms).

One key aspect of the complexity involved is that there may in certain cases be a double dissociation between evaluative norm-based attitudes and norms as part of the social world in which holders of such attitudes are embedded. Speakers sometimes have negative attitudes towards norms that they adapt to in their own speech. This reflects the fact that the complex ontological foundations of norms include two different levels of social and cognitive organization. Norms that underpin cultures and societies do not operate by means of evaluative statements of the kind mentioned above. They constitute features of the social environment in which members of a speech community live. Speakers adapt to such features for the same reason that all organisms adapt (in the evolutionary sense) to features of the environment in which they live.

The most essential property of such norms is that they are "constitutive" (cp. Searle 1969 on "constitutive rules"): such norms are the ontological foundations of the practices that they are concerned with. However, most of the time I am going to use the term "operational" about this aspect of the status of norms, in order to emphasize its causal and de-personalized nature, as part of "the way the world[1] works". The thrust of the argument in this paper is to show what a heightened awareness of this impersonal aspect of norms entails for a full understanding of the role of linguistic norms.

One under-appreciated aspect of this picture concerns linguistic variation. Norms are often assumed to be monolithic, stipulating the one and only correct form. This, again, is simplistic: as emphasized by Labov (1972: 120–1), norms also underlie variational patterns. As with norms for how to drive a car, linguistic norms ratify different outcomes according to who the agent is, what the circumstances are, and what the aim is. This sensitivity towards variation does not entail that norms are necessarily "soft" or "permissive". Rules for what it counts as for "someone like you" to use a particular linguistic form may be very uncompromising, even while they are sensitive to situational circumstances. That the use of the n-word is permitted for African-Americans in certain contexts of use does not imply a lax interpretation of the prohibitive norm for white speakers, for instance.

The basic argument for the force of the distinction between evaluative and operational normativity is predicated on the role of norms in communities as "going concerns", to which the term "operational" applies most naturally. On the basis of that argument, I then try to show how the basic point applies to emergent communities, which are not yet fully "up-and-running" in terms of the rules they play by.

---

[1] In referring to 'the world' in this way, here and elsewhere, I do not necessarily mean 'the whole world'. I use the phrase "the way the world works" to refer to causal mechanisms in the speaker's environment, as distinct from mind-internal mechanisms.

The structure of the chapter is as follows: Section 2 contains an in-depth discussion of the two sides of norms introduced above. Section 3 links up the distinction with two levels of cognitive organization. Section 4 discusses the distinction between individual-level facts and community-level facts, drawing on a theory of evolutionary dynamics. Section 5 takes up the special case of prestige norms while Section 6 discusses the double dissociation between the two sides of norms. Section 7 discusses the implication for emergent communities, and section 8 presents the conclusion.

2 The evaluative and the operational side of norms

The evaluative manifestation of norms is the most visible aspect of the phenomenon. In this capacity, norms are manifested as "opinions". Like other opinions, they can change, because people can "change their minds". Evaluative statements may reflect deep-seated social norms, but they may also be based on purely subjective, idiosyncratic preferences.

That also means they are in principle "negotiable", a phrase often found in variationally oriented forms of linguistics. What is actually negotiable, however, depends on how flexible members of the community are in the relevant situations – it should not be taken for granted that people are actually willing to negotiate on points that one would like to challenge, even when it is in principle feasible.

If successful, such a negotiation brings about a new situation in which participants' conscious evaluation of the relevant features are aligned, after having been different at the outset. We are all familiar with discussions featuring competing evaluative stances – discussions that arise in relation to things like political issues, practices in day care institutions, or food choice (is it wrong to eat meat, for instance?). These competing opinions exemplify norms in this type of ontological manifestation, as explicit mental content.

The operational aspect of norms is much less generally familiar and accepted. This is due to its ontological foundation as an aspect of the way things actually work, rather than as explicitly, consciously manifested opinions. We do not think about norms in this capacity for the same reason that we do not generally think actively about the law of gravity or the fact that the ground offers resistance when we set our feet on it.

Norms in this role were described by Durkheim (1893) as the stuff of which societies were made, and he tried to place them as closely as possible as parallels to laws of physical nature. A core topic for Durkheim was the condition of *anomie*, a condition in which the social universe is disintegrating because its normative foundations have eroded, with increasing suicide rates as one of the consequences.

In more recent times, Searle (1995) has proposed a theory of how social reality is constituted that also includes an account of the social mode of existence of norms. The centrepiece of his theory is the notion of "collective intentionality", whereby members of a community, acting together, can impose so-called "status functions" on features of the natural world – thereby endowing them with causal powers that they do not have by virtue of laws of nature. Thus, when democratic leaders are elected, they acquire new causal powers (i.e., of governmental decision-making). When a judge is appointed, she acquires the causal power to sentence people to jail. When someone is employed as a police officer, she acquires powers of arrest. When a river is assigned the status of border between two nations, crossing the river comes to have consequences over and above the consequences due to the physical properties of the river.

This is what makes possible the rise of cultural differences – and thus the existence of culture as something superimposed on nature. Non-human species live in an environment shaped entirely by natural laws (possibly with exceptions for certain species of primate). They may to some extent create their own environment – like beavers and leaf-cutter ants – but they do it by changing the physical environment, not by assigning additional causal powers to things beyond the causal powers they possess by natural laws.

Such humanly imposed status functions have causal impact via a different route than natural properties. Because they are social norms rather than physical laws, their causal power is inherently linked with a scale of values that determines what is socially right and what is socially wrong. Being a police officer is inherently bound up with norms for what a police officer can and should do. In this, the theory of status functions is compatible with Durkheim's theory of norms as the foundations of human society.

In this capacity, norms are aspects of the way the world, including society, works, and they constitute part of the causal structure which human beings adapt to, along with the causal structure associated with laws of nature. Examples include red and green lights, the penal code, and the rules of football, officially called "The Laws of the Game". Without such norms, there could be no society and no culture – and no football games.

A full account of how this additional, socially imposed layer of norms (or "laws") actually operates must include an account of the mechanisms of adaptation. Regardless of what precise theory of individual adaptive mechanisms one has, however, it is important to note that the force of social laws does not depend on the response (or evaluative stance) of the individual to whom the laws are applied. It is a ground rule of the penal code that ignorance of or disagreement with the law does not mean that the laws do not apply to you.

The mechanism by which adaptation works depends on the attunedness of human subjects towards joint activity. Young children identify with norms even before language acquisition (cp. Warneken & Tomasello 2006): adults are called to order if they deviate from the newly emerged rules of the ball game that adult and child are playing. This orientation toward community entails that being in a community means accepting the normative order according to which things work. If you play football by your own rules, you will be excluded from the collective game (or the game will disintegrate). That is a central factor in giving socially imposed laws a force that is analogous to that of physical laws.

3 Habitus and mental content

The discussion in the previous section raises the question of how social norms are represented in the individual, if they are not conscious mental content. In this context, I am going to rely on concepts introduced by Bourdieu (with occasional supplementary remarks) for my account of what this ontological theory implies for norms as aspects of social dynamics. Following Bourdieu (1977), I am going to stipulate that adaptation works essentially by response patterns ingrained in bodily reactions, rather than by explicit mental representations – the type of status that Bourdieu calls "habitus" (cf. "habituation" as an embodied response); Searle (1992: 177) uses the term "background". In human beings, habitus-based adaptation can be thought of as a feature shared with simpler organisms, with lesser degrees of mental awareness. At a basic level, all organisms accommodate to the world in which we live by embodied, physical adjustment.

Bourdieu (cf. Bourdieu & Passeron 1990) famously argued that the chief effect of education was habituation to a pattern of thinking imposed by the dominant class. Without wishing to eliminate the role of mental activity in education, one can still agree that there is a pervasive element of "getting used to" certain cultural practices in education. Its outcome is that you know how to act in certain types of situations – without necessarily being able to explain or justify the rationale of these practices (knowing *what* exactly it is all about).

An important point about this status is that once norms are embedded in operational practices and endowed with causal efficacy as part of such practices, such norms are not negotiable in the same sense that explicit agreements are negotiable. In claiming this, I am going against a pattern of thinking that is often invoked in discussing social constructions, whereby it is assumed that if something is socially constructed, we can agree to deconstruct it (after negotiating).

Since this is a crucial point, it is necessary to make clear what I understand by "negotiation" and what I think it means to be "negotiable". Negotiation in the sense intended refers strictly to concrete communicative events, localized in space and time, involving specific participants, with outcomes equally localizable in space and time. Thus, roughly speaking, negotiation occurs when A says to B, "how about we do it this way instead?", and B says "OK". This explicitly rules out an extension of the term to processes that include causal adjustments which are only indirectly related to explicit, conscious communication. I am thinking of processes whereby new institutional practices, even if they have been the subject of explicit discussion, only gradually emerge after a period of uncertainty – not in observance of a negotiated agreement, but as a consequence of social changes of which explicit discussion is only one element.

One reason for rejecting this extended sense of what is "negotiable" is that it is at risk of suggesting that it is easier to change undesirable social situations via linguistic communication than it actually is. Another reason is that such an extension would blur the distinction – crucial to my argument – between community-level and individual-level facts. In linguistics, a key example would be the difference between innovation and language change. Individuals can innovate in concrete situations, but they cannot change the language – not even by negotiating about it. There is a relation between innovation and change, but the relationship can only be described if we recognize that the two phenomena are different. Thus "negotiations" can feed into processes of social change, including language change, but they cannot do the trick on their own.

To take an argument from a different social practice: when you hand a ten-dollar bill across the counter, you cannot argue or interpret your way to endowing it with the status of a fifty-dollar bill – even if you persuade a shopkeeper to do you a favour by accepting it as such in a concrete transaction, effectively giving you a cut-price deal.

What you can do, however, is to set about changing the way the world works. Your evaluative stance may motivate you to do that – the point is that it will not do the job on its own. If you want to change the value of money, you have to go via the whole monetary system. If you want to change the role of police officers, you have to change the way law enforcement works. And if you want to change the way languages operate, and the status assigned to different forms of language, you have to find a way to change the way the whole community interacts by linguistic means. This is not impossible, of course; changes occur all the time. But they involve processes that are different from, and more complex than explicit negotiation between parties with different positions. A linguistic example of this complexity is the distinction between the roles of "innovators" and "early adopters" in bringing about linguistic change, cf. Milroy and Milroy (1985: 367), which is not reducible to "let's do this" negotiation.

When I say that social norms are not negotiable, a natural objection is to say that in democratic societies all changes are subject to negotiation. This is of course true – what I point out is that it is not the negotiation itself that brings about the change. Anyone who has been in even the humblest position of power will recognize the following experience: An issue arises that calls for action; you take it up, discuss it with all relevant parties, make a proposal, take it through the proper channels and in the end have your plan approved – and then (if you are new and inexperienced) you think that the matter has been satisfactorily taken care of. To your dismay, you then find that the world goes on exactly as before. What you have then discovered is that for the world to start working differently, explicit agreement is only a beginning: somebody has to change the causal operations in order for even the most consensual and well-thought-out agreement to change the way the world works.

In the best possible case, agreement in each individual *mind* will trigger a *causal change* in the way each individual responds to cases that are affected by the change. It is in principle possible – and we may even agree that this is the way it *should* work among adult, responsible people. But if you assume social norms are negotiable, you are in fact assuming that it works that way one hundred per cent of the time. In the real world, however, negotiation does not have the power to change social norms.

The difference between what is *negotiable* and what is *changeable* can also be brought out by comparing social change with physical change. When Peter the Great of Russia wanted a new capital city bordering on the Baltic, he was faced with the problem that the area was a vast and impenetrable swamp. This was a physical fact and as such not negotiable; no amount of negotiation would in itself bring about a change whereby a city could be built on the site. But although this was not a negotiable fact, it was *changeable*. The Tsar commanded the necessary number of conscripts, convicts and prisoners to dry out the swamp, sink tree trunks into the ground and do whatever was required for preparing the ground for construction. Thousands of people died in the process, but the change was made.

Social change, I argue, has the same causal structure. In democratic societies you can negotiate your way to a conscious decision – but the necessary next step is to change the way the world actually works by a causal implementation procedure. A community of people whose habitus is adapted to a particular set of practices is no more amenable to change by negotiation alone than the swamps that used to occupy the site that is now St. Petersburg.[2]

4 The community level and the individual level – and evolutionary change

The nature of the distinction between the community level and the individual level is essential to understanding the role of norms. The norms associated with the legal system are a feature of the community – not a property of the individual.

It has been a source of mystification where precisely community-level, collective features are found. Especially in the heyday of the cognitive era, one often found statements to the effect that social facts are essentially part of individual minds – because it would be very mysterious if one thought of them as somehow floating around outside people's heads. However, an alternative proposal that has not been widely recognized is that social laws are something that exists only in configurations comprising *more than one* individual mind.

This ontological account shares the insight that if norms did not exist in individual minds, they could not exist at all. But it differs from the individual-based account in pointing explicitly to the role of the community of minds, over and above the content of the individual mind. As an illustration of why this makes a difference, it may be pointed out that this explains why the version of the norm that is embedded in an individual's cognitive system may be *wrong* – because something has gone amiss in the individual's adaptation to the collective norm. Similarly, one cannot destroy a norm by mucking about with an individual mind.

The two levels are linked up by a mechanism of adaptation, as described above, in which the social environment exerts the same kind of adaptive pressures as the physical environment. This is essential to understanding mechanisms of *change*. As in the biological world of mutations, the same laws do not always yield precisely the same concrete outcomes. The way a judge applies the laws of the land may depend on many things, including whether it is before or after lunch (cf. Kahneman 2011). In the legal system, we speak of "precedents"

---

[2] Changes in linguistic and other social practices can be, if not brought about, then spurred on by being addressed explicitly, and may also, in the right circumstances, happen quickly. As an example, when news of the holocaust became public at the end of World War II, it caused a revulsion that rendered (virtually instantly) certain ways of speaking about Jews (which had until then been culturally widespread and well-entrenched) unacceptable across the whole western world.

which are part of the system and which eventually may give rise to changes in the law itself.

The existence of this built-in link between individual-level facts and community-level facts, including a mechanism for change, however, does not mean that one can reduce community-level facts to individual facts and accordingly see them as being in a constant state of flux. Eckert rightly points out that "convention is not a thing but a process" (Eckert 2000: 45), but it does not follow that we cannot speak of convention as existing apart from the ongoing flow. At any given time, there is a state of co-ordination in the community that specifies "how to say things". This state of co-ordination includes variational patterns – but if it did not at the same time allow people to say things in a way recognized across the community, there would not be any speech community (cf. Labov's 1972 definition of the speech community, as discussed by Fabricius, this volume).

Another way of making the same point is that causal factors applying at the individual level and causal factors that bring about change at the community level work on two different time scales. You can cause linguistic change in an individual by making him drink a bottle of whisky, giving rise to "slurred" manifestations of speech sounds, but this will not change the language at community level. For change to take place at community level, more is required – and more *time* is required. The community-level "laws" are *in force*, at the same time as they are *undergoing change* – the two properties are not in contradiction.

Another factor that serves to emphasize the ontological separateness of the community as more than a simple aggregation of individuals is the fact that it is the community that is the source of language change. Labov (2014) illustrates this by reference to the developmental patterns in American English, where a crucial factor is cultural orientation, rather than assumptions based on geographical patterns or density of interaction. New generations do not retain their parents' variety, nor a mixture emerging from who they happen to interact with – they base their speech on the cultural community they identify with.

As we saw above, operational (and hence causally efficacious) norms trigger adaptation, internalized as "habitus" in individual speakers. These may also give rise to explicit internal representations, including representations of values associated with such norms. However, the causal efficacy of such explicit mental representations is far less certain than that of mechanisms of adaptation driven by exposure to the way the world actually works (more on this is section 6). When a rigidly traditional society begins to change, one thing that may happen is that community members become aware of the norms that are beginning to lose their status as unchallenged aspects of the way the world works, and become explicit adherents of them, rather than living automatically by them. They then lose the status of *doxa* ("habituated" norms) and become *orthodoxy* – and that makes them more vulnerable, according to Bourdieu (1977). What works invisibly is simply fact – what is voiced explicitly can be challenged.

5 Norms, variation – and prestige

As mentioned above, norms are often understood as monolithic: X counts as Y, period. However, actually social norms reflect the differentiation inherent in societies: X counts as Y in context C (cp. Searle 1969). Significant *variational* patterns are thus part of the *normative* system – while random variation ("fluctuation") is not norm-sensitive (and that is why it is not significant).

More foundationally, the concept of "variation" makes sense only against the background of a shared system: the zero variant of post-vocalic (–r) would be nothing at all if it did not belong in a system that also included positive variants (cp. Labov 1972). This is also what makes it possible for individual human speakers to recognize *floor* pronounced as [flɔː] as manifesting a zero variant of (–r).

As a by-product of variation, however, complex societies tend to differentiate into practices with higher vs. lower social "rating", cp. Bourdieu (1984) on "distinction". This is reflected in terms like "high culture" and "haute cuisine" – and in language, it is reflected in the form of variation that distinguishes "prestige norms" from "community norms", and also diglossic systems into "H" and "L".

Prestige norms are an add-on to the norms underpinning the linguistic system (e.g., the norm specifying that *cow* means 'cow'). Prestige norms are not necessary for social structure to be possible – and therefore we might in principle be better off without them (at least from a consensual Danish social-democratic point of view). Unfortunately, prestige norms nevertheless tend to sneak in with the same causal anchoring as the norms that are constitutive of human speech communities.

As all sociolinguists are keenly aware, prestige norms are the subject of intense evaluative ("attitudinal") attention. This goes for both sociolinguists and language users in general. One may have a positive attitude to a prestige variant ("good English") or a negative attitude, as do most sociolinguists ("a dialect with an army and a navy"). Evaluative attitudes, however, as we have seen, do not exhaust the topic: a full understanding of what is going on must include the operational (factual, constitutive) aspect.

Crucially, Bourdieu-style "distinction" is a social, community-level fact, not an individual evaluative attitude. The "prestige structure" of a given community is the way it is, regardless of the attitudes you and I may have – just as the law is independent of what we think. For the same reason, the prestige structure may change, just as the law may change – but on a different time scale than the causal patterns of individual usage events.

6 The dissociation between overt attitudes and "subconscious" responses

Kristiansen's (2009) investigations of language attitudes reflect the double nature of linguistic norms. On the basis of experimental studies, he found there was a systematic discrepancy between the forms that Danish informants subconsciously oriented towards as prestigious forms of Danish and the forms that they explicitly liked best (evaluative attitude). In the terminology I have used above, "subconscious" responses reflect the "operational norms" that drive community-level patterns of language change, while overt attitudes correspond to evaluative norms, i.e. "opinions". Kristiansen's used two methods to elicit responses from his participants:

One involved an evaluation of voices in terms of personality traits, which was used to elicit "subconscious" norms. This type of evaluation is familiar from matched-guise-type experiments (cp. Gardner & Lambert 1972), in which a "bi-dialectal" speaker records two versions of the same text, one for each variety, and informants are then asked to evaluate the speaker purely based on listening to such recordings. The findings typically show a recognizable differential profile, so that the recording of the high-status form elicits one set of properties, and the vernacular form a different set. Thus, when a speaker uses the high-status form, he is rated as intelligent and well-educated but perhaps a bit stuck-up, and when he uses his local voice, he is rated as a regular guy, but perhaps not so well-educated and intelligent. In Kristiansen's study, the key cluster of properties is the cluster called "dynamism", which consists of the features "self-assured", "cool", "fascinating" and "nice".

The other method of elicitation involved a "label ranking" task, designed to elicit explicit attitudes, in which informants were simply asked to state which language form they liked best.

It would take us too far to go into the details of this very sophisticated study, but the parameter along which there was a clear dissociation, especially in terms of "dynamism", was the distinction between attitudes to the local form as opposed to the de facto country-wide "modern Copenhagen" form (associated with the capital of Denmark). The basic feature of the pattern found was that the conscious, mentally represented evaluation favoured the local variety, whereas the "subconscious" evaluation that was reflected in responses to the matched guise elicitation ranked the modern Copenhagen variety highest.

The key point for the purposes of this chapter is the double dissociation: You can have conscious attitudes that conflict with your subconscious normative orientation. Even if you may like the local form best, your responses rate the modern Copenhagen norm as more fascinating, cool and nice, and accordingly the Copenhagen norm is what determines the direction of change in the group to which you belong. This norm constitutes the only driver of language change in Denmark.

On two points, my discussion of this dissociation goes beyond what I can cite Kristiansen for, at least terminologically. The first has to do with his use of the term "attitude"; the second with his use of the term "ideology".

Kristiansen distinguishes between conscious and subconscious *attitudes*. I would like to offer an interpretation according to which the responses to the personality trait questions do not unambiguously reflect individual attitudes, but also (or perhaps even primarily) an assessment of social *status*. What the study shows is that the modern Copenhagen form is subconsciously rated by the informants, correctly as it happens, as the form that has the social *status* of being "cool" and "fascinating" (etc.). This is not a case of an individual attitude but an assessment of a social fact. For the same reason, an informant might also *consciously* rate this form as having the status of being "cool" while (also consciously) disliking it.

To avoid confusion, the existence of two senses of the word 'status' should perhaps be addressed explicitly here: the technical sense I introduced above, as in 'status functions', and the everyday sense as found in the collocation 'status symbol'. The everyday sense, however, is a special case of the technical sense: Both the status of being a policeman (the 'status function' sense) and the status of being 'cool' (the 'status symbol' sense) are imposed on their bearers by social consensus. The two senses are seamlessly aligned in the case of prestige. Prestige is not essentially a matter of subjective evaluation, but a matter of social fact. It is unfortunately a fact, for instance, that the humanities, and especially the language courses, currently have low prestige, and are not rated as "cool" in the contemporary Zeitgeist. I recognize this, but I like them nevertheless.

This also implies that there need be no hypocrisy involved in the dissociation – just as there is no hypocrisy involved in obeying the law even if you wished that the law was different. Adaptive pressures cannot be lightly disregarded in favour of standing up for your explicit attitudes at all times. The dynamics of evolution illustrate the advantages of adapting. Professional language advice must reflect an awareness of this type of complexity. It is not always good advice to tell people to "say things in your own way". The causal power of social norms is reflected in selection pressures: a high percentage of job applications may be rejected because of violations of spelling conventions, for instance.

If this is assumed, it has one key implication for the place of overt, conscious attitudes of sociolinguists to linguistic norms in the way the world works: They have essentially no role in shaping the actual speech patterns in the community. "Distinction" (including prestige in relation to language) is assigned by a different causal pathway than the one that starts from explicit and overt attitudes. Even if you could persuade *everybody* to dislike the prestige form, a study analogous to the one discussed above might in principle show that people continued to adapt to the operational prestige pattern in the community.

The two-sided nature of norms also has implications for the understanding of a number of other issues that play a role in critical studies, some of which have been intertwined with the language aspect discussed above. In the following, I attempt to demonstrate the implications for the understanding of the key term *ideology*.

Ideology is closely associated with the discussion of prestige norms in language, since language forms have historically been bound up with ideological formations of various kinds. In direct continuation of the discussion above, Kristiansen regards the dissociation discussed above as involving a contrast between "overt" and "covert" ideology – two conflicting value systems for what language forms are "best". It follows from what I have said about attitudes in the previous section that I think there is an additional dimension in this picture. What is at stake is not solely or even primarily the existence of two discrepant *evaluations* in the minds of the informants, but rather the existence of a community-wide *status* assignment whose existence does not essentially depend on whether an individual informant agrees or not. For that reason, one cannot automatically assume that the word *ideology* applies in the same way at the two levels.

The primary mode of existence of status differences, as argued above, is their embedding in interactive practices in the community. Thus, a standard form is anchored in practices that designate this form as the *appropriate* form for the kind of practices that are associated with official prestige (government, university education, legal documents) etc. Such a status is analogous to a dress code, which may or may not reflect what actual wearers think is the best way to dress. Thus, assessments of standard forms as being associated with being well-educated and possibly a bit stuck up can be understood as stereotypes associated with the kind of people who are standardly involved in such linguistic practices – or, analogously, dressing practices –cp. the book title *Pinstriped parasites*.

Like all off-the-cuff assessments, such judgements reflect social reality imperfectly, in the form of stereotypes and heuristics rather than precise theories about the world. This mode of existence suggests that such judgments would probably not long survive the actual practices that sustain these stereotypes. They do not essentially reflect personal values – although there is a tendency for attitudes to be subject to adaptive pressures as well (thus avoiding cognitive dissonance).

When Kristiansen speaks of "covert" ideology, I would interpret what he refers to as constituting the reflection in individual minds of the normative system that is built into community practices. It thus constitutes a "state of adaptation" to the appropriateness criteria that determine selection pressures in the community. Like all states of adaptation, these are basically not conscious, mental content. However, they can be brought into consciousness, for instance when they are violated – hence the term "subconscious". They thus reflect, albeit only roughly, the way the world is, rather than an individual subject's *opinion* about it. Standard English occupies a certain position in the way the world works, as reflected for example in social stereotypes – whether we like it or not.

7 Norms in emergent communities

The dual role of norms is most naturally understood in relation to communities that are "going concerns". In the context of this volume, however, several chapters focus on communities that are both emergent and transient. The force of the points made above may be less obvious, especially in the case of constitutive or operational norms, when the community in question has not really constituted itself, and the norms are therefore not (yet) operational.

One facet of this type of situation can be captured in terms of what Searle calls the "direction of fit": rather than being a matter of categorizing existing phenomena correctly, an important role for norms is to present themselves as potential aspects of the *strategy* that members can pursue in order to bring a well-functioning community into being – a "directive" rather than a "descriptive" function. In this case, too, an awareness of the role of norms as building blocks of human communities is essential.

A famous example is the rise of communities of slaves in the Americas. Slaveholders had the strategy of putting together slaves with different native languages in order to prevent seditious communication among them. In this situation, creating a shared set of linguistic norms for how to say things is a pre-condition for getting a speech community on its feet. It would be understandable if each individual preferred for their own language to be the shared norm – but if this gave rise to protests against attempts to set up a community norm, motivated by the inalienable right of each individual to speak their own language, no speech community would be possible. This illustrates the enabling rather than the restrictive role of norms.

Even if this is recognized, it is not obvious how an emergent situation can be reconciled with the law-like, causally efficacious status of constitutive norms, which I emphasized above in order to clarify the difference in relation to evaluative statements of personal attitudes. It follows from the "directive" direction of fit, however, that the law-like status is not a present fact, but in the target situation. The strategy of getting a community on its feet implies that the aim is to get operational norms in place, so that the community gets in "working order". So potential constitutive norms are indeed negotiable in the emergent situation – but the aim must be to get beyond that stage. For international student groups, for example, this implies that routines for studying together are in place, so that the groups can achieve their educational aims without spending all their time on discussing how to go about it.

This process, however, is not something that jells once and for all. New questions of how to go about things will continue to arise, and in the process, speakers may invoke a spectrum of norms, which again involves differential takes on actual contexts of speech, cf. Silverstein (2003) on "orders of indexicality". As pointed out by Silverstein, such choices may over time lead to changes in the normative order, also in relatively stable communities – but that takes us back to the different time scales of individual situational choice vis-à-vis social change.

In the emergent situation, this implies that there is no way to tell an emergent constitutive norm from a statement of personal evaluative preference. The only way this can be handled is via the awareness of the members of the different potentials that are involved. There has to be a discussion motivated by the awareness of the enabling potential of norms.

In the following, I am going to attempt to illustrate this in relation to empirical cases discussed in later chapters of this volume (plus an example of my own, involving educational "inclusion"). I am well aware that my interpretations are at risk of being forced and ignoring most of what is going on – they should be understood only as illustrations of the point I wish to make.

An issue that illustrates the importance of distinguishing between the two roles for normative assumptions in emergent communities is the case of national stereotypes, cf. Kraft and Mortensen (this volume). Such stereotypes are classic bogeymen in the critical tradition, direct hindrances to universal humanism. One might expect that the only way for a new-established community to emerge unscathed would be to put all such childish things behind them. However, once again, that would be a bad way to understand what happens in such situations. As all linguists can testify, national stereotypes are a staple feature of cross-cultural conference communication after the working day is over.

The crucial question is how they are used in such situations. They may be a starting point for exchanging information about different customs and traditions, feeling your way mutually towards a sense of who the "other" is. Typically, a bit later down the road, they may serve as a resource for joking and getting a rise out of each other in situations where it is now felt to be safe to do so. This may be regarded as a process of "constitutive hybridisation": what emerges is a person who is at the same time alien (e.g., by being a Swede and not a Norwegian), but who is also becoming "our Swede", a person with a status in the community that depends on the history of discursive construction in the group that cannot be reduced to stereotypical national attributes.

This constitutive use of such normative attributions contrasts sharply with cases where they are used as a source of evaluative, especially negative judgments. As also exemplified in the chapter by Kraft and Mortensen (this volume), this is immediately felt to be an entirely different thing, which is rightly the source of consternation in the community. Without a distinction between constructive build-up of a normative frame of reference and a hostile imposition of alien normativity, this could not be captured. And this would be the case if the only conceptualization was one based on the eminently deconstructible ideological content of national stereotypes.

A normative issue that illustrates the problematic relation between the evaluative and the constitutive role of norms is the question of showing up on time. As empirically demonstrated by Hazel and Lønsmann (this volume), this question may enter into a wider context of socialization, more specifically labour market integration for members of immigrant communities. Let me begin by drawing on my experience as a teacher to illustrate the significance of this as a potential operational and constitutive norm. Teachers are familiar with the gap between learning outcomes in classes in which a norm of being on time becomes operational and in classes where such a norm never takes hold. This also demonstrates the force of Bourdieu's distinction between "doxa" and "orthodoxy": when being on time is a matter of "orthodoxy", it is a far less efficacious state of affairs than when it is an embodied regulatory mechanism that operates without the need for explicit articulation.[3]

In Hazel and Lønsmann's examples, it appears that the situation is one in which being on time is not even particularly orthodox, but is most saliently manifested as evaluative normativity, in the form of negative normative admonitions from teachers. Hazel and Lønsmann rightly point to the relationship between this situation and societal discourses and ideologies for low-paid workers who (unlike highly paid academic workers) always have to start work on time. The lack of direct causal relationships between norms as conscious and explicit evaluations and norms as working practices is particularly striking here – and something that all teachers know from their own experience.

---

[3] I am indebted to Dorte Lønsmann for this observation.

In trying to capture the mode of existence of norms in emergent situations, the notion of "construct resource" (cf. Fabricius & Mortensen 2013; Fabricius, this volume) provides an illuminating approach. A construct resource is

> a mediator between the domain of linguistic practice and emergent linguistic ideology. We define construct resources as ideological postulates about language variation and social meaning, which emerge historically and circulate in society . . . It is located firmly within the domain of language ideology, but emergent in interaction and sometimes crystallized into metalinguistic talk. (Fabricius & Mortensen 2013: 375–376)

Fabricius (this volume) describes a striking case of a construct resource for the use of [r] forms, the trilled and the tapped variants. While the tap is still an extant (albeit conservative and declining) variant, this is less clear for the trill; but there is still a normative aura around it that enables it to serve as a living normative construct, indicating a speech practice associated with what was from a Conservative point of view "the good old days". This was demonstrated when Geoffrey Cox, attorney general, addressed the conservative party conference in a speech liberally studded with conservative variants, which ensured an enthusiastic welcome. Strikingly, however, when he used the same speech style facing an adversarial audience in the House of Commons, the reception was extremely hostile.

The association between Cox's choice of speech forms and classic conservative values was not a law-like force in the community, but something much less well-entrenched. While the Conservative Party might wish for this to be part of the constitutive norms in emerging post-Brexit Britain, it turned into part of the battle, unleashing very unfavourable evaluative normativity. As indicated by the term "construct resource", it is something available for being used, and as such neutral between the potential statuses that norms may come to have – the defining feature is the "ideological" content, while its community status depends on the context of use.

A particular subtype of "emergent" groups is the one in which the explicit (possibly political) aim is to replace an existing norm set with a different set of norms. Those who support this aim are treating the new set of norms as the desired target of a process of emergence – with a top-down agenda attached. The key shared feature is that there are potential norms which are viewed with a "directive" rather than a "descriptive" relation to established practice.

A case in point is the problem of educational "inclusion". Inclusive education is a widespread ideal (to which I personally subscribe), contrasting with divisive class-based education systems. A successful implementation of this ideal entails that students from different backgrounds and with different abilities learn together. The specific case below involves a much-discussed Danish educational measure whereby students with special issues (learning or behavioural challenges) were "included" in normal classrooms, after a period in which an increasing share of students had been assigned to special schools or classes. The distinction between explicit normative attitudes and operational norms is relevant for a full understanding of what such a measure entails.

Attitude problems occur when individual stakeholders (students, parents or teachers) have conscious objections against accepting people that deviate from the in-group stereotype and want to enforce an existing distinction between "us" and "them" based on such objections. Attitude problems can be handled (at least in principle) by explicit arguments and policies, potentially leading stakeholders to accept what at first they did not want. However, inclusion, if it is to become a reality, needs to address the level of operational community practices – including operational norms in the classroom. This means that in the envisaged target situation, newcomers must be part of operational interactive patterns with equal rights and opportunities. This entails that there is an issue of what it takes to ensure that such practices become (and remain) operational – otherwise inclusion cannot succeed. Whether that happens depends not only on attitudes, but also and crucially on achieved participation in the relevant interactive practices.

Hence, it is not enough to require that existing communities have inclusive attitudes – there also has to be a strategy for adapting practices in ways that promise to allow both sides to join in the new enlarged community. A polarized approach, stressing what must be required of one side over the other, is counterproductive in such contexts. It is not fruitful to discuss *who* has to adapt – the essential realization is that *all* parties have to enter into the process of creating a new workable set of norms and corresponding practices. Negotiation is a necessary component at the stage of explicit agreement, but it is never enough – it has to be accompanied by mutual adjustment-in-action. For that reason, it is dangerous to see the inclusion issue as one of attitudes only. Even the most inclusion-positive teachers will not be able make a success of inclusion if resources are such that teachers are defenceless against regular incidents of violence by newly "included" students, as has happened in some cases.

A special case of the same issue is inclusion of marginalized groups especially when coupled with issues of identity politics. A distinction may be made between two versions of identity politics, the "expansive" vs. the "prohibitive" version. In the "expansive" version, the aim is inclusion of a marginalized group in the community (in the operational sense). This version is addressable in the way described above, requiring both positive attitudes (on the individual level) and the building of new interactive norms-and-practices by mutual adjustment (on the collective level).

Sometimes, however, this aim (which most people would support, at least on the explicit evaluative level) has an admixture of something which is more problematic – which brings us to the "prohibitive" version. It occurs when the strategy of the marginalized group involves imposing their own rules on the majority. From the point of view of the marginalized group, the difference between the versions may be hard to detect; after all, both require the majority to change their ways. They differ, however, when it comes to the issue of mutual adjustment.

In the expansive version, the outsiders ask the majority to change their ways to the extent it is necessary in order to make room for newcomers – e.g., to extend marriage regulations to include same-sex couples, without requiring the majority to do things differently. In the prohibitive version, the marginalized group requires the majority to give up existing practices because they want to impose their own rules on the majority. A much-discussed example in Denmark is that of a non-white student who objected to the practice of singing a traditional Danish song because it metaphorically construed the generic "Danish song" as a young, blond girl (which made the student feel excluded). In such a case, a demand made by a minority representative in the name of *diversity*, somewhat paradoxically involves *prohibiting* an existing practice. The alternative, "expansive" approach would be to ask for *new* songs to be included in the curriculum. I think the latter is strategically a more promising avenue. If inclusion of a minority demands that existing practices be prohibited, it is a problematic start for the build-up of a new shared community.

8 Conclusion

I have argued that we need to distinguish more consistently between norms viewed as the source of individual, conscious attitudes, and norms as part of community-level social reality. What tends to be overlooked is the role of norms as part of the fabric of social reality. Even norms that are not in themselves constitutive may have the status of being part of reality, rather than mental attitudes in individual minds. This applies to what may roughly be called prestige norms, or (in Bourdieu's terms) norms imposing "distinction" on certain practices as opposed to others.

While we as speakers or as sociolinguists may like or dislike such norms, they exist as part of the reality we all live in and to some extent adapt our practices to. Thus, they bring about a correlative in individual subjects whose basic mode of being is to be "habitus" rather than explicit mental content. One of the consequences is that individuals may, at the level of "habitus", adapt to norms that they do not subscribe to at the level of evaluative normativity. Although this may appear to be a form of hypocrisy, it merely reflects a built-in complexity in the life form of human beings: being hyper-social animals, we cannot ignore the rules that the community plays by, even if our personal preferences never coincide completely with them. As discussed above, it would be unfair to class as hypocrisy the fact that people most of the time tend to obey (=adapt to) the law even in cases where they do not agree with it.

In cases when individual subjects are habituated to norms that they consciously dislike, research designs of the kind found in Kristiansen (2009) can bring to light a dissociation between conscious and "subconscious" normative orientation in such speakers. The status of the subconscious norms as part of operational social reality is reflected in the fact that they, rather than conscious normative attitudes, are what drives language change (which is a form of adaptation).

Community-level norms are not eternal. They change for a variety of reasons, some of which arise from individual variation among speakers. Even in such cases, however, we cannot reduce the two levels to one: the conditions under which individual changes ultimately cause changes at community level depend on community factors, not on features of individuals.

The same duality can be argued to play a role in phenomena other than language, and I argued that a heightened awareness of it can enhance understanding of ideology and phenomena like inclusion and identity politics. In the context of strategies for bringing about a change in normative orientation, an essential point is that addressing conscious mental attitudes is not sufficient. A strategy for making the world a better place has to include an agenda for changing those community-level patterns that drive adaptive pressures (as exemplified by desegregation in schools in the US).

In emergent cases, the distinction between the evaluative and the constitutive role of norms is essential for understanding the path towards a working community. Here, the primary issue is not to tell them apart – because in emergent groups everything is more or less up for grabs. Rather the issue is how to make use of potentially useful "construct resources" in such a way that the community acquires the best possible foundations for pursuing whatever aims brought members together.

References

Bourdieu, Pierre. 1977. *Outline of a theory of practice*. Translation with revisions of *Esquisse d'une théorie de la pratique, précédé de trois études d'ethnologie kabyle*, Librairie Droz [1972]. Cambridge: Cambridge University Press.

Bourdieu, Pierre. 1984. *Distinction. A social critique of the judgement of taste*. Translation by Richard Nice of *La distinction, Critique sociale du jugement*. Paris: Les editions du minuit. [1979]. New York and London: Routledge

Bourdieu, Pierre & Jean-Claude Passeron. 1990. *Reproduction in education, society and culture*. London: Sage.
Durkheim, Émile. 1996 [1893]. *De la division du travail social*. Paris: Quadrige/Presses Universitaires de France.
Eckert, Penelope. 2000. *Linguistic variation as social practice. The linguistic construction of identity in Belten High*. Oxford: Blackwell.
Fabricius, Anne & Janus Mortensen. 2013. Language ideology and the notion of 'construct resource': a case study of modern RP. In Tore Kristiansen & Stef Grondelaars (eds.), *Language (de)standardisation in Late Modern Europe: Experimental studies*, 375–402. Oslo: Novus forlag.
Gardner, Robert C. & Wallace E. Lambert. 1972. *Attitudes and motivation in second-language learning*. Rowley: Newbury House.
Itkonen, Esa. 2008. The central role of normativity for language and linguistics. In Jordan Zlatev, Timothy P. Racine, Chris Sinha & Esa Itkonen (eds.), *The shared mind: Perspectives on intersubjectivity*, 279–305. Amsterdam: John Benjamins.
Kahnemann, Daniel. 2011. *Thinking, fast and slow*. London: Penguin.
Kristiansen, T. 2009. The macro-social meaning of late-modern Danish accents. In *Acta Linguistica Hafniensia* 41. 167–192.
Labov, William. 1972. *Sociolinguistic patterns*. Philadelphia: University of Pennsylvania Press.
Labov, William. 2014. What is to be learned: The community as the focus of social cognition. In Martin Pütz, Justyna A. Robinson and Monika Reif (eds.), *Cognitive sociolinguistics: Social and cultural variation in cognition and language use*, 23–51. Amsterdam: John Benjamins.
Milroy, James & Lesley Milroy. 1985. Linguistic change, social network and speaker innovation. *Journal of Linguistics* 21 (2): 339–84.
Milroy, James & Leslie Milroy. 1991. *Authority in language*, 2nd edn. London: Routledge.
Searle, John.R. 1969. *Speech acts*. Cambridge: Cambridge University Press.
Searle, John R. 1992. *The rediscovery of the mind*. Cambridge: MIT Press.
Searle, John R.1995. *The construction of social reality*. Harmondsworth: Penguin.
Silverstein, Michael. 2003. Indexical order and the dialectics of sociolinguistic life. *Language & Communication* 23 (3–4), 193–229.
Warneken, Felix & Michael Tomasello. 2006. Altruistic helping in human infants and young chimpanzees. *Science* 311 (5765). 1301–1303.

Spencer Hazel and Dorte Lønsmann
3 Norms, accountability and socialisation in a refugee language classroom

1 Introduction

Social groups such as geographically or socially delimited communities, workplaces and families evidence particular dominant patterns of thought and behaviour across the group. These patterns take on a normative character, with particular instances of conduct treated as variably converging to or diverging from the dominant, model patterns in evidence within the group. In this way, such social norms allow members to evaluate instances of conduct for appropriacy. Where such norms are assumed to be shared by members of a community, they function as taken-for-granted background expentancies that do not require being verbalised. When all participants in a social event are presumed to share the same norms, these are only made explicit in the interaction when there is an orientation to them being violated.

However, in some contexts, norms for social conduct come to the forefront of social interaction. When there is a presupposition that participants do not share the same social norms, talk about norms or indeed socialisation into a particular set of norms may come to occupy a more prominent position in the interaction. The Second Language classroom that we consider in this chapter is one such interactional setting. The students in our dataset are recently arrived refugees in Denmark, participating in a "Danish at work" course. They arrive in the country with a multitude of linguistic and cultural backgrounds, and are *a priori* regarded by gate-keeping authorities as requiring instruction not just in the Danish language but also in local cultural and social norms, and in particular knowledge about the Danish labour market (Ministry of Immigration and Integration 2016). Thus, the teachers in our study have been tasked with the joint aims of instructing the students in the Danish language and preparing them for entry into the Danish workforce.

In situations like this, where participants come together from diverse sociocultural backgrounds, and where students and teachers have very different epistemic rights and institutional positions, talk about social norms comes to the forefront as part of the mandated integration guidance that takes place in the classroom. The dual focus on language learning and teaching of Danish workplace culture

Acknowledgements: We would like to thank Katherine Kappa, Kamilla Kraft and Janus Mortensen for their input to this work during discussions within the TMC project team, and Sirin Eissa, Ida Moth Kej and Solvej Helleshøj Sørensen for invaluable assistance with transcriptions and translations.

https://doi.org/10.1515/9781501511882-003

means that socialisation into classroom norms also becomes an occasion for instructing students in perceived societal norms.

In the current study, our aim is twofold. First, we investigate how students, while attending Danish language classes, are also socialised into norms for appropriate conduct in the classroom setting. Drawing on audio and video recordings of classroom interaction, we analyse episodes where participants explicitly invoke norms for social conduct. The examples we draw on in this chapter all concern conduct around timekeeping and punctuality. We focus on instances where participants orient to a particular action as a deviation from the norms of classroom participation and membership. By focusing on breaches of norms and how participants account for or are made to account for such deviations, we direct attention to the role of "norm talk" as a site of socialisation in the classroom setting and beyond.

Secondly, the analysis also highlights how teachers link norms for classroom participation with students' future participation and belonging in the wider societal context. We are interested in how the interactional setting of a Second Language classroom is used to school students not just in language, but also in other elements of what is deemed socially acceptable behaviour for an imagined future workplace. This leads to a consideration of how the negotiation of norms in local social settings mediates between the immediate interactional context and perceived societal norms and ideologies for the host nation, here Denmark. Finally, the discussion focuses on the study of norms as a way of foregrounding processes of boundary-making, inclusion and exclusion in interaction.

2 Norms and accountability

The normative order underlying much of human behaviour is rarely verbalised. The rules for social conduct are presupposed to be shared, and are therefore to a large extent left unspoken. In this way, a social norm functions as a "scheme of interpretation" (Garfinkel 1967), a kind of "grid" that participants orient to when evaluating social action. In other words, social norms function as landmarks with respect to which social action becomes intelligible, and these "[s]ocial norms account for the orderliness of social life" (Gafaranga & Torras 2001: 198). The existence of norms and the concomitant orderliness does not mean that norms are always followed. But it does mean that people's actions are treated by themselves and others as normatively accountable (Drew 1998). What we refer to as norms in this chapter, Garfinkel (1964: 225) has theorised as making up a social group's moral order:

[A] society's members encounter and know the moral order as perceivedly normal courses of action – familiar scenes of everyday affairs, the world of daily life known in common with others and with others taken for granted.

This understanding highlights the dimension of moral accountability pertaining to norms. When participants choose between alternative courses of action, they consider the normative accountabilities related to these trajectories. In other words, participants are usually aware that if they transgress a norm, they will be held accountable (by themselves and others).

Empirical approaches to the study of morality and moral order as discoverable in social interactional settings have gained ground over recent years. Bergmann (1998) identifies two strands of research on morality and interaction. One strand investigates members' descriptions of moral conduct and of societal actors implicated as (im)moral beings. This strand seeks to address how moral evaluative accounts are produced in interaction (e.g. Aronsson & Cederborg 2012; Potter & Hepburn 2012; Stokoe & Edwards 2012), with the research homing in on the moral reasoning found in such accounts as well as the work of producing them.

A second strand looks to explicate the moral order of interaction itself. This describes how members orient to local interactional conduct as orderly and accountable, and transgressions from the "present but unnoticed organizing properties of talk and action" (Jayyusi 1991: 242) as deviating from a particular perceived moral orderliness, and as potentially open to censure (e.g. Niemi 2016; Niemi & Bateman 2015). For example, looking at classroom interaction, Mortensen and Hazel (2011) show how in cases where a student oversteps the boundaries of turn allocation in a round robin classroom activity, a breach may lead to explicit apologies, accounts for the breach and mitigating conduct such as embodied displays of having committed a faux pas, including laughter tokens and smiling. Elsewhere, Ekström (2009) investigates the accounts made by politicians who have refused to answer a journalist's question, and as such have transgressed against the norm of the interview setting. Such accounts do moral work by providing a basis for evaluating the "rightness" or "wrongness" of whatever action has triggered the account (Drew 1998: 295). Accounts also do social work. They contribute to upholding norms by signalling that transgressions of norms require explanation (Heritage 1988: 140). In this way, accounts contribute to maintaining social orderliness, and like other types of actions, are also in themselves accountable, and may be treated as appropriate and inappropriate.

In any social activity (e.g. sports, games, meetings), deviating from a social norm for how one is expected to conduct oneself can be treated by members of the group as socially transgressive. Relevant here is Bergmann's (1998: 288) work, where he notes how "moral activities frequently are mitigated, covered, and neutralized or are positioned within a nonserious humorous or ironic frame". This demonstrates the consequentiality of appearing to breach the local orderliness of an interaction, and the potential negative impact that this can have on members' moral standing among their peers. Indeed, this can lead to peer-exclusion and possible categorisation as out-group member (Niemi & Bateman 2015). Moments where a breach occurs are a useful resource for the analyst, as they provide a window into the practices that the participants treat as normative. When we focus here on episodes where participants orient to an action as a deviation from the norms of this particular classroom, we do so because such deviations are key to investigating how the underlying "taken-for-granted expectancies" (Garfinkel 1967) are mobilised in the service of socialising newcomers into principles underpinning the social orderliness of the target/host community. These instances where members draw attention to what is perceived to be conduct that deviates from "normal courses of action" draw out for the analyst (and for the members themselves) an underlying moral order, one which is treated by members as "normal".

The study presented here speaks to each of these research strands. In our data, we find the participants both holding one another explicitly accountable for transgressions in the social norms for classroom participation, while at the same time treating social norms for participation in other social contexts as a central pedagogical focus for the particular course in which the students are enrolled.

3 Norms and language socialisation in the language classroom

In settings such as the one we are looking into in this chapter, where members from different sociocultural backgrounds come together, all members may not share the same understandings of what it is to act as a competent, upstanding member of this social group, and what constitutes appropriate conduct for the activity in which they are engaged. Indeed, participants may display an understanding that non-convergent socialised patterns of conduct and thought may be in evidence within the cohort, and that some accommodation between the two (or more) sets may need to be negotiated. The Second Language classroom specifically is a setting where such accommodation is on the agenda. Second Language classrooms are sites of language socialisation (Ochs & Schieffelin 2011). The explicit aim is to socialise students into the linguistic norms of the target language, that is, not only those pertaining to the language itself, but also the appropriate use of the language within social engagements. In addition, however, students are also socialised into norms for social conduct, including norms for classroom participation. In a classroom setting, social norms include where to sit, how to sit, when to stand, who to face, when to move around, who speaks when, for how long, who has the right to allocate turns at talk, to set the agenda, to open or close down a conversation. While most of us are socialised from an early age into classroom participation practices, classrooms are not uniform, and the patterns of conduct not universal. As pointed out by Mortensen and Hazel (2017), "although members are socialized from an early age into the order of the classroom, how classroom management is actually organized is locally contingent". Especially in cases where participants come from diverse sociocultural backgrounds, there may be a perceived need to socialise students into not just linguistic norms, but also social norms of the classroom.

This points to the deontic dimension in how such institutional settings are organised. Whereas teachers are conventionally afforded greater epistemic primacy over course content, teacher authority (e.g. Macbeth 1991) is also premised on teachers being accorded superior rights to direct the actions of others in class, or to articulate and verbalise matters of responsibility, obligation and duty. Such orientations to respective members' authoritative status – asymmetrical rights and responsibilities afforded to members to demarcate domains of action into what should and what should not be a course of action – relate to deonticity in social interaction (see e.g. Stevanovic & Svennevig 2015). Studies of deontic modality in a variety of settings (e.g. Antaki & Kent 2015; Dalby, Gulbrandsen & Svennevig 2015; Stevanovic & Peräkylä 2012) seek to uncover the processes through which members constrain the actions of others, both through the adoption of a *deontic stance* – a display of authority or power in a particular domain of action – and *deontic status* – the relative position of authority a member is deemed to have in a group, regardless of their claim (Stevanovic & Peräkylä 2014). The focus of these studies is equally relevant for the classroom settings that we study here, as the interactional management of the classroom involves teachers being afforded rights to not only direct the actions of the student participants, including maintaining discipline in class (see e.g. Margutti & Piirainen-Marsh 2011), but also to instruct them in how they should conduct themselves in future workplace settings.

Gay (2000) stresses how "school performance takes place within a complex sociocultural ecology and is filtered through cultural screens both students and teachers bring to the classroom" (2000: 54), arguing that teachers should develop awareness of their students' sociocultural backgrounds in order to "make learning encounters more relevant to and effective for them" (2000: 29). Hence, we may find both teacher and student participants orienting to a particular normative order as legitimate and needing to be adopted, and an orientation to others' conduct – rooted perhaps in other normative frameworks – as needing to be made compliant with the dominant one; in this case, that pertaining to the host setting, namely Denmark (cf. Harder's discussion, this volume, of the need to establish a normative order in emergent communities).

4 Socialisation into Danish language and Danish norms

The Second Language classroom we investigate here is particularly interesting in relation to norm negotiation and socialisation, because the aim of the classroom activities is not just socialisation into the linguistic norms of the Danish language but also socialisation into perceived cultural norms of the Danish labour market (see Piippo this volume for a similar case from the Finnish context). The language classes form part of an integration programme that the refugee students are obligated to follow as part of their integration contract with the Danish state. This integration programme, and Danish and European immigration policy in general, was (and still is at the time of writing) heavily anchored in ideologies of integration (Flubacher & Yeung 2016) and employability (Flubacher, Coray & Duchêne 2017) that construct refugees as a burden on society that needs to be alleviated through their contribution to the labour market. Consequently, integration measures focus on increasing migrants' marketability (Del Percio 2018). While this way of viewing refugees is largely unquestioned in the current political climate, it is worth pointing out the contrast with earlier discourses constructing refugees primarily as people in need of help and safety, focusing on the humanitarian obligations of the welfare state, as can be found e.g. in the UN Refugee Convention from 1951 that had Denmark as the first signatory (see also Pöyhönen & Tarnanen 2015 on shifting discourses of integration in the Finnish context).

Despite an existing focus on "Danish for the labour market", a new law was passed in 2017 (just before the fieldwork) that emphasised that "education in labor market relations – together with education in culture and social conditions – must be a common element in the three Danish programmes"[1] (Ministry of Immigration and Integration 2017, our translation), including information about Danish meeting culture and hygiene in workplaces. Within this remit, the work of the language teacher extends beyond the facilitation of language learning; it also involves associating the use of the target language with particular social norms. Moreover, in this language school, teachers have to report on students who are late or absent so that case workers in the local municipality can decide on appropriate sanctions, which may take the form of a monetary deduction from the student's monthly allowance for days when he or she is absent or late.

---

[1] Original: "undervisning i arbejdsmarkedsforhold – sammen med undervisning i kultur og samfundsforhold – skal være et gennemgående element på de tre danskuddannelser". The 'three Danish programmes' mentioned here refer to three different pathways available for students, based on what educational experience they have had prior to entering Denmark.

Pennycook (1989: 46) has argued in the context of second language pedagogy that an adopted method for teaching "reflects a particular view of the world and is articulated in the interests of unequal power relationships". In addition to the current construction of refugees as potential workers as discussed above, we note how the ideology pertaining to an intimate connection between language and nation-state – and the presumed social norms for that nation-state – underlies the pedagogical framework. Indeed, the framework bears some hallmarks of Content and Language Integrated Learning (CLIL) approaches to curriculum design. In our case, the Danish language and the social norms for Danish (workplace) culture constitute the "content" of the pedagogy, with Danish also acting as the language through which the content is delivered and learned. This kind of instruction in perceived social norms for membership of a Danish workplace may be said to promote increased intercultural sensitivity and ethno-relativity (following Bennett's model, 1986) among students (and arguably teachers too), by exposing participants to alternative cultural models that differ from their own. However, with the institutionally prescribed logic behind the programme provision being solely to prepare refugees for entry into a workplace in Denmark, there is an element of ethnocentrism embedded within the curriculum: The students' cultural understandings and practices are treated as needing to be brought into line with the practices, attitudes and expectactions of the target/host community.

5 This study

The data for this chapter was generated during fieldwork in a programme called *Dansk på Arbejde* (translated as 'Danish at Work') at a language centre in Denmark. In this five-month programme, students alternate between periods of two-three weeks in Danish class and two-three weeks in internships in local workplaces, typically supermarkets or daycare centres. Danish language classes as well as internships are required activities for refugees who have been granted asylum in Denmark, with financial sanctions being imposed if the refugees do not attend. As mentioned above, the Danish education for foreigners has the explicit double aims of teaching the students Danish and socialising them into the Danish labour market, and Danish cultural and societal conditions more generally. This means that norms for how to behave in a Danish workplace form a central part of the teaching, with classes set aside to focus on this aspect, e.g. with exercises in "how to call in sick for work", and "how to do small talk with co-workers during breaks". As we will see, socialisation into Danish workplace norms also takes place during other classroom activities.

All the students in the programme were refugees or had come under the family reunification scheme as the spouse of a refugee. Most had been in Denmark between one and three years, and had been learning Danish for most of this period. The majority of the group were from Syria and were Arabic speaking, but the group also included students from South Sudan and Chechnya. Students ranged in age from early twenties to mid-fifties, with big differences in educational background and work experience. While 19 students were signed up for the class when it started in August, usually between four and eight were present, and talk about attendance and punctuality turned up frequently in the data set.

The fieldwork was carried out by the second author who conducted participant observation in the classroom from March to November 2017. The full data set includes participant observation and fieldnotes of two groups of students (Spring and Autumn), audio and video recordings of classroom interaction (Autumn group), interviews with teachers, students and case workers as well as photos and documents. For the analysis presented in this chapter, we focus on interactional data from the audio and video recordings of classroom interaction during the autumn. We have located in the data episodes where an action is oriented to as a breach of a social norm, in turn leading to some form of reproach (Macbeth 1991). The large majority of these episodes were related to attendance and punctuality which subsequently became the focus of the analysis. In addition to episodes where participants turn up late for class, we have also included episodes where participants discuss attendance and punctuality, e.g. while waiting for more students to turn up, and excerpts from the feedback session with the two teachers where attendance and punctuality are discussed. These episodes have been transcribed in CLAN (MacWhinney 2000) by student transcribers and checked by the authors as the first round of analysis. Subsequent analyses have focused on identifying the conversational routine (Coulmas 1981) surrounding lateness. In Coulmas' understanding,

> Routines are a means of guiding a person's normal participation in social interaction. Viewed from the interpretive side, they constitute standardized links between what people actually say and what sort of communicative functions their addresses serve to perform. Literal meanings and functions of utterances – i.e., the verbal acts that they accomplish – are not bi-uniquely mapped on each other. (1981: 6–7)

In our study, we have selected a particular recurrent conversational routine which occurs when a student arrives late to class. The routine includes an explicit verbal orientation to the lateness, as well as subsequent accounts and accountability related to attendance and punctuality.

6 Analysis

6.1 The "You're late" conversational routine

In the first example, we see how a norm for punctuality is made relevant. On this day, 14 weeks into the programme, only two students had shown up when the session started. Sirin and another student enter ten minutes later.

Excerpt 1

```
01   *SIR:     godmorgen↗
02   %tra:     good morning
03   *CAM:     godmorgen:::→
04   %tra:     good morning
05   *SAR:     godmorgen↗ ne:j↘
06   %tra:     goodmorning o:h
07             (0.5)
08   *CAM:     I kommer for sent↗
09   %tra:     you're late
10   *SIR:     men øh ↑bussen meget→
11   %tra:     but uh the bus a lot
12             (1.7)
13   *SIR:     et men bussen↘
14   %tra:     a but the bussen
```

Sirin (*SIR) enters the classroom with a greeting. She is greeted first by the teacher, Camilla (*CAM), then by the other teacher Sara (*SAR) who adds a prolonged expression of surprise or perhaps joy at seeing more students arrive. After a short pause, Camilla produces the formulation "you're late" with rising intonation. Sirin immediately starts to account for her being late with an account of what happened to her on her way to class. By invoking what Heritage (1988: 138) has called the "no-fault quality" of accounts, Sirin makes it clear that her being late should not be seen as a hostile or careless act. In this way, such accounts are used by latecomers to negotiate their relationship with the other participants, specifically by constructing the lateness in a way that does not appear face-threatening to them.

This pattern is repeated throughout the data set: Students turn up late, they are greeted by the teachers, followed by the statement "You're late". But students do not always produce accounts the way Sirin does.

Excerpt 2

```
01    *SAR:     kom ind↗
02    %tra:     come in
03              (0.3)
04    *CAM:     hej↗
05    %tra:     hi
06    *SAR:     godmorgen↗
07              (0.3)
08              godmorgen kom ind↗
09    %tra:     good morning (0.3) good morning come in
10              (0.5)
11    *FAW:     ja↗
12    %tra:     yes
13    *CAM:     I kommer for sent↗
14    %tra:     you're late
15    *FAW:     ja↗ ja→
16    %tra:     yes yes
17    *CAM:     (laughter?)
18    *FAW:     vi kommer for sent↘≈
19    %tra:     we're late
```

In this sequence, taken from the second week of class, Fawzi (*FAW) and three other students, including Mohammad (*MOH, who does not speak in this excerpt), arrive at class when the session has already started, and teacher Sara tells them to come in. Camilla, the other teacher, initiates a greeting sequence, matched by Sara, who adds further words of welcome to the salutation in her restating of the invitation to enter. At this point, the classroom activity could be resumed. However, we note that Camilla instead produces the formulation "you're late", formatted with rising intonation. This is simply a statement of fact, and not treated as new information by Fawzi who answers with "yes yes", which simply confirms the statement, marking it without any form of change-of-state token like "oh" or "really".

These types of statements of fact are interesting. Verbally formulating something that is already self-evident to those present opens for inference of the social action being performed by the utterance (Sacks 1992/1966, lecture 14). It can for example act as a warning, "I'm behind you" or a caution "I'm watching you"; as an assessment, "That sky's so blue", or as a tease, "You were really drunk last night". None of these observations of fact provide new information to the recipient. Rather, whatever social action is embodied by the statement requires a different type of response by the addressee than a simple information receipt. A statement of fact regarding someone arriving at a later time than expected may lead to an inference that this is a complaint, or in an institutional setting such as this classroom, an admonishment even (Hazel & Mortensen 2017; Mortensen & Hazel 2017;

see also Macbeth 1991; Stokoe & Edwards 2014). Complaints and admonishments normatively require as response one of a range of types of actions or response formats. These could be rejections, apologies, displays of contrition, elements of mitigation or other forms of accounting for the perceived transgression contained in the admonishment. In this way, the formulations act as directives (Searle 1979), prompting the recipient to produce one of a range of acceptable response types. In turn, this allows the teacher to monitor the student's understanding of what kind of reponse is appropriate. Drew (1998: 295) argues that "our descriptions are themselves accountable phenomena through which we recognizably display an action's (im)propriety, (in)correctness, (un)suitability, (in)appropriateness, (in)justice, (dis)honesty, and so forth. Hence they may, always and irretrievably, be understood as doing moral work". The way the account is formatted by the "offending" party is therefore relevant for displaying their understanding of the action and in what way it deviates from what is socially acceptable for this interactional setting.

In Excerpt 2, however, we note that Fawzi simply offers a confirmation of the statement of fact. It is arguable that this response accounts for Camilla's laughter in line 17. There is nothing inherently funny in what Fawzi says here, so this in itself may not warrant such laughter. However, in terms of sequential organisation, if what is projected by the statement of fact is an invitation to account for the student's lateness, then the student producing an alternative response type may result in the kind of incongruity that could prompt laughter. Indeed, much situational comedy is built using this interactional pattern as a technique to engender laughter (Stokoe 2008).

It is not clear how Fawzi reads this, but he follows the laughter by expanding on the minimal response confirmation with an expanded confirmation, "we're late", reformatting Camilla's account as a 1st person formulation. Still, this does not provide anything in the way of a type-fitted response to an admonishment, and in Excerpt 3 below we see Camilla subsequently pursuing this further.

6.2 Requests for accounts and acceptable accounts

We see in what follows that Camilla does not treat the type of response produced by Fawzi as sufficient, rather pursuing a fuller explanation from the student.

Excerpt 3

```
18    *FAW:    vi kommer for sent↘≈
19    %tra:    we're late
20    *CAM:    ≈ hvorfor kommer I for sent↗
21    %tra:    why are you late
```

22	*FAW:	fordi vi har problemer med øh nogle personer her↘
23	%tra:	*because we have problems with uh some persons here*
24	*CAM:	↑nå→
25	%tra:	*oh*
26	*FAW:	ja→
27	%tra:	*yes*
28	*CAM:	med nogle per↑soner↘
29	%tra:	*with some persons*
30	*FAW:	ja↗
31	%tra:	*yes*
32	*CAM:	hvad er det for nogle personer↘
33	%tra:	*what kind of persons*
34	*UNK:	(hedder xxx)
35	%tra:	*name xxx*
36	*MOH:	xxx (0.9) xxx ha ha ha
37		(0.8)
38	*CAM:	I har problemer med per↑soner↘
39	%tra:	*you have problems with persons*
40		(0.8)
41	*FAW:	⌈ja→⌉
42	%tra:	*yes*
43	*CAM:	⌊er det⌋ poli↑tiet I har problemer med→
44	%tra:	*is it the police that you have problems with*
45	*FAW:	nej↘
46	%tra:	*no*
47	*CAM:	nej↗
48	%tra:	*no*

Here, in between lines 20–32, Camilla enquires after the reason for Fawzi and the others' lateness, and treats the reason provided by Fawzi – that they had "some problems with some persons" – as being an insufficient account. Fawzi however treats her turns as information seeking questions (line 22) or confirmation requests of her understanding (lines 26 and 30), rather than as a request for providing a response to a complaint or admonishment. It rests with Camilla to reformulate the statement again in a question format ("what kind of persons"), and to pursue a response again in line 38 by recycling his initial account ("you have problems with persons"). Again, however, this does not elicit any further specificities regarding the reason; rather, Fawzi produces yet another minimal response token, "yes", confirming Camilla's statement.

Not giving up, Camilla then produces yet another question, this time modelling the kind of information that would suffice as responding to a complaint. She specifies a person category, "the police", and links it to the problems which were embedded in Fawzi's account. Fawzi rejects the candidate category ("no"), and when Camilla produces yet another confirmation check, "no?" (see Excerpt 4),

Fawzi finally gives a little more detail as to the identity of the person who he had problems with (Excerpt 4).

Excerpt 4

47	*CAM:	nej↗
48	%tra:	no
49	*FAW:	han øh (1.2) han er: (1.0) studerer↘ (0.3)
50		med sammen med↘
51	%tra:	he uh (1.2) he is (1.0) studies (0.3) with together with
52		(0.7)
53	*CAM:	nå det er en ↑klassekammerat↘
54	%tra:	oh it is a classmate
55	*FAW:	nej ikke [klasse]kammerat→
56	%tra:	no not classmate
57	*CAM:	⌊nej⌋ okay↘(0.3) men det er en anden kursist↘
58	%tra:	no okay (0.3) but it is another student
59	*FAW:	ja→
60	%tra:	yes
61	*CAM:	ja→
62	%tra:	yes
63		(0.5)
64	*CAM:	okay↘

We see how Camilla here guides Fawzi to identify the person in question, at least to a specification deemed sufficient for building the account for the lateness, "another student", though not from the same class. Camilla and Sara then move on to collaborate on pursuing the account further.

Excerpt 5

65	*SAR:	kører I med ham→
66	%tra:	do you get a ride from him
67		(0.4)
68	*FAW:	hvad↗
69	%tra:	what
70	*CAM:	ah det kan være [en forklaring]
71	%tra:	ah that could be an explanation
72	*SAR:	⌊kører I i bil⌋ med ham→
73	%tra:	do you get a ride from him in his car
74	*MOH:	ja→
75	%tra:	yes
76	*FAW:	nej→
77	%tra:	no
78		(0.7)

79	*SAR:	nå→
80	%tra:	oh
81	*FAW:	jeg kører min din bil min bil og (1.2) han kører (0.4) sin bil↘
82	%tra:	*I drive my your car my car and (1.2) he drives his car*
83	*CAM:	okay↘
84	*FAW:	ja→
85	%tra:	*yes*

Building on the information that the person in question is a fellow student, Sara asks Fawzi whether he shares a ride with the other student, which leads Camilla to propose that this could be an explanation ("forklaring", line 70). An explanation is a particular kind of action, but one which can serve different functions, including, as we argue here, providing justification or excuse for an action, and particularly an action that has occasioned some form of complaint or admonishment. We see that Fawzi rejects this candidate explanation, first with a bare "no", then expanded with a more elaborated account for how both he and the others come to class.

At this point, Camilla abandons the pursuit of a full account for the reasons behind the students being late to class, and instead produces a turn which in this sequential context can be heard as a request, namely that they ask the "person" in question to get up earlier.

Excerpt 6

86	*CAM:	kan I sige til ham han skal stå tidligere op↗
87	%tra:	*can you tell him that he needs to get up earlier*
88		(2.6)
89	*MOH:	igen↗
90	%tra:	*again*
91	*CAM:	kan I sige til ham han skal han skal tage sit
92		øh sin alarm sit vækkeur↘ og så skal han stå tidligere op↗
93		ti minutter (0.3) tidligere↘
94		(0.5)
95	%tra:	*can you tell him he has to he has to take his uh*
96		*his alarm his alarm clock and then he has to get up earlier*
97		*ten minutes (0.3) earlier*
98	*FAW:	ja→
99	%tra:	*yes*
100		(1.0)
101	*CAM:	he he he ja↗
102	%tra:	*ha ha ha yes*

Again, this draws on what Sacks has called the "inference making machine", namely a cognitive analytic capacity to "deal with and categorize and make statements about an event [the person] has not seen" (1992: 116), one which "provides for the *local* social organization of facts, observations and relevances of a particular set of conditions and predicated inferences" (Housley & Fitzgerald 2002: 79). The argument here is that people draw on their understandings of how the world works in order to draw reasonable conclusions regarding events which they did not witness, and for which they have only partial evidence. In this case, it allows for Camilla to propose one logical reason for the other "person" making Fawzi late, namely that this person got up late. It also relies on inference from the addressees, who are being asked to activate bodies of knowledge in order to infer why this particular request is being made. Mohammad orients to difficulties in understanding Camilla's talk (line 89), and the teacher subsequently reformulates it (lines 91–93), adding greater detail. Fawzi then acknowledges the request, which Camilla responds to with laughter tokens, possibly orienting to the sensitive nature of the public reprimand, and the mitigation required in such instances. Such reprimands occur several times in the data set and include direct orders to leave home earlier and to take into account the regularly occurring problem with finding parking space at the school.

In the analysis, we see how social norms for punctuality are worked up as a focal topic in classroom talk, including appropriate practices for providing an account in the event of a transgression of the norm. At the same time, the normative use of Danish for the conversational "you're late" routine allows for authentic talk in the target language. In this way, the routine works both as an opportunity for authentic language production and as language socialisation into classroom norms. But the talk around attendance and punctuality also does another type of social work. By pointing out breaches of norms and requesting accounts for them, the teachers position themselves as those with the "right" norms, and the students as those who have to be socialised into these norms. In this way, norm talk becomes a process of differentiation where teachers draw on and make relevant their institutional role as well as their epistemic primacy status pertaining to their own sociocultural background as Danes with superior authority to pronounce on others' conduct. As we show in more detail below, the students are, in contrast to the teachers, positioned not just as learners of Danish, but also as outsiders who require instruction in local norms. This type of positioning and differentiation work becomes particularly obvious when the transgression of classroom norms is used as an occasion to instruct students in what is deemed socially acceptable behaviour for a hypothetical future workplace in the host country.

6.3 Norms for the classroom as norms for the workplace

The need for regular attendance and punctuality in the classroom is frequently emphasised by reference to classroom-internal concerns, such as making the best use of the relatively short amount of time the teachers have to work with this group of students, or the inconvenience to the teachers who have to change their plans if far fewer students show up than expected. But in addition to these concerns, the teachers also frequently point out that appreciating and adhering to these norms for attendance and punctuality is important in relation to the world outside the classroom, in particular the workplaces where the students hopefully will work in the future. This point is made already from the beginning of the semester. In week 2, five days into the programme, teacher Sara makes a point of the fact that she is the only one of the group who has been present all five days, in this way flagging attendance as an important issue. Later in the same interaction, Sara and Camilla introduce an attendance sheet. They explain to the students that they will put this up on the wall, and the students will then fill out when they arrived and when they left school each day "fordi så kan I selv se (0.5) hvordan går det med at komme i skole" ("because this way you can see yourselves how it's going with getting to school"). When a student tries to provide an account for why he is sometimes late, Camilla first counters this by saying that she cannot relay all the various excuses to the case workers, and then Sara adds:

Excerpt 7

01	*SAR:	og en chef som betaler for de ti minutter I kommer for sent
02		(0.4) han er heller ikke glad
03	%tra	*and a boss who pays for those ten minutes you are late*
04		*(0.4) he is not happy either*

By introducing the attendance sheet, the teachers emphasise the importance of this particular norm. While it is not made explicit in the interaction, the punctuality norm is in fact an institutionalised norm. The teachers have to report it to case workers if students turn up late, which Camilla hints at in her response that she cannot relay all the excuses to the case workers. Sara further emphasises the severity of transgressing the punctuality norm when she connects the norms for the classroom with norms for an (imagined future) workplace. She does this by drawing a parallel between the consequence of being late for class and being late for work: In one case they will make their teacher angry, in the other they risk angering the boss who pays them for their time. Keeping in mind that the focus of the educational programme is to prepare refugees for entering the Danish labour market, and that the teaching of Danish workplace culture is an explicit part of the curriculum – with one day per week set aside for teaching "Arbejde i DK" (translated as "Work in Denmark") – the inference here is that the norm in question is one relevant for a Danish workplace, rather than workplaces more generally.

In this next sequence, from week 6 of the programme, several students have again turned up late for class. They try to provide accounts for why they were late, but Sara does not accept these as valid reasons, responding, for instance, that problems finding parking is not a new issue, but something that happens all the time. She then comments that the teachers have changed the plan for the day since only four students showed up, and now that four more have arrived, they are forced to change the plan again. When Adnan (*ADN) again tries to provide an account,[2] Sara interrupts him with the following reply:

Excerpt 8

```
01    *ADN:    men ⌈men men          ⌉
02    %tra     but but  but
03    *SAR:         ⌊men der er man⌋- prøv og hør
04                 prøv og hør der er mange undskyldninger
05                 ⌈jeg kan ikke parkere mine bør- mine børn skal i sko⌉le
06    %tra     but there are a lot- listen
07                 listen there are many excuses
08                 I can't park my chil- my children have to go to school
09    *ADN:        ⌊allah wakilek abu ali ana ma eli alaqa         ⌋ xxx
10    %tra:    honestly that's abu ali's fault not mine xxx
11    *HUD:    laughs
12                 ⌈siarti atlane⌉
13    %tra:    my car has crashed
14    *SAR:    ⌊jeg          ⌋ (.) hvis jeg er chef
15                 på arbejde så siger jeg
16                 jeg er ligeglad
17                 (1.0) du er fyret
18    %tra     I (.) if I'm the boss
19                 at work then I say
20                 I don't care
21                 you are fired
22                 (1.6)
23    *SAR:    jeg forstår godt at på i skole
24                 der bliver I ikke fyret
25                 I mister ikke et arbejde
```

---

2 While most of this excerpt is in Danish, lines 9 and 12 are in Arabic. It is clear from the subsequent interaction that Adnan and his wife Huda (who speaks in lines 11–12) got a ride from another student, referred to here as "Abu Ali", and that they were late because he picked them up late.

26		men I gør mit arbejde meget svært
27	%tra	*I understand that going to school*
28		*you won't get fired there*
29		*you won't lose a job*
30		*but you are making my job very difficult*
31		(2.6)
32	*SAR:	så derfor så siger jeg
33		kom til tiden i skolen
34		kom til tiden i praktik
35		kom til tiden (.) på arbejde
36	%tra	*so that's why I say*
37		*be on time for school*
38		*be on time for internship*
39		*be on time (.) for work*
40		(1.5)
41	*SAR:	det er meget meget vigtigt
42	%tra	*it is very very important*

In this excerpt, Sara provides two reasons for why the teachers focus on norms for punctuality. As Sara makes clear in line 26, students being late for school is very inconvenient for teachers because it requires them to change their plans, sometimes several times. This then is an example of how actions that have a greater effect on others may be more likely to be subject to disapproval (Horne 2001). Most of the excerpt focuses on another reason, however, that failure to uphold the norm for punctuality will have consequences outside of the classroom. Sara here (lines 14–17) links classroom norms with Danish workplace norms where, according to her, being late will get someone fired. In this imagined workplace, Sara argues, the employer will not care about excuses for tardiness, but simply terminate the employment.

In both of these examples, the teachers draw on (supposed) larger-scale norms to impose order in the local interactional setting. By painting a picture of the hypothetical "boss" in these examples, the breaching of a classroom norm is used as an occasion for teaching "Danish workplace culture". At the same time, drawing attention to "real world" (as opposed to classroom) consequences of being late functions as a way of emphasising the severity of the transgression and underlining the importance of being socialised into the norm: Breaching the norm may have consequences beyond the immediate interaction, it may even endanger the future livelihood of the students. In this way, bringing larger-scale social norms into the classroom serves the dual purpose of socialising the students into specific positions on the labour market and of emphasising the importance of being socialised into the local norm. Echoing Stokoe and Edwards (2012: 185), in this educational programme, one which aims to prepare refugees for entry into the Danish labour market, we note how students-as-prospective-workers "are accountable for behaving in certain ways, where "accountable" means both being describable (their actions can be placed under a range of vernacular descriptions) and being held to account (mundane morality)".

7 Discussion and conclusion: Norms, accountability and processes of differentiation

Second Language classrooms may have as primary purpose the development of language competences in a target language, focusing on grammar, fluency, lexis, listening and speaking. They also, however, offer opportunities for exposure to and socialisation into social norms that are deemed relevant to the projected future social settings participants may seek to enter. In the Danish language education for adult migrants, socialisation into such norms is indeed part of the explicit aims of the programme. The excerpts that we have looked at illustrate the language socialisation taking place on several levels in a language classroom for refugee students. First of all, students are socialised into linguistic norms. Here we have seen how they are taught to respond to the assertion "you're late". By using the same conversational routine repeatedly, the teachers provide an opportunity for students to learn how to respond appropriately to the statement in Danish, including the form and extent an account must take to be treated as sufficient and appropriate. Secondly, by pointing out a breach and making the students morally – and publicly – accountable for it, the routine also serves as a way of socialising the students into a particular classroom norm ("Being on time is part of the social contract for participating in the class"). Third, this norm is explicitly linked with participation in the wider societal context, more specifically in the labour market. The teachers compare being late in class with being late in a future imagined workplace. By doing this, the teachers emphasise the gravity of transgressing the norm for being on time, while also socialising the students into a particular kind of work and a particular part of the Danish labour market (where being on time is proposed as crucial). Whether or not being late for work will get someone fired in a Danish workplace can be questioned. While being on time is important for many jobs, not all types of workplaces have rigid work hours with a fixed starting time, including for instance many academic workplaces and other white-collar workplaces. As pointed out elsewhere (Lønsmann 2020), the students in the Danish integration programme are being socialised not just into the Danish labour market but to specific positions in the labour market, viz. low-status and low-skilled work. Telling students that their imagined future workplace will be of the type that sanctions latecomers by terminating employment contributes to this type of positioning. Also, by linking classroom transgressions with wider societal norms, the teachers invoke a particular deontic status, where they simultaneously produce what Stevanovic (2015) has termed proximal and distal deontic claims. The former (proximal) sees the teacher instructing students in how to keep time and how to respond to an admonshiment for being late (for this class). The latter refers to how the teacher uses these sequences to imply that they have the right to pronounce on future action for how the latecomer should behave (in the workplace) in order to be accepted as a morally upright member of the community.

The classroom context entails an asymmetrical relationship between the teacher(s), who are afforded superior epistemic rights to adjudicate on matters of language and local social norms, and the students, who supposedly lack this knowledge and hence the rights. In a Danish language classroom for refugees, this asymmetry is increased by the unequal access to locally valued linguistic resources, unequal legal status in Denmark and unequal access to the Danish labour market. In our data, the teachers occupy positions not only as those who know the Danish language, but also as those who are deemed to know "Danish workplace culture". By contrast, the students are positioned as needing instruction not just in the Danish language, but also in Danish social norms. Specifically, by tying classroom norms for punctuality to labour market norms, and by treating the refugee students as requiring instruction in these norms, the interactions concerning breaches of norms and accounting for these breaches contribute to constructing the refugee participants as outsiders in relation to the Danish labour market. Previous work on integration programmes for migrant workers finds that rather than taking the point of departure in migrants' existing educational and linguistic capital or their previous work experience, such programmes focus on what migrants lack, e.g. local language competence, soft skills etc., and that through this focus, migrants are constructed as "abnormal" and in need of fixing (Allan 2013; Diedrich & Styhre 2013). In our study, by treating the students' breaches of classroom norms as a lack of knowledge about labour market norms, the students are arguably similarly positioned as lacking knowledge about "how to work" in general. By orienting to the students as requiring this form of instruction into moral conduct, the teachers position the students as deficient in relation to participation, not just in the classroom, but in Danish society. In other words, while Danish language education for adult migrants ostensibly is about turning the students into ingroup members, the way this is done continually constructs the students as outsiders. While it can be argued that recently arrived migrants *are* outsiders in Danish society, our point is that emphasising their otherness is a counterintuitive way of attempting to include them.

Also, other types of migrants, such as transnationally mobile knowledge workers, are not to the same extent constructed as deficient in relation to societal and labour market participation. Their lack of Danish competence and knowledge of the Danish labour market is not seen as a gap that requires political intervention and societal resources. This comparison highlights the construction of certain types of migrants as deficient in relation to societal participation and reveals that "outsiderness" is contingent upon other factors than just cultural and linguistic "otherness". Highly educated work migrants with no Danish competence and no knowledge of the Danish labour market are nevertheless seen as attractive outsiders who need to be drawn to Denmark e.g. by incentivising tax schemes. And while refugees are forced to adapt linguistically to the Danish labour market, many international workplaces are more than happy to adapt linguistically to other types of migrants by introducing English language policies (Lønsmann 2017). Juxtaposing the language ideologies and policies surrounding these two types of migrants reveals a contrast between problematic and attractive linguistic diversity, and underscores Barakos and Selleck's point that "not all 'multilingualisms' are equal" (2019: 364).

In this chapter, we have investigated norm talk in a classroom for adult migrants from the perspective of norms as they relate to moral accountability and group membership. From this perspective, it becomes clear that an investigation of norms necessarily becomes an investigation into the social work done by participants' orientations to norms in a social setting. By focussing on norm talk, and particularly *breaches* of norms, we gain a lens through which we can study how participants perceive the social world to be organised, and what is considered appropriate conduct for someone to be treated as a legitimate member. Investigating how norms are used by participants, for what purpose and with what consequences, we can see processes of differentiation play out. In the case examined here, where some participants are treated as needing instruction in certain norms, and other participants are positioned as those who can give instruction in those norms, a focus on norms leads to a focus on assumptions of sharedness and non-sharedness. The programme of language education for adult migrants with its built-in focus on Danish workplace culture assumes that migrants who need language instruction also need instruction in socially acceptable conduct. In other words, a study of norms becomes a study of assumptions of sharedness and processes of differentiations. By looking at who is constructed as needing to be taught acceptable patterns of conduct, we can identify who is being constructed as insiders and outsiders. From this perspective, it becomes clear that norm talk is not inconsequential for the participants, but may rather have wide-ranging consequences in terms of identity construction and positionality, and material consequences in terms of the types of employment the migrant may be able to access. Consequently, the study of how the social conduct of certain migrants is policed as part and parcel of the induction into the local language demonstrates some of the dynamics involved in the local implementation of integration policies. Drawing on a "one nation, one language" ideology, here the learning of a language is used as an opportunity to roll out a parallel ideology, namely "one nation, one set of social norms of conduct". Similarly, where language learners are treated according to a deficiency model with a focus on what they lack rather than what they have, they are equally treated as (as yet) deficient social actors.

From a language classroom perspective, this study raises the question of what kinds of norms are being taught in the classroom for refugee students (beyond linguistic norms). In our data, certain norms (such as the norm for being on time, but also norms for language choice and gender norms, which we have not discussed in this chapter) are clearly foregrounded either in the laws and guidelines for language education for adult migrants or by the teachers in this particular classroom. While this has been beyond the scope of the present investigation, we propose that future investigations of norms should include a consideration of why certain norms are foregrounded in particular local settings, and whose authority and agenda drive this. Such investigations should also consider the extent to which some norms have a stronger force than others, e.g. because these norms have become institutionalised. A close analysis of which social norms are made relevant in particular interactional settings, the degree to which they are enforced, and how they are connected to societal discourses and ideologies can be a way of linking local concerns with larger societal concerns.

This study has taken an interactional perspective on social norms, investigating how participants in a Second Language classroom orient to breaches in norms for punctuality, and how for this setting it may also lead to the norms becoming topics for explicit instruction. This interactional approach contributes to our understanding of social norms by explicating how, when and by whom norms are made relevant in social interaction. Attention to how participants make norms relevant in interaction, in particular how they orient to breaches of norms as moral transgressions, aids our understanding of how deontic status is conferred and constructed in a local social setting. Finally, by including considerations of how participants draw on more widespread social norms as part of the language socialisation process, the chapter highlights the social work done by participants' attention to norms. In this way, the chapter contributes to the study of language in social life by showing how the invoking of social norms contributes to processes of differentiation by assigning status and group membership to social actors.

Transcription conventions

↗	rising intonation
↘	falling intonation
→	flat or continuing intonation
↑	pitch shift
:	prolonged sound
≈	latching
(0.5)	pause measured in seconds
(.)	pause measuring less than 0.2 seconds
xxx	unintelligible
⌈ ⌉	overlap
⌊ ⌋	overlap
%tra: *italics*	English paraphrase

References

Allan, Kori. 2013. Skilling the self: The communicability of immigrants as flexible labour. In Alexandre Duchêne, Melissa Moyer & Celia Roberts (eds.), *Language, migration and social inequalities: A critical sociolinguistic perspective on institutions and work*, 56–78. Bristol: Multilingual Matters.

Antaki, Charles & Alexandra Kent. 2012. Telling people what to do (and, sometimes, why): Contingency, entitlement and explanation in staff requests to adults with intellectual impairments. *Journal of Pragmatics* 44 (6–7). 876–889.

Aronsson, Karin & Ann-Christin Cederborg. 2012. Family therapy and accountability. *Journal of Applied Linguistics and Professional Practice* 9 (2). 193–212.

Barakos, Elisabeth & Charlotte Selleck. 2019. Elite multilingualism: Discourses, practices, and debates. *Journal of Multilingual and Multicultural Development*, 40 (5). 361–374.

Bennett, Milton J. 1986. A developmental approach to training for intercultural sensitivity. *International Journal of Intercultural Relations* 10 (2). 179–95.

Bergmann, Jorg R. 1998. Introduction: Morality in discourse. *Research on Language and Social Interaction* 331 (3–4). 279–294.

Coulmas, Florian. 1981. *Conversational routines: Explorations in standardized communication situations and prepatterned speech*. The Hague: Mouton de Gruyter.

Dalby, Anne Marie Landmark, Pål Gulbrandsen & Jan Svennevig. 2015. Whose decision? Negotiating epistemic and deontic rights in medical treatment decisions. *Journal of Pragmatics* 78. 54–69.

Del Percio, Alfonso. 2018. Engineering commodifiable workers: Language, migration and the governmentality of the self. *Language Policy* 17. 239–259.

Diedrich, Andreas & Alexander Styhre. 2013. Constructing the employable immigrant: The uses of validation practices in Sweden. *Ephemera* 13(4). 759–783.

Drew, Paul. 1998. Complaints about transgressions and misconduct. *Research on Language and Social Interaction* 31 (3–4). 295–325.

Ekström, Mats. 2009. Announced refusal to answer: A study of norms and accountability in broadcast political interviews. *Discourse Studies* 11 (6). 681–702.

Flubacher, Mi-Cha & Shirley Yeung. 2016. Discourses of integration: Language, skills, and the politics of difference. *Multilingua* 35 (6). 599–616.

Flubacher, Mi-Cha, Renata Coray & Alexandre Duchêne. 2017. *Language investment and employability*. London: Palgrave.

Gafaranga, Joseph & Maria-Carme Torras i Calvo. 2001. Language versus medium in the study of bilingual conversation. *International Journal of Bilingualism* 5 (2). 195–219.

Garfinkel, Harold. 1964. Studies of the routine grounds of everyday activities. *Social Problems* 11 (3). 225–250.

Garfinkel, Harold. 1967. *Studies in ethnomethodology*. Oxford: Polity Press.

Gay, Geneva. 2000. *Culturally responsive teaching: Theory, research, and practice*. New York, NY: Teachers College Press.

Hazel, Spencer & Kristian Mortensen. 2017. The classroom moral compass – participation, engagement and transgression in classroom interaction. *Classroom Discourse* 8 (3). 214–234.

Heritage, John. 1988. Explanations as accounts: A conversation analytic perspective. In Charles Antaki (ed.), *Analysing everyday explanation: A casebook of methods*, 127–144. London: Sage.

Horne, Christine. 2001. Sociological perspectives on the emergence of norms. In Michael Hechter & Karl-Dieter Opp (eds.), *Social norms*, 3–34. New York: Russell Sage Foundation.

Housley, William & Richard Fitzgerald. 2002. The reconsidered model of membership categorization analysis. *Qualitative Research* 2 (1). 59–83.

Jayyusi, Lena. 1991. Values and moral judgement: Communicative praxis as a moral order. In Graham Button (ed.), *Ethnomethodology and the human sciences*, 227–251. Cambridge: Cambridge University Press.

Lønsmann, Dorte. 2020. Language, employability and positioning in a Danish integration programme. *International Journal of the Sociology of Language* 264. 49–71. [Special issue on Multilingualism betwixt empowerment and the reproduction of inequality]

Lønsmann, Dorte. 2017. A catalyst for change: Language socialization and norm negotiation in a transient multilingual workplace. *Journal of Linguistic Anthropology* 27 (3). 326–343. [Special issue Transience: Emerging norms of language use].

Macbeth, Douglas H. 1991. Teacher authority as practical action. *Linguistics and Education* 3. 281–313.

MacWhinney, Brian. 2000. *The CHILDES Project: Tools for analyzing talk*. 3rd edn. Mahwah, NJ: Lawrence Erlbaum Associates.

Margutti, Piera & Arja Piirainen-Marsh. 2011. The interactional management of discipline and morality in the classroom: An introduction. *Linguistics and Education* 22. 305–309.

Ministry of Immigration and Integration. 2016. *Bekendtgørelse om danskuddannelse til voksne udlændinge m.fl. LBK nr 981 af 28/06/2016*. [Consolidation Act on Danish education for adult foreigners and others no. 981 on 28/06/2016].

Ministry of Immigration and Integration. 2017. *Orienteringsskrivelse om ændringer af lov om danskuddannelse for udlændinge*. [Briefing note on changes of the law concerning Danish education for foreigners].

Mortensen, Kristian & Spencer Hazel. 2011. Initiating round robins in the L2 classroom – preliminary observations. *Novitas-ROYAL (Research on Youth and Language)* 5 (1). 55–70.

Mortensen, Kristian & Spencer Hazel. 2017. Navigating the moral maze. Order and transgression in language classroom participation. In Götz Schwab, Sabine Hoffmann & Almut Schön (eds.), *Interaktion im Fremdsprachenunterricht. Beiträge aus der empirischen Forschung*, 113–132. Münster: LIT Verlag.

Niemi, Kreeta. 2016. *Moral beings and becomings: Children's moral practices in classroom peer interaction*. PhD dissertation, University of Jyväskylä.

Niemi, Kreeta & Amanda Bateman. 2015. Cheaters and stalkers: Accusations in a classroom. *Discourse Studies* 17 (1). 83–98.

Ochs, Elinor & Bambi B. Schieffelin. 2011. The theory of language socialization. In Alessandro Duranti, Elinor Ochs & Bambi B. Schieffelin (eds.), *The handbook of language socialization*, 1–21. Malden: Wiley Blackwell.

Pennycook, Alastair 1989. The concept of method, interested knowledge and the politics of language teaching. *TESOL Quarterly* 23 (4). 589–618.

Potter, Jonathan & Alexa Hepburn. 2012. Somewhere between evil and normal: Traces of morality in a child-protection helpline. *Journal of Applied Linguistics and Professional Practice* 9 (2). 245–262.

Pöyhönen, Sari & Mirja Tarnanen. 2015. Integration policies and adult second language learning in Finland. In James Simpson and Anne Whiteside (eds.), *Adult language education and migration: Challenging agendas in policy and practice*, 107–118. London: Routledge.

Sacks, Harvey, 1992. *Lectures on conversation*. Oxford: Blackwell.

Searle, John R. 1979. *Expression and meaning: Studies in the theory of speech acts*. Cambridge: Cambridge University Press.

Stevanovic, Melisa. 2015. Displays of uncertainty and proximal deontic claims: The case of proposal sequences. *Journal of Pragmatics* 78. 84–97.

Stevanovic, Melisa & Anssi Peräkylä. 2012. Deontic authority in interaction: The right to announce, propose, and decide. *Research on Language and Social Interaction* 45 (3). 297–321.

Stevanovic, Melisa & Anssi Peräkylä. 2014. Three orders in the organization of human action: On the interface between knowledge, power, and emotion in interaction and social relations. *Language in Society* 43 (2). 185–207.

Stevanovic, Melisa & Jan Svennevig. 2015. Introduction: Epistemics and deontics in conversational directives. *Journal of Pragmatics* 78. 1–6.

Stokoe, Elizabeth. 2008. Dispreferred actions and other interactional breaches as devices for occasioning audience laughter in television "sitcoms". *Social Semiotics,* 18 (3). 289–307.

Stokoe, Elizabeth & Derek Edwards. 2012. Mundane morality: Gender, categories and complaints in familial neighbour disputes. *Journal of Applied Linguistics and Professional Practice* 9 (2). 165–192.

Irina Piippo
4 Norms in the making – exploring the norms of the teaching register *selkosuomi* in immigrant integration training classrooms in Finland

1 Introduction: Norms as objects of sociolinguistic enquiry

Understanding the patterned nature of human conduct is central to the humanities and the social sciences, and for a long time the notion of "norm" has been an important theoretical part of this endeavor. However, norms have proven quite elusive as objects of empirical enquiry (e.g. Parsons 1949: 396–397), and this has led some scholars to question the usefulness of the notion altogether. Especially scholars who favor so-called micro-level approaches have often been reluctant to use the notion of norms, dismissing it as simplistic and static (cf. Garfinkel 1967: 68). As the current sociolinguistic toolbox offers other conceptual tools which allow us to approach the patterned and discursively constructed nature of social life, such as the notions of language ideologies (Silverstein 1979; Woolard 1998) and enregisterment (Agha 2007), one might even question whether "norms" have any currency in poststructuralist or postmodern sociolinguistics at all.

In this chapter, I explore the norms of the teaching register *selkosuomi* ("easy to understand Finnish") in adult literacy training classrooms in Finland in order to discuss the role and relevance of norms in sociolinguistic theory and practice. My approach emphasizes the importance of reflexivity in theorizing norms of social conduct (see Piippo 2012), and it takes inspiration from linguistic anthropological research with a similar focus (Lucy 1993; Agha 2007). Despite the empirical element in the chapter, my main argument is metatheoretical: rather than providing an extensive description of the norms of the teaching register *selkosuomi*, my aim is to use this particular educational context as an illustrative case, which will allow me to discuss some central preconceptions concerning social and sociolinguistic norms.

Acknowledgements: I wish to thank the two anonymous reviewers for their helpful comments on an earlier draft of this chapter.

https://doi.org/10.1515/9781501511882-004

One of the common preconceptions about social norms is that they are a macro-level concept, a part of abstract structures that keep communities and cultures together. Especially in earlier structuralist sociology (cf. Durkheim 1938; Parsons 1949) this conception meant that norms were often approached from an etic, researcher-driven perspective. However, since the early days of sociology, perspectives have changed. Especially the linguistic turn in the social sciences and humanities in the 1960s and 1970s paved the way for approaches that were more deeply grounded in participants' own ways of perceiving, organizing and navigating their everyday lives (see e.g. Berger & Luckmann 1966). Constructivist perspectives on social life have also made the distinction between "macro" and "micro" less dichotomous: after all, even the existence of durable social institutions that are considered as part of the macro-context depends on micro-scale, situated events where actors re- and co-create their social worlds. What does this type of discursively oriented reflexive outlook mean for studying norms in social life? The focus has in many ways shifted to participants, but this does not mean that the ideologies, normative expectations and perspectives of the researcher do not matter.

In this chapter, I will explore these issues based on ethnographic fieldwork I have conducted in a Finnish educational organization that provides literacy training for adults. In particular, I explore the local practices that the teachers label *selkosuomi* and discuss their interlinkage with *selkokieli*, "easy to understand language", an institutionally theorized and partly standardized variety of Finnish that the *Finnish Center for Easy to Read* develops and promotes. I argue for the importance of studying norms as situationally grounded reflexive models. This type of perspective enables seeing beyond the preconception that norms need to be uniform and socially shared and provides access to the complex semiotic processes from which norms emerge. Based on the multimodal meaning-making practices in the literacy classrooms, I also argue for a broader sociolinguistic conception of norms.

2 From norms and ideologies to reflexivity and (en)register(ment)

I approach norms as reflexive models of meaningful, expected and appropriate conduct (cf. Piippo 2012). For me norms are *reflexive processes* whereby actors organize and make sense of the world around them. This initial definition is broad enough to warrant a more detailed discussion of a number of other socially routinized metapragmatic constructs (Agha 2007: 29) that can be encountered while observing social behavior.

First, it is useful to clarify how norms differ from and, at the same time, are interlinked with ideologies. The notion of norms is sometimes used as a label for relatively general ideals of behavior. For instance, Jørgensen (2008), in his discussion of polylingual languaging, speaks about norms of linguistic behavior and identifies such entities as "a monolingualism norm" and "a multilingualism norm" that describe people's stances towards multilingualism. Rather than norms, I would call such recognizable general tendencies *ideologies* of linguistic conduct. In contrast to this perspective, I regard norms as detailed situation-bound yet routinized reflexive models that allow actors to interpret social conduct as a flow of recognizable signs (see also Agha 2007: 8). In other words, instead of seeing norms as abstract ideals of behavior, I see norms as routinized reflexive models embedded in particular practices where members of a social group deploy and interpret semiotic tokens as part of specific participation frameworks. This is to say that when it comes to norms, in addition to the context, such issues as the actors' roles and relationships matter. For instance, in educational contexts, the norms concerning teachers' and students' linguistic and other social conduct differ in many respects.

Ideologies of language (see e.g. Woolard 1998) can be understood as beliefs and conceptualizations of languages, their speakers and discursive practices. Within linguistic anthropology, the study of language ideologies has often focused on how these conceptualizations are inherently socially and culturally positioned and politically loaded (see Silverstein 1979; Irvine 1989), and often employed in regimenting social behavior (see Kroskrity 2000; also Costa 2019). The definition at the beginning of this paragraph might give the impression that language ideologies will always surface as explicit metalinguistic comments. Sometimes they do, but on the whole, they can also be considered a more implicit and inextricable part of social life. They are a way to conceptualize the inherently positioned nature of linguistic conduct. In this sense norms are also ideological: they represent a perspective and might serve some interests and social groups better than others.

While I approach norms primarily as a grid against which actors interpret social conduct, norms are often also associated with the idea of social pressure to act in a certain way. This dimension of norms is often called normativity. In this chapter, normativity is understood as the way and extent to which certain kinds of conduct are recognized as normal for a particular social group and guarded against breaches by social sanctions (see e.g. Weber 1962: 67–68, 75–76; also von Wright 1963: 9; Agha 2007: 124–127). Norms vary according to how closely they are monitored and how aware social actors are of their existence. Often, normative expectations related to a situation become visible when they are violated, and actors are held accountable for their actions (see Garfinkel 1967; Heritage 1984: 115–120; also Hazel & Lønsmann in this volume).

What connects the notions presented above – norms, ideology and normativity – is that they all, when used in relation to language, involve various kinds of reflexive metapragmatic or metasemiotic behavior (Lucy 1993; Urban 2006), i.e. behavior that focuses on, interprets and evaluates linguistic and other semiotic conduct. Studying reflexive metalinguistic activities has always been a part of sociolinguistic research, although approaches differ in how much emphasis is given to the ways in which language users categorize and evaluate aspects of linguistic and other semiotic behavior (see Jaworski, Coupland & Galasìnki 2004). In linguistic anthropological research, reflexive behavior is seen as an inextricable part of the semiotic processes through which the social world as we know it is created, maintained and fractionally changed, and this is also the approach I adopt here. Metasemiotic conduct is ubiquitous, and it is not restricted to occasions of explicit metapragmatic descriptions of how certain types of people speak or how one typically conducts oneself in a certain type of situation. It also includes nonlinguistic and less explicit activities that can range from a raised eyebrow as a response to what someone just said to sequential uptake where the next speaker orients to the previous turn in a certain way. In other words, metasemiotic conduct is a constant feature of interaction by which participants signal how they frame (Goffman 1974) their own contributions and interpret the contributions of others in interaction.

Defining norms as situation-bound reflexive models entails that it is important that norms are explored from a participant perspective. To achieve this, I use Agha's (2007) concept of *enregisterment* to analyze the norms of the teaching register *selkosuomi* as expressed through metapragmatic behavior and social interaction in the fieldwork site. Agha (2007) describes enregisterment as a social process in which "diverse behavioral signs (whether, linguistic, non-linguistic or both) are functionally reanalysed as cultural models of action, as behaviors capable of indexing stereotypic characteristics of particular interactional roles, and relations among them" (Agha 2007: 55). His perspective thus highlights the role of metasemiotic conduct in consolidating registers into nameable and describable entities – entities that from the lect-based and grammar-oriented view have often been associated with a single, homogenous pre-existing norm (for criticism, see Hymes 1989: 433).

In the analysis below, I focus on select occasions where the teaching register under investigation and its features become visible, nameable and describable in interaction. My focus is mainly on metasemiotic conduct, but I also analyze an excerpt from my recordings of classroom interaction in order to illustrate the meaning-making mechanisms of the teaching register in action. This two-pronged approach allows me to explore the norms of the register from multiple perspectives and illustrate how translocal educational ideals, language ideologies and locally relevant social categories and identities are all part of the semiotic processes whereby the norms and normativity of *selkosuomi* are locally produced in interaction.

3 Research context – ethnographic fieldwork in literacy classrooms for adults

The material I use in this chapter comes from eleven months of ethnographic fieldwork in a private educational organization in Finland that provides immigrant integration training. The fieldwork was conducted in 2017. Because of my background in Arabic sociolinguistics, I entered the field to study adult language socialization of this particular language group, but since then the ongoing research project has gained a more multilingual emphasis. During my time in the organization, I focused on what is called literacy training for adults, a ten-month study programme that is provided prior to immigrant integration training proper for those students that need support in their literacy skills in the Latin alphabet. In the Helsinki metropolitan area, the training consisted of three smaller modules that lasted 75, 75 and 50 days, respectively.[1] In terms of language socialization, these modules provide a chance to study the early stages of institutional language learning. Most of the students had arrived in Finland 1.5–2 years prior to the fieldwork, but since adult immigrants to Finland do not start their integration training until they have been granted asylum or received a residence permit, the literacy courses constituted their first contact with institutional language training in Finland.

I had a chance to follow two different multilingual groups through their ten months of training. The students came from a variety of social backgrounds. Some had university degrees while others had no or very little formal schooling. Age-wise the students ranged from barely twenty to their late fifties. Many of them were literate in their mother tongue or some other medium of schooling, but usually these languages would be written in a non-Latin alphabet. In each of the groups, however, some students started their literacy training from the very basics. The majority of the students came from Arabic-speaking countries.

---

[1] Since 2018, literacy training for adults has been provided either as the first module of basic education for adults or as courses organized by liberal adult education institutions. The aim has been to better adapt the training to students' varying life situations and educational paths. Because of the changes, the courses described in this chapter do not have exact equivalents in the current system.

This situation reflected the demographics of immigration to Finland in the two-year period before my fieldwork. Although Arabic-speakers formed the majority, most of the groups were linguistically heterogeneous so that in a group of 15 students there were often at least five different first languages represented. These additional first languages included Somali, Tigrinya, Amharic, Malayam, Dari, Sorani, Kurmanji, Bulgarian and Chinese. Although some teachers had learned some Arabic, generally the students' first languages were not part of the teachers' repertoires.

As part of my fieldwork, I participated in the classroom activities of each group once a week for a full day. On each of these days, I video-recorded a full lesson to collect longitudinal material on the early stages of adult second language socialization. In addition to these recordings, my material consists of field notes as well as teaching materials and other documents given to the students. At the end of each module, when participants were about to move on to other groups, I also conducted interviews with teachers and students. In terms of recorded material, I have 63 lessons and 48 interviews. The recorded material provides a chance to examine the everyday semiotic practices in the classrooms in detail. However, when it comes to material on metapragmatic conduct, I also rely on observations that I made off-camera and recorded in my field notes.

The literacy courses partly resemble courses in later stages of immigrant integration training. Despite their specific focus on literacy skills, the scope of the courses is relatively broad and includes study skills and socialization into Finnish society and work life as an integrated part of the courses (see Hazel & Lønsmann this volume for a similar example from the Danish context). The teachers themselves, however, often commented that teaching these courses differed considerably from other kinds of Finnish as a second language teaching. These differences had to do with the ways in which interaction and teaching practices were affected by a lack of shared linguistic resources and shared literacy practices with the students in the literacy courses.

At this point, a short methodological note is in order. Below, I will mainly be approaching norms of *selkosuomi* through ethnographic vignettes and observations from my fieldwork material. However, I will also analyze an excerpt of classroom interaction to illustrate meaning-making practices in the classroom setting. This dual approach allows me to consider norms (defined as reflexive models that allow actors to interpret social conduct as a flow of recognizable signs) through analyses of metapragmatic conduct as well as observable patterns in social behavior.

4 Analysis

A challenge in studying norms in any social group of people is that in the flow of perceivably normal everyday life, norms often go unnoticed. Interaction that proceeds without anyone being held accountable for perceived misconduct might provide insights into habitualized ways of acting and interpreting actions, but observing a situation that proceeds smoothly does not help identify the boundaries of normality, nor does it allow an analyst to determine whether observed patterned ways of acting are considered *normative* by the participants themselves. This is why normativity is often studied through cases in which participants orient to breaches of the social order.

The normativity of interactional practices in the classrooms I studied became evident during my first day of classroom observation when I unintentionally breached the local norms by speaking Finnish in a way that was considered "too difficult" for the students. When I introduced myself and my research project to the students, my introduction got translated[2] by the course teacher into "easier to understand language". Later on, I observed a similar instance during a school-wide career day when a presentation given by a visitor from a nearby catering school was similarly spontaneously translated into a form of Finnish that was perceived to be more suited to the audience.

These instances were the first indication that for the language teachers, the semiotic practices in the classroom constituted *a normalized model of behavior* (Agha 2007: 126), a reflexive model specifying that a certain type of behavior was normal or typical for certain kind of actors, in this case for more experienced Finnish-speaking participants interacting with the learners. Especially on the second occasion I observed this, where a considerable portion of the teaching staff was present, it became quite clear that the normative orientation was at some level shared: the teachers present seemed to view the spontaneous translatory practices of their colleague as an ordinary part of the situation. These explicit instances of "correction" also indicate that the ways of interacting in these situations constitute a *semiotic register* (Agha 2007: 81), a cultural model of action in

---

2 Translation often refers to written texts and interpretation to oral forms of translation. Here, I use translation as a notion that also covers occasions where prior talk is represented in another language or register. While both translation and interpreting can be professional practices, they are ubiquitous phenomena also in everyday interaction (see e.g., Harjunpää 2017). This was also the case in the organization in which this study was conducted. Students from similar language backgrounds often spontaneously translated the teacher's speech and activities to each other. In addition, both teachers and students utilized students with stronger language skills as interpreters, sometimes so that multilingual mediation involved more than two languages.

which a semiotic repertoire is linked with stereotypic indexical values and recognized by a certain population. What this repertoire is, what kind of indexical values it has, and by whom it is recognized as a register will be discussed next when I explore more instances where the teaching register *selkosuomi* is made visible in interaction, often through metapragmatic commentary.

4.1 *Selkosuomi* and its enregisterment as a teaching register

My first day in the classrooms had implied that there was a specific, normative way of interacting in the classroom setting. By the following week, I had already learned that the expected way of conducting oneself also had a metalinguistic label. The teachers called the register that they deployed with their students *selkokieli* or *selkosuomi*, "easy to understand language" or "easy to understand Finnish". By using these labels, the teachers explicitly associated their practices with the institutionally theorized and partly standardized variety of Finnish that the *Finnish Center for Easy to Read (Selkokeskus)*[3] develops and promotes.

Let us consider, for instance, the following excerpt from an interview with Miika, one of the staff members who worked as a social counsellor at the school. I had asked him what the biggest linguistic challenges outside the school context were for his clients in the early phases of being socialized into a new language and socio-cultural context. Without being prompted, Miika immediately identified the lacking knowledge of *selkosuomi*, "easy to understand Finnish", in the surrounding society as one of the major challenges:

> [. . .] ja käsitys selkokielestä esimerkiks virastoissa ja muualla nii on hyvin erilainen et tai siis se käsitys, sitä käsitystä ei oikeastaan ole. et niinkun musta on välillä niinku hyvin niinku mielenkiintosta että kun ihmiset kokee puhuvansa helppoa suomea, ja tota et se että sä puhut ne liirum laarumit niinku hitaasti ni se ei oo sama kuin et se on helppoa suomea, niin se on silloin hidasta suomen kieltä ja tota ja niin edelleen. niin niitä tulkintoja siitä selkosuomesta on niinku yhtä paljon kuin sen puhujia. et varmasti niinku moni pyrkii selkiyttämään sitä suomen kieltä, mutta tota aa ei se oikein suju.

---

[3] The Finnish Center for Easy to Read is a part of the Finnish Association on Intellectual and Developmental Disabilities, and it is funded by the Finnish Ministry of Social Affairs and Health. Although in this chapter the focus is on second language socialization, the target audience of easy to understand language also includes those whose language skills have been affected due to aphasia or memory loss and those with neurobiological disorders. Unlike in some other countries, in Finland easy to understand language is developed without focusing on the specific needs of its various audiences.

> [. . .] *and in public services and such, understanding of what easy to understand language is, is very different, or the understanding, the understanding does not exist. I find it very interesting that when people think that they are speaking easy Finnish, when they produce their gobbledygook slowly, that is not the same thing as easy Finnish, it is then merely slow Finnish and so forth. So, there are as many interpretations of easy to understand Finnish as there are its users. Surely a lot of people try to make their Finnish clearer, but they are not really succeeding in it.* Interview 20.10.2017

Here Miika describes *selkokieli*, "easy to understand language", as a register that should in principle be used in public services. However, officials in these services have a very different, and as he later amends, in fact *nonexistent* understanding of how to effectively interact with those that are still at the early stages of second language socialization. By criticizing those that do not succeed in adjusting their Finnish, Miika simultaneously portrays himself as someone who knows how to do it. *Selkosuomi* is not treated as a constant entity, but as a set of practices that may vary depending on one's understanding, experience and expertise. In this way, by focusing on participants' metasemiotic work where register formations become bounded, describable objects, it is possible to see how registers are more than simply sets of linguistic features. In this case for instance, Miika's reported good command of *selkosuomi* functions as an emblem of his expertise as someone who works with multilingual learners of Finnish.

This instance thus provides us with a glimpse of how the process of enregisterment works, while also being an example of how norms in the sense of reflexive models of meaningful, expected and appropriate conduct are upheld and molded in interaction. While analytically it is reasonable to keep the concepts separate, in everyday interaction registers and their norms are discursively produced side by side. For example, in this excerpt Miika identifies a particular way of speaking and associates it with a group of people – those who encounter newly arrived immigrants in their work. He also expresses a normative expectation that this is the appropriate way of speaking and acting with individuals who are still being socialized into Finnish.

4.2 The teaching register *selkosuomi* and its links to *selkokieli* as an institutionalized register

For ease of reference, I call the oral register encountered in the observed classrooms *selkosuomi*, "easy to understand Finnish". As indicated above, this register is related to *selkokieli* "easy to understand language[4]", though the relationship is not a straightforward one. As an institutionally theorized and promulgated register, *selkokieli* represents an attempt at standardization. With regards to written "easy to understand Finnish" this development is well on its way. There are guides for *selkokieli* (Leskelä 2019; Virtanen 2009) and recently, the Finnish Center for Easy to Read published a detailed measurement tool for determining whether a text fulfills the criteria of basic level "easy to understand language" (Center for Easy to Read 2018). *Selkokieli* is also present in media. The Finnish Broadcasting Company YLE regularly broadcasts news in easy to understand Finnish both in radio and in television. Some public services have adapted parts of their websites into "easy to understand language" and some municipalities have carried out campaigns where parts of their communication with relevant population groups have been produced in easy Finnish (for examples see Sainio 2013). Still, although "easy to understand language" is relatively widely used and promoted, written *selkokieli* remains somewhat of an expert register. The Finnish Center for Easy to Read for instance regulates the use of the register label by awarding *selkotunnus*, a specific logo certifying that a publication (or a video) conforms to the criteria for "easy to understand language".

When it comes to spoken communication in *selkokieli*, the register is less explicitly described and codified. Guidelines for which communicative practices to adopt in order to support this type of asymmetric communication[5] do exist (see e.g. Kartio 2009: 8–24), and the Center organizes training "in easy to understand interaction", but on the whole, multichannel interaction does not lend itself to standardization in the same way as written language, textual objects or videos do. For instance, the guidelines (Kartio 2009) mention briefness, everyday vocabulary, questions, repetition, emphasis, slow speech rate, gestures, facial expressions and pictures as features that facilitate asymmetric interaction but does not provide that much detail.

Yet, it is interesting to note that although spoken *selkokieli* is not a strongly standardized register, it is a quite heavily theorized one. The relationship between *selkokieli* and linguistic research is tight and especially spoken "easy to under-

---

[4] As can be seen already in Miika's excerpt above, *selkosuomi* "easy to understand Finnish" and *selkokieli* "easy to understand language" are often used synonymously. While it is more common to refer to the institutionalized, standardized register as *selkokieli* and hear the teachers speak about their own practices as *selkosuomi*, the difference is not a categorical one.

[5] *Selkokieli* is being developed with insights from conversation analytic tradition. In conversation analysis, asymmetric communication is understood as asymmetries between participants for instance in knowledge, participation – and languages. These asymmetries are visible at the micro-level of communication.

stand Finnish" is developed and promulgated through conversation analytic research (see e.g. Leskelä & Lindholm 2012). Among other things, this research has sought to address conversational practices that emphasize the asymmetric role of the interactants (see e.g. Leskelä 2009).[6] The range of possible audiences of "easy to understand language" is broad, but so far, *selkokieli* in learning contexts has received less attention than "easy to understand Finnish" used with and among individuals with neurobiological disorders.

The organization where I conducted my fieldwork also had an institutional role in promulgating *selkokieli* to the wider public. At the time of my fieldwork, it had a responsibility of producing material for *Selkosanomat*, a biweekly newspaper and its accompanying website in "easy to understand Finnish". In addition to this, the teachers regularly produced study materials in written "easy to understand Finnish" that were utilized in the classrooms. In other words, this more standardized dimension of *selkokieli* was also part of everyday life in the organization. Indeed, the relationship between the standardized *selkokieli* and the oral teaching register is a dialogical one: the standardized register provides an identifiable institutionalized frame of reference for the non-standardized language socialization practices upon which it has been developed. "Easy to understand Finnish" as a classroom norm is therefore reliant on semiotic processes with both local and translocal dimensions.

4.3 *Selkosuomi* as a multimodal semiotic register

Often when the teachers spoke about their work in the literacy courses, they noted that interaction in literacy classrooms was markedly different even from other kinds of immigrant integration training. This difference was often located in the ways in which meaning-making in the classrooms relied on multimodal semiotic resources, with teachers and other staff members often engaging in intensive visual communicative work to overcome the lack of common linguistic resources. The following excerpt from my field notes illustrates this type of interaction. The snippet was written down two weeks after the beginning of the first study module.

> The teacher has a message for Ilyas from the social worker about a meeting tomorrow to sort out day care issues with the help of an interpreter. Intensive eye contact, time written on

---

[6] *Selkokieli* originates in everyday accommodative practices that in sociolinguistics have been studied as "simplified" registers such as *motherese* and *foreigner talk* (Ferguson 1971, 1981), and it may on occasion be construed as "talking down" to the recipient.

a paper and the orally conducted message and gestures support each other. For instance, tomorrow was produced simultaneously with a hand gesture where a semi-circle is drawn forward.   Field notes 1.3.2017

This same multi-channeled nature of meaning-making was also repeatedly brought up as the teachers described their own practices in the classroom. The explicitness of the descriptions varied, but on the whole, multimodality can be considered a recognized feature of the teaching register. Below, I examine two excerpts from my material. The first one illustrates how enregistered ways of acting are intermingled with ideologies. The second one presents in more detail some stereotypic features of the teaching register.

The first excerpt is from an interview with a teacher called Otso. I had just asked him about utilizing students' earlier languages in the classroom. At the time of my fieldwork, translanguaging pedagogies (García & Li 2014) were making their way into this organization with management's support.[7] Quite often, however, the ratified presence of languages other than Finnish was not self-evident in the classroom, and for instance students' translatory practices were considered at times counterproductive for learning Finnish. In his answer, Otso contrasts occasions of multilingual interaction for purposes of relaying information with his preferred method of teaching that includes deploying multimodal means.

> niin siis ei siis niiku kyllähän sitä voi jotenki niinku varsinkin jos pitää tiedottaa jotain. niin tottakai siitä on hyötyä että siellä on se yks joka ymmärtää hyvin ja tulkkaa muille. kaikki tämmöset huomenna testi tämä ja tämä kello ja sellaset asiat. ni sillonku on kysymys niinku viestinnästä tai informaation välittämisestä niin mun mielestä ilman muuta tulkki. se ei oo suomen kielen opetustilanne vaan se on tiedon välitystilanne ja siin kohtaa kaikki kielet on sallittuja ja kaikki keinot tavallaan et se informaatio välittyy mahdollisimman oikein. Mut sitten kun on kysymys kielen opiskelusta niin sitten niin (.) sit se kyllä menee vähän hankalammaksi että että, miten sitä vois siinä sit hyödyntää. Mahdollisesti sitä vois ajatella myös niin-, mutta tää on nyt, koululla on valittu linja että mistä mäkään en voi niin livetä että mä noudatan niinku [organisaation nimi] toimintasuunnitelmaa, että sitä vois ajatella että vois sitä myös opettaa silleen kun meillekin on kieliä opetettu. [. . .]
>
> kyllä mä opetuksessa oon yrittänyt pitää linjaa siinä että se jollain kuvalla tai jollain päällä seisonnalla saadaan se asia, vaikka mä tiedän että se on siinä vaiheessa tulkattu miljoonaan kertaan kun mä sitä kuvaa etin, niin silti, koska siellä voi olla se yks eritrealainen ja sit muutenkin kun mä en ymmärrä mitä he tulkkaa ni mä en oo ihan varma että kuinka oikein ja lähelle se menee aina. ni sit jos mä saan sen kuvan kuitenkin ja pystyn sen vielä ikään kuin rautalangasta vääntämään ni sitten musta onnistumisen edellytykset on parhaimmat.

---

7 There were, for instance, groups that consisted solely of Arabic-speaking students so that utilizing multilingual pedagogies would be easier.

Well, they can be utilized somehow, especially if you need to inform [the group] about something. It is definitely useful if there is someone who understands well and acts as an interpreter to others. All these kinds of "tomorrow test this and this time" and so forth. When it's about conveying information, I think that then interpreting is ok. It is not a situation where you teach Finnish but a situation where you convey information and at that point all languages and all means are permitted so that the information is conveyed as correctly as possible. But when it is about studying Finnish, then it gets a bit trickier to think of how to utilize [the earlier languages]. It could be possible to think so-, but it is, there is a chosen policy at the school that I cannot abandon just like that, that I follow the strategy of [name of organization], that you could think that you could also teach languages the way they've been taught to us. [. . .]

I have tried to maintain a policy in my teaching that the matter is conveyed with the help of a picture and by something like standing on your head, although I know that while I'm looking for the picture, the matter has been interpreted at least a million times. Nevertheless, because there might be the one Eritrean [who does not speak Arabic] and also because I don't understand what they are interpreting, I can't be sure how close and correct the translation is. So, if I find the picture and if I can explain it in plain language, then I think that the possibilities for success are the greatest. Interview 30.11.2017

The excerpt illustrates the way in which the teaching register and its norms are intertwined with language ideologies, in this case the ideology of monolingualism. Otso describes this ideal as the official policy in the organization and notes that the policy restricts his possibilities of utilizing students' other languages in the classroom.[8] He then goes on and describes how his teaching practice, in addition to "plain or easy to understand Finnish", also involves other semiotic means, namely pictures and what he describes as "standing on one's head". Otso produces "standing on one's head" with smiley voice accompanied by a hand gesture in which he twists his hands, probably mimicking the multimodal nature of interaction.[9] In Otso's answer, teaching events proper are contrasted with situations where the students are simply informed about something. In the latter case, all languages and all linguistic resources are permitted, thus portraying the multimodal, partly non-linguistic teaching practices as practices that comply with the monolingual ideals identified as the organizational policy.

The monolingual ideology present in this excerpt is not in itself surprising – monolingual ideals are still a persistent part of language education; when it comes to institutional structures of education as well as teachers' beliefs (see Piippo 2021;

---

8 There was no official language policy in the organization. However, some of the teachers that had a longer history in the organization reported these types of strong normative expectations of monolingual teaching (for the monolingual principle in teaching, see e.g. Cummins 2007).
9 In Finnish, *(vaikka) päällään seisten* '(even) while standing on one's head' is an idiom that refers to readiness to tolerate hardship. In the excerpt, standing on one's head is not produced exactly in the idiomatic form, yet I'm inclined to interpret Otso's choice of words as a reference to the challenging nature of communication.

Alisaari, Heikkola, Commins & Acquah 2019). What is noteworthy here is that the ideological lens affects the way the multimodal nature of *selkosuomi* is interpreted. The multimodality of interaction that in translanguaging studies is seen as going beyond named languages (see e.g. Li 2018) is seen here as a way of staying within the confines of a single "language", and hence as a way of complying with the normative expectations identified as the institutional language policy. In this manner, the excerpt illustrates how classrooms are often multifaceted crossroads of language policy (Lilja, Mård-Miettinen & Nikula 2019). Besides participants' ideologies and norms, the practices in the classrooms are shaped by standards and normative expectations attributed to parties outside the immediate context.

The next excerpt illustrates in more detail some stereotypic features of the teaching register *selkosuomi*. With this excerpt, I will discuss the role of explicit metapragmatic comments in exploring the norms of *selkosuomi*. The snippet is from my field notes and it describes a conversation in the teacher's lounge one day when I had come to meet the head of division, Minna, to discuss some practicalities regarding a new teaching module that was about to start. While we are chatting, Enni, a teacher who participates in my project, comes in and hands in a consent form from Namdar, a Dari-speaking student who had just recently joined the group. There are also other teachers present in the lounge.

> Minna asks whether Namdar speaks Arabic. I reply that not to my knowledge, although some of the Arabic-speaking students do address him in Arabic. At this point, someone quips that Dari and Arabic *sama sama*. I act on the joke and say that the classroom situations have made me re-evaluate a linguists' relatively strict understanding of similarity and difference between things. I continue that just the previous day in Tiina's class the students had had an intensive discussion on the way in which the Finnish word *kaupunki* 'city, town' should be translated into Arabic. Both city (*madīna*) and province (*muqāṭaʿa*) had been proposed as translations. To this discussion one of the students had noted partly in Arabic and partly in Finnish that city, province *sama sama*. [. . .] Enni who is still standing by the door notes that the previous week she had taught family words to students. In that context she had told the students that in Finland, families can be of many kinds. *Naimisissa normaali* 'married normal', *eronnut normaali* 'divorced normal', *äiti ja isä normaali* 'mother and father normal', *äiti ja äiti normaali* 'mother and mother normal', *isä ja isä normaali* 'father and father normal'. She continues that in literacy courses many things are taught by cutting corners. She, for instance, teaches that [Finnish] *alas* 'downwards' and *alhaalla* 'down' *sama sama* (simultaneously Enni first squats down and then makes a gesture where she presses her hand down). She laughs that, at the point when students reach module three of the literacy training, they notice that they have been fooled. The teacher has taught that *kissa ja koira sama sama* 'cat and dog same same'. "That is the way it goes in these literacy courses".
>
> Field notes 22.3.2017

In this excerpt, we may note several things of relevance for the teaching register and its norms. First, Enni's description of her conduct in the classroom provides explicit examples of the multimodal nature of *selkosuomi*. The description that she provides for the way in which she teaches *alas*, 'downwards', and *alhaalla*, 'down', is not restricted to describing only her linguistic conduct. Enni's illustration also includes a metasemiotic typification of concurrent embodied action and gestures, squatting down and lowering her hand, both actions presented as something typical for literacy teaching. Similar animated instances of self-reported speech were fairly common in the teacher's lounge and they also occur in recorded teacher interviews (see Otso's answer above). The field note excerpt and similar observations indicate that the actors themselves explicitly orient to the multimodality of the register as something that is pertinent to the meaning-making practices and the norms of this context.

The excerpt also illustrates that the teaching register exists as more than a mere register label. For instance, Enni's animated examples of her teaching practices provide evidence of the *semiotic repertoire* of the register. In her self-reported speech, Enni formulates a contrast between her everyday speech and the typical practices of the classroom, and this distinction is clearly recognizable to the other staff members, judging by their reactions. Enni further describes "cutting corners" as something especially characteristic of literacy training, thereby creating a contrast between literacy teachers and other Finnish as a second language teachers. All these details indicate that *selkosuomi* is a *semiotic register* with a semiotic repertoire that is recognized by the teachers in this organization. It also seems to be a *normalized model of behavior,* i.e. a reflexive model of interaction that a larger group recognize regarding the normal or typical ways of communicating with the students.

Despite these observations, the norms of the teaching register *selkosuomi* cannot be located solely by examining teachers' metapragmatic and metasemiotic comments. Self-reported speech, even when it includes seemingly detailed examples of conduct, often only provides access to fairly stereotypic features of the register. For instance, in the excerpt above, the formulations *x and y same same* and *x and y normal* give the impression that the loss of copula is a prominent feature of the teaching register (see also instances of Otso's reported speech). While these features do occur in classroom interaction, they are arguably exacerbated in this type of reported speech. Hence, exploring the norms of the teaching register also requires a closer look at the interactive practices in the classroom.

4.4 The teaching register *selkosuomi* in use

The following excerpt is from a lesson approximately halfway through the first 75-day module of literacy training. In the first module, one of the overarching learning goals is for students to become acquainted with Finnish phonemes and their graphemic equivalents. At this point of the course, the group is focusing on Finnish /r/. The teacher has also recently introduced the notion of syllable to the students, and the group has practiced /r/'s and syllables with a dictation where the students have used letter cards to form words read aloud by the teacher. The excerpt is from a situation where the teacher starts to bring the dictation to an end, compliments the group for work well done, and gives instructions on how to collect the cards used in the assignment. The last dictated word repeated in lines 1–8 is *surullinen*, 'sad'. In the transcript below, I have also transcribed some of the teacher's embodied actions that are relevant to the analysis. These are included as the third line of the transcription. The asterisks (*) mark beginnings and ends of the described action and hashes (#) mark the points where the gestures illustrated in the figures appear in the flow of interaction (see the transcription key at the end of the chapter and Mondada 2016 for details). For gestures reiterated in a similar manner superscript numbering is used (e.g. #[1] #[2] #[3] all indicate the same gesture).

Excerpt 1. "Four syllables"

Teacher = T; Faadil = F; Ilyas = I

```
01  T:  No niin (0.8)   *su (1.4) rul (0.5)       [li (0.2) nen    *(.) * neljä *    *tavua. (1.1)
        Well then (0.8) *su (1.4) rul (0.5)       [li (0.2) nen    *(.) * four *     *syllables.(1.1)
    t                        * with each syllable lifts one more finger *   *4 fingers up* *walks--------
02  F:                                            [li nen
                                                  [li nen
03  F:  su rul li **nen
        su rul li **nen
    t   -------> **writes on smart board
04  T:  su (0.4) [            [rul           [li        [nen (0.4) neljä tavua.     *
        su (0.4) [            [rul           [li        [nen (0.4)four syllables.   *
    t       ------------------------------------------------------------------->    *
05  F:            [su (0.6) ru [   [rul(0.5) [li (0.5) nen [
                  [su (0.6) ru [   [rul(0.5) [li (0.5) nen [
06  F:  joo
        yeah
07      (1.3)
08  T:  *su (0.2) rul (0.4) li (.) nen*
        *su (0.2) rul (0.4) li (.) nen  *
    t   *with each syllable points the text in question*
09      *(1.1)*
    t   * walks *
10  T:  ↑ hyvä (0.3)    ↑ tosi hyvä    (.)  kiitos teille
        ↑ good (0.3)    ↑ really good  (.)  thank you
11      (1.0)
```

12	T:	laita nyt sinun	(.) #¹a (.)	#²i		
		put now your	(.) #¹a (.)	#²i		
	fig		#fig.1	#fig.1		

figure 1

13		laita aina	#¹sama	#²sama nippuun niin	#minä kerään pois.
		put always	#¹same	#²same into a stack so	#I collect away.
	fig		#fig. 2	#fig. 2	#fig.3

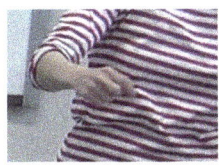   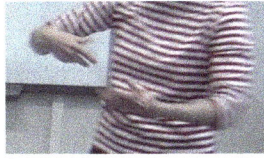

figure 2   figure 3

14	F:	joo.
		yeah.

15	T:	laita sama	#kirjain aina	[#¹a #²a #³i #⁴i niin minä kerään sit pois.	*
		put the same	#letter always	[#¹a #²a #³i #⁴i so I collect then away.	*
	t				*walks-->
	fig		#fig.4	#fig.5	

16	F:		[okei joo okei. okei okei okei okei	*opeetaja.
			[okay yeah okay. okay okay okay okay	*teacher.

figure 4   figure 5

17	T:	te olitte tosi hyvät.	*
		you were really good.	*
	t	with letter box ------>	*

18		*(1.2)*
	t	* nods her head*

```
19        tosi hyvä.
          really good.
20   I:   kiitos opettaja, kiitos.
          Thank you teacher, thank you.
21        (0.7)
22   T:   joo.  *eli     laita   uut       samaan ja  (0.7) ja n sama    *
          yeah. *so put your     u's together and     (0.7) and n together. *
     t         *stacks letters on x:s desk                                *
23        *(2.7) niin minä kerään sit nopeasti pois.  *
          *(2.7) so I'll collect then quickly away.    *
          *moves the letter box to x:s desk            *
24        (1.1)
25        *uut, jes *
          *the u's, yep*
     t    * takes a stack of letters from F's desk*
26        (4.4)  ja voit ottaa sit sen sinun r-sivun kirjasta
          (4.4) and you can take then that r-page from the book
     t    * organizes letter cards into the box----------------------
27        kun on (0.4) kaikki (0.5) kerätty.          *
          when everything has been collected.          *
          ----------------------------------------------->  *
```

Earlier subsections have already identified some stereotypic features of *selkosuomi*: simpler vocabulary and structures, repetition, pauses, emphasis, gestures and the use of visualizations. The excerpt above illustrates most of these stereotypic features. The teacher's overall rate of speech delivery is slow, and pauses are utilized more frequently to organize the delivery. There are also frequent repetitions. In the excerpt, for instance, the compliment for work well done is repeated three times (lines 10 and 17–18) and the instructions to stack the cards four times (lines 12–13, 15, 22–23). Also pitch range is partly exaggerated, especially in line 10 where she compliments the class for the first time. The sentence structure is simple throughout and occasionally inflections such as case endings are left out so that words are easier to recognize.[10] On other occasions, ease of comprehension is supported with more overt marking of grammatical relations. For instance,

---

[10] Teachers had different views on the use of structurally simplified language in the classroom. Analyzing teacher's understandings of the appropriate ways of "simplifying" language is beyond the bounds of the current chapter. In written *selkokieli* there is an expectation of linguistic correctness. Leskelä (2019: 95) describes *selkokieli* as a truncated, artificial variety of Finnish that as a principle cannot have any features that are against the rules of "standard" language. In spoken *selkosuomi* the boundaries of appropriateness were often more lenient.

person deixis is more prominently displayed: The teacher uses standard register forms *minä* (I) and *sinun* (you, sg. gen.) to emphasize who needs to do the stacking and who collects the cards (see e.g. lines 12–13).

These observations, however, do not offer a full account of the norms of the teaching register. This is partly because the non-linguistic dimensions of *selkosuomi* are difficult to capture in metapragmatic typifications. If we take another look at the situation in Excerpt 1, we may note that multimodality is at play. For instance, the iterations of the word *surullinen,* 'sad', in lines 1, 4 and 8 look fairly similar in terms of verbal production. However, when the accompanying embodied action is taken into consideration, it becomes clear that the teacher with each iteration orients to a different modality of language. First the focus is on listening to the word and identifying the syllables that she simultaneously counts with her fingers (line 1). Then the focus shifts to making the connection between the spoken and written form of the word, which she demonstrates by writing the syllables on the smartboard (line 4). When the text is ready, she reads the text aloud syllable by syllable and simultaneously points to each of them and thus illustrates the process of interpreting a written text (line 8). Although the teacher's explicit metalinguistic comments are restricted to stating the number of syllables, other actions function as meta-signs of how the students are to proceed with assignments like this. In other words, the way the teacher's activities are sequentially ordered in this instance socializes the participants into the sequence of actions known as "doing a dictation". At this point, all of the students have finished their assignment and they watch and listen seemingly attentively while the teacher recapitulates the process. One of the students, Faadil even repeats the syllables after the teacher (lines 2, 3 and 5) and produces a confirmative *joo,* 'yeah', (line 6) once the teacher has finished writing the word. With their uptake the students co-construct the activity as something expected in the classroom context – as part of a reflexive model of meaningful, expected and appropriate conduct.

The multimodal nature of meaning-making is also evident when the teacher provides instructions on how to collect the letter cards. In this part of the transcript, the teacher's verbal directives are accompanied by gestures that can be interpreted as mimicking the process of stacking letter cards and retrieving the cards from the students. In line 12, the directive *laita nyt sinun a i*, 'put now your a i', is produced with an iterated hand gesture where the teacher's hand mimics a card that is placed on a table (Figure 1). At this point, the act of stacking is merely introduced through the iterative gestures as the imperative verb *laita*, 'put', on its own does not specify where or how the letter cards should be placed. Next (line 13), the teacher iterates the directive by producing *laita aina sama sama nippuun*, 'put always same same into a stack'. This time the verbal message contains an adverb *nippuun*, 'into a stack'. However, also this time the object of the imperative verb, the reduplicative *sama sama* is accompanied by an iterated hand gesture (Figure 2). Gesturing also supports the delivery of *niin minä kerään sit pois* 'so [that] I collect away' (line 13) as the teacher brings both her arms towards her torso in a sweeping motion (Figure 3). The directive is produced yet a third time in line 15 as *laita sama kirjain aina a a i i*, 'put the same letter always a a i i'. Now, the object of the imperative verb *sama kirjain*, 'same letter', is an NP with the term *kirjain*, 'letter'. The teacher seems to orient to the possibility that the word might not yet be familiar to all the students and completes the directive with *aina a a i i*, 'always a a i i', a re-wording parallel to the one she used in line 12. With her gestures, the teacher indicates that *kirjain*, 'letter', and the letter names *a* and *i* refer to the same thing by producing on each occasion a similar gesture where she closes her palms on top of each other (Figures 4 and 5).

This brief analysis illustrates how the meaning-making mechanisms in this excerpt, which can be identified as an instance of *selkosuomi*, rely heavily on non-linguistic resources and multimodal interaction. The concurrent use of linguistic, textual, aural, visual and spatial resources enables the teachers to utilize iconicity and indexicality as sign modes that are less tied to language-specific knowledge and which can more readily be interpreted by relying on one's experience and the immediate surroundings. While such signs are inherently meaningful, they can also be quite ambiguous (see Goodwin 2014: 200). Excerpt 1, for instance, shows how gestures can be utilized to further specify what kind of activity was meant by the imperative *laita*, 'put'. These gestures are iconic in the sense that they resemble the activity of stacking, yet they are at the same time utilized indexically to point to connections between meanings emerging through different channels. It is also relevant to note that in this example, the gestures are an integral part of the referential content of the utterance and provide a more detailed representation (Kendon 2004: 158–160) of the activity of stacking something. According to my ethnographic experience, this reliance on gestures as well as visual and spatial resources in establishing the referential meaning of the utterance was a particularly prominent feature of interaction in these classrooms, especially in the early stages of second language socialization when common linguistic resources were still limited.

5 Discussion – The norms of *selkosuomi*

In this chapter, I have explored the teaching register *selkosuomi* and its associated norms by focusing on metapragmatic discourses and multimodal teaching practices in literacy classrooms in the metropolitan area of Helsinki. The starting point of the discussion was my claim that norms should be conceptualized as semiotic processes rather than static products. I also argued that norms, if we want to approach them as objects of sociolinguistic enquiry, should be studied in their local context by examining both the metapragmatic conduct of the participants and their actual everyday practices. I focused on the teaching register *selkosuomi,* a register that is associated with the standardized register of *selkokieli* ("easy to understand language") and which bears resemblance to other registers of linguistically asymmetric communication.

As Agha (2007: 168) notes, registers exist as bounded objects only to the extent that they are "treated by their users as functionally recognized partitions within the total inventory of its expressive means". With the examples discussed throughout Section 4, I illustrated that for the teachers "easy to understand Finnish" was a functionally recognized partition that was explicitly described as their typical classroom conduct. The descriptions were of varying elaborateness, but whether or not they made explicit reference to the register labels *selkosuomi* or *selkokieli,* the use of "easier language" and simultaneous intensive use of other semiotic channels were elements that were repeated in the teachers' portrayals. This indicates that *selkosuomi* was fairly strongly enregistered among the teachers, and this enregisterment enabled the teachers to engage in local identity work and to position their own practices *vis-à-vis* perceived institutional standards and changing global and translocal educational ideals. The discourses surrounding the register also shaped the teachers' understandings of what the norms of *selkokieli* are, and for whom they are norms.

My discussion of "easy to understand Finnish" has almost exclusively been from the teachers' perspective. This has been for a reason – the teaching register *selkosuomi* is an asymmetric register stereotypically deployed by the linguistically more expert interactant. For the teachers, *selkosuomi* is a professional register, the norms of which are molded by their constant practice of the register and a variety of discourses they participate in. This does not mean, however, that the students would not have a reflexive understanding of the register and social personae connected to it. The observation that certain features of the teaching register were not reciprocated by the students could be taken to indicate that the division of labor associated with this register was recognized on some level. For instance, slowed down tempo of speech, exceedingly clear articulation and strategically placed pauses were some of the features to which also the students seemed to orient in their practices as part of didactic speech that was not utilized when speaking with more proficient Finnish speakers. However, this should not be taken as a categorical difference. The norms of the teaching register also provide the possibility for tropes, i.e. metaphorical uses (Parmentier 1994: 102) of the register tokens. A student could, for instance, deploy features of the teaching register in addressing a fellow student thus presenting herself as the more knowledgeable party. These types of tropic uses deploying stereotypically "teacher's" resources did occur in the classrooms. I did, for instance, observe the students produce other-corrections (Schegloff, Jefferson & Sacks 1977: 380–381; Macbeth 2004) early on in their studies.

Although the students seemed to display a reflexive understanding of the teaching register and the social personae it is connected to, it is safe to say that their access to the semiotic processes that mold the teaching register *selkosuomi* was quite different from that of the teachers. While *selkosuomi* in one way or another was part of the everyday life of the classrooms, the explicit metasemiotic discourses on the register took place mostly elsewhere. Many students became aware of the differences between the classroom language and language outside of the school early on in their studies, but when these issues were discussed in the classroom setting, the teachers usually explained them as differences between standard Finnish and spoken varieties.

The potentially problematic social indexicalities of *selkosuomi* did not escape the awareness of the teachers. Although *selkosuomi* is promulgated as a medium that promotes equality and equal possibilities to participate, the teachers were cognizant of the fact that instead of well-intentioned consideration of recipients' possibilities to participate, addressing someone in *selkosuomi* can be interpreted negatively, for instance as belittling recipients' language skills or treating one's co-participant patronizingly. The teachers were well aware of the potential indexicalities of the setting, where the very activities and artifacts connected with learning literacy skills could invoke problematic connotations of pursuits more typical to children than grown-ups. The teachers often verbalized this by emphasizing the importance of remembering that the students were adults.

Occasionally, also the students seemed to orient to these features as indexes of asymmetry.[11] However, it is also worth noting that many of the stereotypic elements of the register are not exclusive to didactic talk, nor other kinds of asymmetric interaction. For instance, in any kind of interaction, excessive repetition can quite easily be interpreted as undermining or drawing into question the recipient's ability to understand. Therefore, if we think for example of Faadil's uptake of the teacher's repetitions (Section 4.4), the uptake does not rely on him recog-

---

11 The notion of enregisterment also allows us to see *selkosuomi* in a broader sociohistorical context. In terms of its metapragmatic typifications (simpler, easier to understand language) and metapragmatic stereotypes, *selkosuomi* is discursively linked to a wider variety of practices in linguistically asymmetric interaction. While an individual might not recognize *selkosuomi* as a register, they still might recognize some of its stereotypic features as typical for asymmetric situations. For conversation on analytic perspectives on these kinds of indexes of asymmetry, see e.g. Leskelä 2009.

nizing the repetitions as a stereotypic instance of "easy to understand language". Even if we assume that Faadil interprets the repetition as a potential index of asymmetry, such interpretation could well rely on norms that are not that register or language specific.

When registers are understood as discursively produced distinctions, this entails that a register is not "the same" to all participants. Participants' effective command of the register might vary, they might valorize the register or its parts differently, and have a fairly different sense of what is transpiring through register use (see Agha 2007: 147–150 for discussion). This was also the case with *selkosuomi* in the context I have examined here. Teachers differed from each other, for instance, in the way they oriented to simplified structures of Finnish or the expression *sama sama* that characteristically belonged to the classroom language. There were also individual differences in preferred modalities utilized for teaching. Also, the way the register use was justified by various ideologies differed from teacher to teacher.

The differences in participation in and valorization of the register also mean that the participants do not share exactly the same norms. According to the definition I have offered in this chapter, norms are reflexive models that allow semiotic conduct to be interpreted as meaningful signs. If norms are defined in this way as pertaining to the ways in which participants deploy and interpret actual semiotic tokens, the norms of *selkosuomi* inevitably vary between participants, across different settings and different channels. However, this lack of uniformity did not prevent the teaching register *selkosuomi* from being normative for the teachers. This observation has important theoretical implications: just as norms emerge from a complex set of interlinked semiotic processes, so does normativity. In these classrooms normativity of spoken *selkosuomi* seemed to be a result of a more complex set of interlinked semiotic processes that shaped the language policies in the classroom. Normativity is often connected with standardization, a process whereby a certain kind of behavior gets codified (Agha 2007: 125). While the teaching register *selkosuomi* is normative in the sense of being recognized as typical for these classrooms, and even though it was guarded against breaches by social sanctions (see Section 4), the register is by no means standardized in the sense of having an explicit set of codified practices. Rather, although the stereotypic features connected with oral *selkosuomi* are easily recognizable, its semiotic range is such that the register has defied standardization.

The semiotic range of the various resources utilized in the classrooms I have studied also poses a challenge for describing in detail the norms of the teaching register. In my analysis of Excerpt 1, I illustrated how conveying even the referential content of the teacher's turns relied heavily on multimodal means. In the literacy classrooms, the multimodal means were various and included not only gestures but also bodily actions and visual media, for instance pictures. More variation was brought by the fact that only some of these means were conventionalized into habitualized, socially shared practices among the teachers. For instance, the referential gesture indicating a future point in time that I described in one of the excerpts from my field work diary (see Section 4.2) was this type of conventionalized resource that the teachers utilized throughout the organization. The gesture also had a parallel for indicating past. However, this observation alone does not yet fully describe a norm, if norms are understood as reflexive habitualized models that allow semiotic conduct to be interpreted as meaningful signs. We would need to know, for instance, with what kinds of linguistic signs (verbs, adverbs of time) the gesture is utilized, and how established and widely shared these usages are. In studying norms, it is these kinds of habitualized practices of meaning-making that are of interest. In the case of *selkosuomi* it is likely that these habitualized ways include larger configurations of mutually interacting resources. Many of the mutually interacting resources, however, did not necessarily reoccur in a similar form or with the same linguistic element ever again. The gestures that Enni produced in conjunction with her directives to stack the letter cards were most likely these kinds of more ephemeral multimodal sign configurations.

A telltale sign of the potentially diverse norms that the students were socialized into was the observation that it often took a while for the students to adjust to the communicative style of a new teacher. Students that had participated effortlessly in classroom activities in the end of the previous teaching module would suddenly comment, "I don't understand a word the teacher says", in the beginning of the next one. Reasons for this could of course be various and could include teacher's "accents" or didactic language that became suddenly considerably more difficult. However, I would say that these were not the reasons for students' bewilderment. Rather, I suspect that students' difficulties could be explained at least partly by the multiplicity, multimodality and individual differences in those practices that in this chapter have been called the teaching register *selkosuomi*.

Such findings are also relevant to the study of multilingual classrooms where multimodal perspectives on interaction have existed for a while. For instance, gestures, facial expressions and touches are examined as a part of classroom practices (see e.g. contributions in McCafferty & Stam 2008; Jakonen & Evnitskaya 2020; Heinonen, Karvonen & Tainio 2020) and the various modes of interaction are recognized as affordances (van Lier 2000) that support the process of being socialized in a new language. However, metatheoretical perspectives on multimodality are changing (see Dufva 2020; Block 2013), and instead of just a useful element in language learning, multimodality and embodiment are increasingly understood as an integral part of language skills (Dufva 2020). The implications of this perspective for language pedagogy are considerable because instead of just "language" classroom teaching needs to orient to a more holistic way of seeing the processes of meaning-making – and norms of language.

6 Concluding remarks

I began this chapter by asking whether the notion of norms still has currency in poststructuralist and postmodern sociolinguistics. My answer is that the usefulness of the notion depends on the theoretical frameworks it is embedded in. In this chapter, I have used the conceptual tools of reflexive theorizing to tease out various discursive processes that mold the norms of the teaching register *selkosuomi*. My observations suggest that despite the normativity of the teaching register, the norms of the register are far from uniform. These types of observations invite us to reconsider our understanding of social and sociolinguistic norms. Norms have been considered to be the glue that hold communities together (cf. the Introduction to this volume), but when the perspective is shifted from products to the ways in which actors re- and co-create their social worlds, it becomes clear that much of that work is accomplished by a wide variety of discursive processes. In studying norms, also one's metatheoretical view of "language" matters (for details, see Piippo 2012). A closer look at the meaning-making strategies in the literacy training classrooms suggested that a fuller understanding of the norms of *selkosuomi* would require exploring potentially habitualized ways of multimodal meaning making. Such research would widen our understanding of interactional norms and challenge the linguistically biased perspectives which continue to dominate the field.

Transcription conventions

.	Falling intonation
,	Level intonation
↑	Intonation rises
(.)	Micropause
(0.5)	Length of pause
[ ]	Overlap
**	Point and descriptions of embodied actions
---	Duration of the embodied action when it continues across subsequent lines
fig	Figure
#	Indicates the exact moment within the turn of talk at which a screen shot is taken
t	Identification of the participant doing the embodied action

References

Agha, Asif. 2007. *Language and social relations*. Cambridge: Cambridge University Press.
Alisaari, Jenni, Leena Maria Heikkola, Nancy Commins & Emmanuel O. Acquah. 2019. Monolingual ideologies confronting multilingual realities: Finnish teachers' beliefs about linguistic diversity. *Teaching and Teacher Education 80*. 48–58.
Block, David. 2013. Moving beyond "lingualism": Multilingual embodiment and multimodality in SLA. In Stephen May (ed.), *The multilingual turn: Implications for SLA, TESOL, and bilingual education*. London: Routledge. 54–77.
Berger, Peter & Thomas Luckmann. 1966. *The social construction of reality: A treatise in the sociology of knowledge*. London: Penguin.
Center for Easy to Read. 2018. *Selkeästi kaikille: selkomittari* [Understandable for all: measurement tool for easy to read]. Published 11.10.2018. Retrieved from https://selkokeskus.fi/selkokieli/selkokielen-mittari/. (accessed 10 July 2020).
Costa, James. 2019. Introduction: Regimes of language and the social, hierarchized organization of ideologies. *Language & Communication 66*. 1–5.
Cummins, Jim. 2007. Rethinking monolingual instructional strategies in multilingual classrooms. *Canadian Journal of Applied Linguistics/Revue Canadienne de Linguistique Appliquée* 10 (2). 221–240.
Durkheim, Émile. 1938 [1895]. *The rules of sociological method*. (Ed.) George E. G. Catlin. (Trans.) Sarah A. Solovay & John H. Mueller. New York: Free Press.
Dufva, Hannele. 2020. Mitä ihmiset osaavat, kun he osaavat kieltä? Henkilökohtainen repertoaari ja sen multimodaalisuus. [What people know when they know language? Personal repertoire and its multimodality]. In Sabine Grasz, Tiina Keisanen, Florence Oloff, Mirka Rauniomaa, Iira Rautiainen & Maarit Siromaa (eds.), *Menetelmällisiä käänteitä soveltavassa kielentutkimuksessa – Methodological turns in applied language studies. AFinLA Yearbook 2020*, 17–32. Publications of the Finnish Association of Applied Linguistics 78. Jyväskylä.
Ferguson, Charles. 1971. Absence of copula and the notion of simplicity: A study of normal speech, baby talk, foreigner talk and pidgins. In Dell Hymes (ed.), *Pidginisation and creolization of languages*, 141–50. Cambridge: Cambridge University Press.
Ferguson, Charles. 1981. Foreigner talk as the name of a simplified register. *International Journal of the Sociology of Language* 28. 9–18.
García, Ofelia & Li Wei 2014. *Translanguaging: Language, bilingualism and education*. New York: Palgrave Macmillan.
Garfinkel, Harold. 1967. *Studies in ethnomethodology*. Englewood Cliffs, NJ: Prentice-Hall.
Goffman, Erving. 1974. *Frame analysis*. New York: Harper Colophon.
Goodwin, Charles. 2014. Intelligibility of gesture within a framework of co-operative action. In Mandana Seyfeddinipur & Marianne Gullberg (eds.), *From gesture in conversation to visible action as utterance: Essays in honor of Adam Kendon,* 199–216. Amsterdam: John Benjamins Publishing Company.
Harjunpää, Katariina. 2017. *Translatory practices in everyday conversation: Bilingual mediating in Finnish–Brazilian Portuguese interaction*. PhD dissertation. Helsinki: University of Helsinki.
Heinonen, Pilvi, Ulla Karvonen & Liisa Tainio. 2020. Hand on shoulder touch as a resource for constructing a pedagogically relevant participation framework. *Linguistics and Education* 56. 1–10.

Heritage, John. 1984. *Garfinkel and ethnomethodology*. Cambridge: Polity Press.
Hymes, Dell. 1989. Ways of speaking. In Richard Bauman & Joel Sherzer (ed.), *Explorations in the ethnography of speaking*, 433–451. Cambridge: Cambridge University Press.
Irvine, Judith T. 1989. When talk isn't cheap: Language and political economy. *American Ethnologist* 16. 248–267.
Jakonen, Teppo & Natalia Evnitskaya. 2020. Teacher smiles as an interactional and pedagogical resource in the classroom. *Journal of Pragmatics 163*. 18–31.
Jaworski, Adam, Nikolas Coupland & Dariusz Galasiński (eds.). 2004. *Metalanguage: Social and ideological perspectives*. Berlin: Mouton de Gruyter.
Jørgensen, J. Normann. 2008. Polylingual languaging around and among children and adolescents. *International Journal of Multilingualism* 5 (3). 161–176.
Kartio, Johanna. 2009. Kohti selkokielistä vuorovaikutusta. [Towards interaction in easy to understand language.]. In Johanna Kartio (ed.), *Selkokieli ja vuorovaikutus* [Easy to understand language and interaction], 1–24. Helsinki: The Finnish Association on Intellectual and Developmental Disabilities.
Kendon, Adam. 2004. *Gesture: Visible action as utterance*. Cambridge: Cambridge University Press.
Kroskrity, Paul V. (ed.). 2000. *Regimes of language: Ideologies, polities and identities*. Santa Fe: School of American Research Press.
Leskelä, Leea-Laura. 2019. *Selkokieli – Saavutettavan kielen opas*. [Easy to understand language: guide for accessible language]. Helsinki: The Finnish Association on Intellectual and Developmental Disabilities, Opike.
Leskelä, Leea-Laura & Camilla Lindholm. 2012. *Haavoittuva keskustelu: Keskustelunanalyyttisia tutkimuksia kielellisesti epäsymmetrisestä vuorovaikutuksesta* [Vulnerable conversation: conversation analytic studies on asymmetric interaction]. Helsinki: The Finnish Association on Intellectual and Developmental Disabilities.
Leskelä, Leea-Laura. 2009. Selkokieli kahdenkeskisessä keskustelussa. [Easy to understand language in in dyadic converstation]. In Johanna Kartio (ed.). *Selkokieli ja vuorovaikutus* [Easy to understand language and interaction], 25–45. Helsinki: The Finnish Association on Intellectual and Developmental Disabilities.
Li, Wei. 2018. Translanguaging as a practical theory of language. *Applied Linguistics* 39 (1). 9–39.
Lilja, Niina, Karita Mård-Miettinen & Tarja Nikula 2019. Luokkahuone kielipoliittisena ja kielikoulutuspoliittisena tilana. [Classroom as a space of language policy and language education policy]. In Taina Saarinen, Pirkko Nuolijärvi, Sari Pöyhönen & Teija Kangasvieri (eds.), *Kieli, koulutus, politiikka: monipaikkaisia käytänteitä ja tulkintoja* [Language, education, policy: translocal practices and interpretations], 175–197. Tampere: Vastapaino.
Lucy, John A. (ed.) 1993. *Reflexive language: Reported speech and metapragmatics*. Cambridge: Cambridge University Press.
Macbeth, Douglas. 2004. The relevance of repair for classroom correction. *Language in Society* 33. 703–736.
McCafferty, Steven G. & Gale Stam. 2008. *Gesture: Second language acquisition and classroom research*. New York: Routledge.
Mondada, Lorenza. 2016. Conventions for multimodal transcription. Retrieved from https://franzoesistik.philhist.unibas.ch/fileadmin/user_upload/franzoesistik/mondada_multimodal_conventions.pdf. (accessed 10 July 2020).

Parmentier, Richard J. 1994. *Signs in society: Studies in semiotic anthropology.* Bloomington: Indiana University Press.
Parsons, Talcott. 1949 [1937]. *The structure of social action: A study in social theory with special reference to a group of recent European writers.* New York, NY: Free Press.
Piippo, Irina. 2012. *Viewing norms dialogically: An action-oriented approach to sociolinguistic metatheory.* PhD dissertation. Helsinki: University of Helsinki.
Piippo, Irina.2021. Muuttuvat näkökulmat monikielisyyteen. [Changing perspectives on multilingualism]. In Maria Ahlholm, Irina Piippo & Päivi Portaankorva-Koivisto (eds.), Koulun monet kielet – Plurilingualism in the school, 21–43. AFinLA-e. Soveltavan kielitieteen tutkimuksia 13. Jyväskylä: The Finnish Association for Applied Linguistics, AFinLA.
Sainio, Ari (ed.). 2013. Viesti perille – selko-opas kunnille [Getting the message: a guide to easy to understand language for municipalities]. Helsinki: KAKS – Kunnallisalan kehittämissäätiö.
Schegloff, Emanuel A., Gail Jefferson & Harvey Sacks. 1977. The preference for self-correction in the organization of repair in conversation. *Language* 53. 361–382.
Silverstein, Michael. 1979. Language structure and linguistic ideology. In Paul R. Clyne, William F. Hanks & Carol L. Hofbauer (eds.), *The elements: A parasession in linguistic units and levels,* 193–247. Chicago, IL: Chicago Linguistic Society.
Urban, Greg. 2006. Metasemiosis and metapragmatics. In Keith Brown (ed.) *Encyclopedia of language and linguistics*, 88–91. Oxford: Pergamon Press.
Weber, Max. 1962. *Basic concepts in sociology.* Translated by H. P. Secher. Secaucus, NJ: Citadel Press.
Woolard, Kathryn. 1998. Language ideology as a field of inquiry. In Bambi Schieffelin, Kathryn Woolard & Paul Kroskrity (eds.), *Language ideologies: Practice and theory*, 3–49. New York: Oxford University Press
Virtanen, Hannu. 2009. *Selkokielen käsikirja* [Handbook of easy to understand language]. Helsinki: The Finnish Association on Intellectual and Developmental Disabilities, Opike.
Van Lier, Leo. 2000. From input to affordance: Social interactive learning from an ecological perspective. In James P. Lantolf (ed.), *Sociocultural theory and second language learning: Recent advances*, 245–259. Oxford: Oxford Universtity Press.
Von Wright, Georg Henrik. 1963. *Norm and action: A logical enquiry.* London: Routledge and Kegan Paul.

Kamilla Kraft and Janus Mortensen
5 Norms and stereotypes: Studying the emergence and sedimentation of social meaning

1 Introduction

In the sociolinguistic literature, norms are often invoked as conceptual primes that help explain how and why languages vary according to context and situation. The underlying idea is that language use varies because there are different norms for how language *is* or *should be* used in specific contexts. Thus, Jørgensen (2008: 169) argues that young Danish urban language users operate according to what he calls a *polylingual norm*, in which speakers "consistently and creatively" combine features from what are commonly considered distinct languages. This polylingual norm, Jørgensen argues, is in opposition to a distinct *monolingual norm* otherwise dominant in Danish society, particularly among older language users. Observed differences in linguistic behavior between the two groups of speakers can in this way be explained with reference to the existence of different norms.

Norms are believed to be in operation at multiple levels of linguistic description, from the levels of phonetics and lexico-grammar to pragmatics and social interaction more broadly. An interest in norms at a rather detailed level of linguistic description can be exemplified by Meyerhoff and Niedzielski's (2003: 534) discussion of a potential "shift from older, more British-like norms to newer, more American-like ones" in the realisation of particular lexical and phonetic variables in New Zealand English. The broader pragmatic interest can be illustrated with reference to work on transnational call centres where Hultgren (2011) argues that Danish and British call centre workers design their "rapport-building speech styles" in different ways due to "the predominance of different *politeness norms* in the two cultures" (Hultgren 2011: 36, our emphasis).

Acknowledgements: Work on this chapter has been supported by The Danish Council for Independent Research | Humanities through grant no. 6107-00351, *Transient Multilingual Communities and the Formation of Social and Linguistic Norms* (2016–2019). The analyses we present have benefitted from discussions within the TMC project group (www.tmc.ku.dk). We would like to thank Dorte Lønsmann, Katherine Kappa, Spencer Hazel and Nikolas Coupland for their input, as well as Ida Moth Kej and Jorunn Simonsen Thingnes for their work on and help with the transcriptions. All remaining shortcomings remain our responsibility.

Despite its limited size, this selection of examples from the literature illustrates how central the notion of norms is within several areas of sociolinguistics. Despite their differences, the examples also illustrate that in sociolinguistics, linguistic norms are often seen to establish links between linguistic form and social meaning. We consider this normative relationship between form and meaning to be reflexive (cf. Piippo, this volume), historically contingent and interactionally emergent. As other social norms, linguistic norms are not negotiable in any fundamental sense in the here-and-now (cf. Harder, this volume), but human interaction may nevertheless be said to constitute the primordial and primary site for the emergence and maintenance of social norms.

In this chapter, we set out to shed light on the process of *norm formation* through a micro-longitudinal study of how members of a transient community develop ways of *using* and *ascribing meaning to* labels related to different national categories. As part of investigating how group members collectively develop situated norms, we also explore what pre-existing meanings members bring with them into their local interactions, and how they can be seen to use these in the development of the local norms. The transient community under study is the management team of a construction site in the Norwegian capital, Oslo, and the analysis focuses on how members of the group, as part of their everyday interaction, employ – and create meaning around – the categories "Norwegians" and "Swedes".

By drawing on ethnographic observations and analyses of video recordings of naturally occurring interaction on the site, we explore how the members of the management team (1) develop stereotypes based on national categories and (2) establish discursive norms for the use of these stereotypes within the group. Based on our analyses, we argue that the participants draw on and reproduce an interactional norm of "othering" through the use of national stereotypes which comes to function as a resource for negotiating interpersonal relationships in the group, while also allowing the group members to position themselves *vis-à-vis* outsiders. In order to describe how the national categories are imbued with meaning and become stereotypes, we explore how the participants, through a process of indexicalisation (cf. Jaffe 2016), gradually saturate the stereotype labels with layers of social meaning. As part of this process, the participants draw on normative frameworks which must be assumed to be in place beyond the scale of the immediate, local group, although their existence arguably, and somewhat paradoxically, ultimately relies on their perpetual (re)production in specific social settings like the one we explore here.

The chapter is organised as follows. We begin by offering an account of the three central theoretical concepts employed in the chapter: norms, stereotypes and indexicalisation (Section 2). In Section 3, we present our data in more detail and offer some reflections on the methodological advantages and challenges involved in studying norm formation in the context of transient social configurations. In Section 4 we present our analysis, in which we explore the interactional work done around the stereotypes and show how they gradually come to be imbued with meaning. Section 5 discusses the process of norm formation as a dialectic process, providing a critical discussion of the implications of the norm formation process identified in the analysis. Finally, the overall argument of the chapter is summed up in Section 6.

2 Norms, stereotypes and indexicalisation

Etymologically, both norms and stereotypes refer to a standard: *Norma*, the Latin etymon for the English 'norm', refers to a carpenter's square, a tool used to measure out right angles; a stereotype is a metal cast used in printing presses to print identical characters on paper (Augoustinos & Walker 1995: 209). Both terms can thus be seen to invoke connotations related to orderliness and (re)production. In their contemporary uses, the terms refer to social constructs, internalized by individuals but shared within a group, that guide expectations concerning human behaviour. Thus, behaviour, either one's own or that of others, can be experienced as norm-conforming or deviant – not conforming to a specific cast (cf. the examples of perceived deviant behaviour discussed by Hazel & Lønsmann, this volume). While we do not want to pursue this etymological reading too far, we believe that this form of "backtranslation" of current metaphorical usage offers a good starting point for teasing out the differences and similarities between the two concepts.

In the social domain, norms can be thought of as "reflexive models of meaningful, expected and appropriate conduct" (Piippo 2012; Piippo, this volume) that guide individual and collective behaviour and thus help shape social order. In contrast to laws of nature which exist independently of human influence, norms are social constructions that are historically contingent and contextually malleable. Moreover, social norms are of a dual nature: they may be used simply to *describe* the common state of affairs in some context, but they may also be used to pre- or proscribe particular forms of social behaviour – defining what is acceptable or unacceptable. Used descriptively, norms provide an account of what may be considered "normal" behaviour in a particular context. When used prescriptively, they *mandate* particular forms of behaviour, based on normative models "linked to standards whose breach results in sanctions" (Agha 2007: 126). Of course, in some activity types, breaking the norm is the norm. This is clearly seen in certain styles of joking where the humorous outcome relies on speakers violating a general norm that is suspended for the duration of the joke, cf. Labov's (1972) work on ritual insults in which breaking a norm – performing an insult – *is* the norm. A related example is Delfino's (2016) study of "joning", a stigmatised register used by AAVE speakers to negotiate social relations through mock teasing and insults. The studies by Labov and Delfino exemplify how discursive practices (in both cases incidentally including the use of stereotypes) and their associated social meanings often rely on multiple and multi-layered normative frameworks.

Moving from norms to stereotypes, we may begin by asking what the relationship is between the two. In this chapter, we take stereotypes and the use of stereotypes in interaction to be underpinned by norms and at the same time indicative of norms. For something to be considered stereotypical behaviour, it must conform to some norm, and perhaps even constitute an exaggerated version of that type of behaviour. In this way, stereotypes can be thought of as ideological and normative "common sense" perceptions about particular groups of people and their attributes. They are "construct resources" (Fabricius & Mortensen 2013; cf. Fabricius, this volume) that provide a convenient (if simplistic) mapping of social space, based on shared representations. As Hewstone and Giles (1986) point out, stereotypes provide the content of social categories, as the end-result of cognitive processes which segment and organize "the social world into social categories or groups" (1986: 11).

In Allport's definition, a stereotype is "an exaggerated belief associated with a category" whose "function is to justify (rationalize) our conduct in relation to that category" (1979: 191). Tajfel omits the idea of "*exaggerated* beliefs" but similarly maintains that a "social stereotype consists of assigning certain traits in common to individuals who are members of a group and also of attributing to them certain differences in common from members of other groups" (Tajfel 1981: 115). Viewed in this way, social stereotypes are constructs that perform social, evaluative and ideological work, thereby "explaining or justifying a variety of social actions" (Tajfel 1981: 146). They are social representations that may be based on knowledge, experiences and beliefs (Tajfel 1981: 117).

Augoustinos and Walker (1995) further characterise stereotypes as individual cognitive schema *as well as* shared social representations that "emerge and proliferate within the particular social and political milieu of a given historical moment" (Augoustinos & Walker 1995: 222). As such, stereotypes have individual as well as collective functions (cf. Tajfel 1981). For the individual, stereotypes help organize social reality, while the collective function is to produce and maintain social explanations and group ideologies. These ideologies serve to rationalise relations and attitudes towards outgroups and may help produce, maintain or enhance "differentiations between the ingroup and relevant outgroups" (Hewstone & Giles 1986: 19).

While norms may *describe* as well as *pre-* and *proscribe* expected behaviour in various contexts, stereotypes are rarely used prescriptively. People can be ridiculed (or more rarely, perhaps, praised) for behaving "stereotypically" (i.e. in accordance with a particular social stereotype), but it is uncommon for someone, comedians and actors excluded, to be asked to behave according to a particular stereotype. Possible exceptions could be reproaches like "be a man" or "don't be childish" where a person is asked to behave in a particular way. In such cases, we might say that stereotypes are embedded within proscriptive norms. In more general terms, we would argue that a stereotype is something we recognize *with reference to* socially shared norms, and the meaning of stereotypes is dependent on the existence of such shared norms (cf. Alexander, Brewer & Livingston 2005). Another way of putting this would be to say that stereotypes carry pragmatic presuppositions (Caffi 2006) about social norms, about what is "normal" and what is "abnormal".

While the body of work reviewed above helps us understand how norms and stereotypes *work* in social and psychological terms, it does not account for how particular norms and stereotypes come to acquire specific meaning. Here the notion of indexicalisation (Jaffe 2016) offers some help. Jaffe uses indexicalisation as a general term for the process whereby linguistic signs are imbued with social meaning, in a process quite similar to the way styles or "ways of speaking" come to acquire meaning through processes of "enregisterment" (Agha 2003; Agha 2007; cf. Jaspers & Van Hoof 2019; Mortensen & Coupland 2018). Studying indexicalisation involves an interest in examining "how indexical meanings accrue to particular forms, how indexicals at one level (or 'order') are projected onto subsequent orders (Silverstein 2003), and how indexicals are organized into fields (Eckert 2008)" (Jaffe 2016: 86). In cases where an indexical field comes to exist in relation to a specific social group or a label designating such a group, this may lead to the formation of stereotypes, i.e. widespread social evaluations in relation to the designated group. Such processes of indexicalisation can be explored by observing how speakers over time use and attribute meaning to particular social objects, in our case the national categories referenced by the labels "Swedes" and "Norwegians".

In sum, we take social stereotypes to consist of culturally salient indexical links between idealised or "imagined" groups of people and the range of social meanings and behaviours conventionally associated with these groups. As such, stereotypes can help establish and maintain perceived differences between social groups, "them" and "us", and at the same time also be used to create in-group affiliation across stereotyped groups. Social stereotypes are premised on the existence of social norms, and they also reflect these norms. Studying how stereotypes are used interactionally and how they come to be imbued with social meaning may therefore be seen as one way in which we can approach the study of norms in language and social life, since it allows us to track the emergence of normative meaning in interaction.

3 Method

3.1 Data and participants

The analysis presented below is based on ethnographic fieldwork carried out by the chapter's first author in a Norwegian construction site between September 2017 and March 2018. The construction project itself was carried out from September 2017 to August 2018, i.e. the fieldwork commenced at the same time as work on the construction site began. The fieldwork was focused on the day-to-day activities of the site's management team, based on fieldnotes, observations, and video-recordings of interactions.

Figure 1 provides an overview of the members of the management team. As indicated, the participants had different organisational roles. The project leader Jon had the overall responsibility for the project, while the other members were divided into three specific domains: administration, project planning and production.

At the beginning of the project, the team had a total of six members: Jon, Luisa, Nils, Pia, Erik and Hans. Four of these individuals, Jon, Erik, Luisa and Hans, all worked for the main contractor on the site, and had some previous knowledge of each other. However, Luisa and Jon were the only ones who had worked together on projects before. Nils and Pia were both on lease from other companies and hence entirely new to each other and to the rest of the group. Pia was even new to the construction industry. After a week, the group was joined by Anne who was also employed by the main contractor and knew of some of the others but had so far been working on quite different tasks at the contractor's headquarters. Linus joined the project approximately a month after start-up to replace Erik. He had no prior experience of working with the others in the management team. Anders joined approximately three months into the project. He does not feature in our analysis below (and he is not the Anders referred to on page 117).

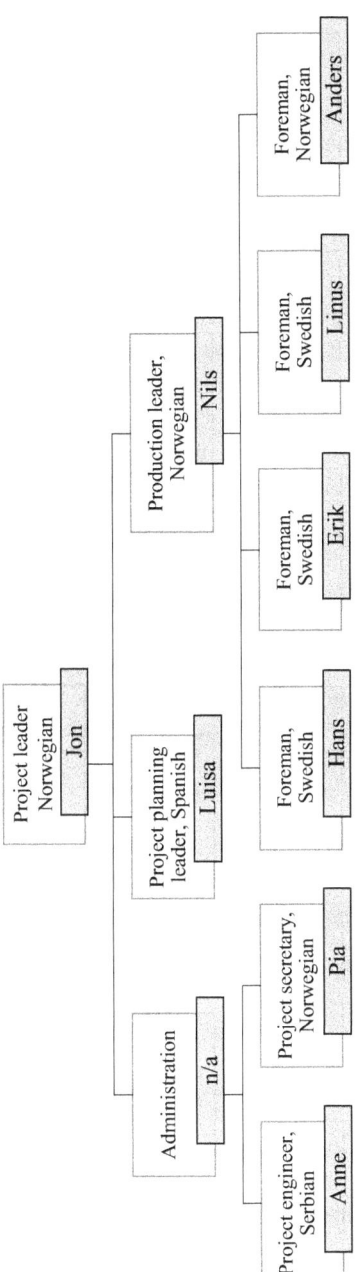

Figure 1: The participants (pseudonyms), their nationalities and organisational roles.

3.2 Analytical approach

The data excerpts we analyse below are part of a collection of instances where one or more participants in the data set invoke a national category during their day-to-day interaction. The interest in national categories and stereotypes as an analytical object was based on early noticings during the fieldwork, as well as on earlier work on construction sites and stereotypes (Kraft 2017). The examples in the collection were identified through a chronological examination of the recorded data, supported by fieldnote entries. Identified sequences were subsequently transcribed in CLAN (MacWhinney 2000), and salient excerpts were discussed and co-analysed at data sessions with colleagues within the TMC project.[1] The excerpts we focus on in this chapter are all taken from the beginning of the project, and as mentioned above, they all concern two national categories, *viz.* "Norwegians" and "Swedes", which are also the most frequently occurring labels in the data set.

Aligning with the framework of linguistic ethnography (Copland & Creese 2015; Rampton, Maybin & Roberts 2015), our analysis consists of micro-analyses of recorded interaction informed by ethnographic observations and knowledge of the general field and the particular site. By adopting this approach we are able to explore the emergence of social meaning in interaction in an ethnographically informed manner (Cicourel 1987; Day 2008; Moerman 1988), while at the same time considering the wider spatio-temporal and multi-scalar context of the interaction and its relevance for the local discursive practices and their meaning (Blommaert 2010; Carr & Lempert 2016).

4 Analysis: National categories and stereotypes in a Norwegian construction site

As mentioned above, the analysis we present in this section focusses on the national categories "Swedes" and "Norwegians" and their function as stereotypes. We pay particular attention to the synergies between the two sets of stereotypes and how they are actively part of constructing the cultural "other" (Jenkins 1994; Said 2003). In section 4.2 we will demonstrate how these national categories are gradually imbued with meanings through interaction amongst the members

---

[1] The TMC project (*Transient Multilingual Communities and the Formation of Social and Linguistic Norms*) was funded by The Danish Council for Independent Research | Humanities, from 2016 to 2019. Apart from the authors of this chapter, project participants included Spencer Hazel, Katherine Kappa and Dorte Lønsmann. See www.tmc.ku.dk.

of the management team. However, by way of setting the scene for this analysis, we begin in section 4.1 by discussing an interview excerpt from Kamilla's earlier fieldwork in the Norwegian construction industry.

4.1 A vignette

In 2015, Kamilla interviewed Jakob, a Norwegian manager who was part of another building project where Kamilla did fieldwork. They had been talking about migrant workers, and Kamilla had mentioned Poles as an example of this category. Jakob corrected her, stating that Swedes were also "foreign workers". This led to the following exchange.[2]

1	Kamilla:	det er interessant ha ha ha	this is interesting ha ha ha
2		er de udlændinge	are they foreigners
3	Jakob:	de er Nordens østeuropæere	they are the Eastern Europeans of the North
4	Kamilla:	ha ha ha okay	ha ha ha ok
5	Jakob:	vi må ikke la dem glemme det	we can't allow them to forget that
6	Kamilla:	ha ha ha	ha ha ha
7		(1.2)	(1.2)
8	Jakob:	nei der har alltid vært litt	there has always been a bit of
9		kniving mellom Norge og Sverige	backstabbing between Norway and Sweden
10		vet du for de har vært storebror	you know they have been the big brother
11	Kamilla:	ja	yeah
12	Jakob:	så vi syns det er veldig gøy	so we think it's great fun
13		at de må komme hit å jobbe	that they have to come here to work
14	Kamilla:	ja	yes

We include this interview excerpt as an illustration of what we believe to constitute commonly held ideas concerning (1) the relationship between Norway/Norwegians and Sweden/Swedes, and (2) the kind of banter that is often found in inter-Scandinavian interactions based on this relationship.[3] In lines 8-10, Jakob

---

2 The original language of the interaction is transcribed on the left, and we provide an English paraphrase on the right, line by line. A detailed transcription key is included as an appendix.
3 For 'folk' discussions of this relationship see e.g. https://www.quora.com/What-do-Norwegians-think-of-Swedes (last accessed 3 July 2019) or the popular web comic Scandinavia and the World (https://satwcomic.com/sweden-denmark-and-norway, last accessed 3 December 2019). Furthermore, music videos like Partysvenske (https://www.youtube.com/watch?v=tRRS8iH-4Qo8, last accessed 3 December 2019) and parodies such as kamelåså (https://www.youtube.

argues that Sweden, historically speaking at least, has been seen as the elder sibling, perhaps implying a more advanced, privileged or even superior status. Regardless of the intended meaning, it seems obvious that Jakob establishes – or refers to – a hierarchy between Norway and Sweden, and the reversal of this hierarchy (realised by Swedes having to take up work at Norwegian construction sites) constitutes "great fun" according to Jakob (line 12). The humorous nature of Jakob's remarks is supported by Kamilla's laughter in lines 1, 4 and 6.

Yet, it is worth noticing that Kamilla laughs *before* Jakob provides his explanation in line 8 onwards. This suggests that Kamilla might be attuned to the fact that "a joke" is in the making even before Jakob explicates its premises. Whether Kamilla's laughter is designed to support or somehow mitigate the upcoming "joke" and its stereotypical underpinnings is difficult to tell from the transcript. However, the fact that the laughter to some extent pre-empts the joke can be taken to indicate that Kamilla and Jakob share a degree of pre-established understanding concerning the stereotypes in play, as well as the underlying social norms for how they can be activated in interaction.

It is hard to pinpoint exactly *why* it should be funny to describe Swedes as "the Eastern Europeans of the North". However, based on ethnographic knowledge of the Norwegian construction industry, we suggest that the label "Eastern European" indexes a high degree of mobility and may also index a perceived professional skills deficit. Thus, by characterising Swedish workers as "the Eastern Europeans of the North", Jakob creates an incongruous category which clashes with and playfully subverts the high status stereotypically attributed to Swedes. In their interaction, Jakob and Kamilla are thus relying on shared knowledge of these stereotypes and their associated social meanings, while at the same time perpetuating the stereotypes and locally ratifying (or possibly reappraising) their meanings through humour. As such, the interview excerpt encapsulates the themes we will be pursuing in the analysis below, providing a first, condensed illustration of how stereotypes about Norwegians and Swedes (as well as Eastern Europeans though these will not be the focus of this chapter) circulate as productive meaning-making resources in the context of the Norwegian construction industry, and how the use of these stereotypes is related to certain norms for social interaction, i.e. "reflexive models of meaningful, expected and appropriate conduct" (Piippo 2012) that in our case pertain to prosocial humour as well as boundary-making.

---

com/watch?v=s-mOy8VUEBk, last accessed 3 December 2019) and Norway 200 years (https://www.youtube.com/watch?v=FqgRC5sfCaQ, accessed 3 December 2019) depict stereotypes of the Scandinavians and their relationships and have been extremely popular.

4.2 'The Swede': Stereotyping as a multifunctional tool

The timeline in Figure 2 illustrates a selection of cases where the national category "Swedes", or alternatively "Sweden", was activated as a stereotype during the life cycle of the management team. The first four examples are all from the first month of collaboration (days 8, 9, 10 and 15), and the last example is towards the end of the fieldwork period, some five months later (day 155). The early instances of stereotyping can be seen to serve interpersonal goals, helping the participants in the process of "getting acquainted" through prosocial banter. The last example also has interpersonal functions, but it demonstrates a more alienating use of stereotypes about Swedes.

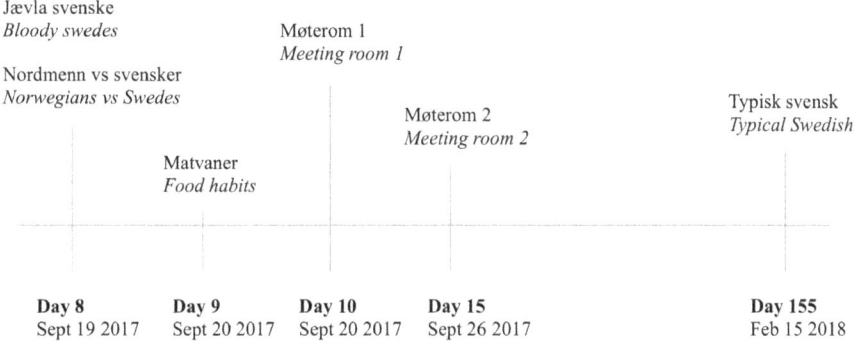

Figure 2: Timeline illustrating when the 'Swede'/'Swedes'/'Sweden' stereotype is activated in the data excerpts.

In the following we will treat the examples in turn.

4.2.1 Launching the stereotype

Excerpt 1, *Jævla svenske*, is from the group's very first internal meeting, about a week into their collaboration. The meeting is the first in a series of meetings that the project leader, Jon, has decided the team should have on a weekly basis, enabling them to coordinate their individual tasks and ensure that everyone has a general idea of what is going on everywhere in the site. At this point in time, Jon is in the process of selling his private flat (which is somewhat urgent since he has already bought a new house). As the excerpt begins, he is re-entering the meeting room after having been outside to answer a call from his estate agent. Besides Jon, the meeting involves Hans, Nils, Pia and Anne (who has just joined the team on this very day).

Excerpt 1: Jævla svenske / Bloody Swede

1		((Jon re-enters the room. Hans raises both arms over his head))	
2	Jon:	ingen salg	no sale
3		(0.4)	(0.4)
4	Hans:	[nei:::]	[no:::]
5	Anne:	[nei:::]	[no:::]
6	Jon:	der er sånn der (eh:) (0.7)	it was just like (eh:) (0.7)
7		jævla svenske	bloody Swedes
8	Pia:	ha ha ha	ha ha ha
9		(0.4)	(0.4)
10	Jon:	som æh: eller to svens [ker]	who erm: or rather two Swed [es]
11	Hans:	[sa-]	[say-]
12		((Hans turns towards Anne who is sitting to his right))	
13		han også (0.3) [ss-]	he also (0.3) [ss-]
14	Anne:	[ha]	[ha]
15	Hans:	(ej) det høres som om	(what) it sounds like it is
16		[mi- min] [feil]	[my- my] [mistake]
17	Anne:	[ja ja]	[yea yea]
18	Jon:	[som æh:]	[who erh:]
19		sitter på gjerdet og venter	sit on the fence and wait
20		er interessert men	are interested but

As he re-enters the room, Jon reveals the disappointing news that his flat has not yet been sold, and Hans and Anne immediately express their sympathy by producing co-occurring "no:::"'s (lines 4 and 5). In line 6, Jon begins to explain the situation in greater detail, pauses, and then introduces the national category "Swede" pre-modified by the negative evaluative adjective *jævla* ('bloody'). Pia chuckles at this (line 9), and Jon then reactivates the national category in line 10 by indicating that it was in fact not only one but *two* Swedes who would not go ahead with the deal. At this point, Hans orients to Anne and complains, smilingly, that Jon makes it sound as if the situation is *his* fault. In line 17, Anne laughingly agrees with Hans.

The expression "bloody Swede" that Jon uses in this excerpt arguably invokes a general stereotype that can be used as part of social banter. The expression may also, in less benign ways, be used as an explicitly derogatory label. In the case of this example, the uptake Jon receives from Pia suggests that she understands the term to be used in jest. Indeed, Jon may be heard as performing a stylised version of "a Norwegian mocking a Swede", a cultural trope which we argue is in wide circulation in the popular Norwegian/Swedish imagination, cf. the vignette above. In the context of the group, this culturally familiar framing of Swedes – and indeed the *relationship* between Norwegians and Swedes – takes on a local significance because one of the team members, Hans, is a Swede.

After Jon has activated the category of "Swedes" twice, Hans takes up the gauntlet and makes his Swedishness relevant by performing what may be heard as an equally stylised role as "the offended Swede", tongue-in-cheek. Together with Anne, Hans creates a specific meaning for Jon's category of "bloody Swede", namely that it is about himself, since he is a Swede and as such becomes a representative of the category but also responsible for the actions of his fellow countrymen. While Hans and Anne's exchange only involves the two of them as speakers, it is obviously available to everyone in the room, making it akin to a performance with actors and an audience. Taking on the role of "the offended Swede", Hans actively positions himself as the implied "butt" of Jon's sarcastic comment, even though there is no on-the-record indication that Jon was necessarily hinting at Hans when he made the remark. While insulting categories that have co-members present is a common sociolinguistic phenomenon (their existence reflected in formulations like, "present company excluded, of course"),[4] the very active co-construction by the "insulted" party is perhaps less common.

Interestingly, Hans seems to select Anne as the audience for his performance through the direction of his gaze. While this may be completely coincidental, it could also be seen as an attempt on Hans' part to build an allegiance between himself and Anne (who has a Serbian background) as two non-Norwegian outsiders. Thus, using the stereotype of "bloody Swedes" as a springboard, Hans simultaneously manages to position himself *vis-à-vis* Jon, performing what we might describe as *mock disalignment*, and possibly indicating an affiliative stance towards Anne as a fellow non-Norwegian.

In this excerpt, the category "Swede" is imbued with different meanings. In Jon's account a Swede is annoying because s/he is passively waiting rather than actively bidding. Hans in turn builds on Jon's stereotyping and potential othering by building an alliance with Anne based on outsiderness, a trait they have in common even if it is only Hans' national group membership which is made explicitly relevant here. Together, Jon and Hans produce a performance that the other team members may laugh at, thereby – as we shall see – launching the performance of jokes based on a stereotypical Norwegian-Swedish relationship as an emerging discursive norm in the group.

---

[4] We are indebted to Nikolas Coupland for this observation.

4.2.2 Introducing 'the other half'

A little later, approximately 20 minutes into the same meeting, a similar situation arises. Once more, the primary interactants are Jon and Hans, and once again it is Jon who is the first to introduce a national category, though this time he refers to "Norwegians" rather than "Swedes" (Excerpt 2). In the conversation leading up to this excerpt, Hans has raised a technical issue for the group to consider. He argues that the way they have planned to carry out a particular elevator shaft is flawed, since the worker finalising the shaft will have no way of getting out of the shaft once he is done with his work. Hans therefore proposes a rather demanding solution. However, it eventually turns out that Hans has seemingly misinterpreted the technical drawings. Excerpt 2 shows Jon pointing this out to Hans while offering an alternative suggestion for how to handle the situation. As he speaks, Jon points to different details on the technical drawing on the table in front of them.

Excerpt 2: Nordmenn og svenskere / *Norwegians and Swedes*

1	Jon:	så mitt forslag da er (.)	so my suggestion then is (.)
2		nordmenn hadde liksom	a Norwegian would kinda have been
3		stått her	standing here
4	Pia:	ha	ha
5		(0.3)	(0.3)
6	Anne:	hah	hah
7	Jon:	så hadde dem krabba opp der	and then they would have climbed up there
8		(0.8)	(0.8)
9	Nils:	[ha]	[ha]
10	Anne:	[ha]	[ha]
11	Pia:	[ha]	[ha]
12		((Hans turns his head, looking directly into the camera))	
13	Hans:	jag hoppas det blir registret	I hope it is getting recorded
14		den här i filmkamera med øh eh	on the video this erm erh
15		den här rasistiske ??pååkningen??	this racist ??tackle??
16		((all participants laugh, chuckle or smile during	
17		Hans' turn and he too ends his turn smiling at Jon))	

As Jon proposes his solution in lines 1–3, he activates the national category "Norwegians" which in this particular context may be interpreted as forming an opposition to the category of "Swedes" – seeing that Hans, who is the primary recipient of Jon's comment, is a Swede. He then describes a rather straightforward solution, creating an indexical link between Norwegians and logical action. This explicit construction also makes an implicit representation of Swedes as not behaving logically, but rather making unnecessarily complicated suggestions. The immediate uptake from Anne, Pia and Nils is laughter (lines 9–11), showing that they treat Jon's comment as a laughable. Hans is (once again) the first one to explicitly turn Jon's utterance into a matter of stereotyping, as he in lines 12–15 turns towards the camera and says that he hopes this "racist tackle" is being recorded. This too makes everybody laugh, chuckle or smile.

If this exchange had played out in an entirely serious key, Hans would be making very strong accusations here, expressing a feeling of being discriminated against on the grounds of his nationality. However, once again, it is quite clear that Jon and Hans are to some extent playing out roles where they can use the invoked national stereotypes for jocular "attacks" against each other. Through this process, the abstract categories of "Norwegians" and "Swedes" become imbued with local meaning, both relating to what the terms "mean" (their indexical value) and how they can be used within the context of the group: Norwegians, personified by Jon, are positioned as the logically thinking in-group, while Swedes, personified by Hans, are positioned as a "not-so-clever" out-group. Interestingly, these meanings are quite different from the ones activated only 20 minutes earlier, yet they are arguably based on the exact same relationship between the two groups.

The participants' use of national stereotypes gradually creates an indexical field (Eckert 2008) of conflicting meanings. On the one hand, the act of stereotyping is framed as a playful activity; on the other the participants also orient to an alternative interpretation, namely discrimination, which however seems to become part of the playful activity. The interactional work done around the stereotypes functions as a display of shared humour while *at the same time* constructing hierarchies between the national categories being invoked and between the speakers in the room who fall under their labels. As such, the use of stereotypes has at this point come to be established as an element of the group's discursive practice which is used for the negotiation of interpersonal relations and individual stances.

On a practical level, the act of stereotyping as part of a jocular frame is in this particular case deployed as an interactional resource that allows Jon as the project leader to point out to his foreman (20 years older and much more experienced than him) that he has made a professional blunder *without* addressing this directly in an authoritarian style. In this way, the potential for stereotypes to be enlisted as a resource in delivering critique emerges as a part of the discursive practices within the group, which we argue helps maintain a norm of relative equality amongst the members. The importance of having a "flat structure" was repeatedly brought up by Jon in conversation with the other team members. In this case, by substituting a professional hierarchy with one of nationality, the "Swedish" stereotype comes in as a handy resource for "doing having" a flat structure at a point in the interaction where the organisational hierarchy of the team is otherwise hard to ignore, with Jon as the manager effectively correcting a subordinate. The state of inferiority/superiority is removed from the individual relation and resettled as part of a membership category.

While the particular meanings and interactional functions of the stereotypes we see in action here are clearly local to this group, we would argue that they nevertheless rely on and reproduce pre-existing stereotypic ideas about Norwegians and Swedes and their relationship, cf. the vignette discussed above. Moreover, we would suggest that the way the stereotypes are used relies on a pre-established shared norm which positions this type of banter as expected and permissible social behaviour.

Taken together, the two first excerpts have demonstrated how the national stereotypes of Swedes and Norwegians and the way they are used in the interaction rest on a normative expectation that making fun of and with each other through the use of stereotypes is a legitimate social activity. The excerpts also illustrate that there is an underlying assumption of a dichotomous relationship between Norwegians and Swedes, where one group is positioned as valuable in some respect and the other less so. The participants mutually orient to the Norwegian-Swedish stereotypes as being "funny", displaying that there is already a norm for how to interpret these stereotypes in place: an example of productive reflexivity around norms and stereotypes. Ultimately, this shared "norm of interpretation" (Hymes 1974) helps legitimise and contribute to the reproduction of these stereotypes.

4.2.3 The plot thickens

In the third excerpt, which takes place during a lunch break the following day, the banter and playful othering continues, this time to discuss the relative "normality" of Swedish and Norwegian food habits. It begins as Erik, one of the Swedish foremen who has also been part of the team from the start, asks for the cheese cutter, and Jon is quick to enquire if Erik is going to put *brunost* (a Norwegian caramelised cheese) on top of his other food, clearly marking the proposed combination as unusual.

Excerpt 3: Matvaner / *Food habits*

1	Erik:	får jeg låna høvlen	can I have the cutter, please
2		(3.1)	(3.1)
3		osthyvel	cheese cutter
4		(1.4)	(1.4)
5	Jon:	du vil ha høvel	you want the cutter

6	Erik:	ja	yes
7		(0.9)	(0.9)
8		tack	thanks
9		(1.1)	(1.1)
10	Jon:	skal brunost opp [på den]	is the brown cheese going on top [of that]
11	Pia:	[hdr]	[hdr]
12	Anne:	ha [ha ha]	ha [ha ha]
13	Erik:	[jeg: skal bare ha ved] sida	[I'm: just having it on] the side
14		(0.5)	(0.5)
15	Pia:	ha ha ha	ha ha ha
16		(1.2)	(1.2)
17	Erik:	ingon fara	no danger
18	Pia:	ha (0.2) ha ha	ha (0.2) ha ha
19		(4.6)	(4.6)
20	Erik:	hva- man må prøva alt	hva- you have to try everything
21		(1.9)	(1.9)
22		for å få frem den perfekte smaken	to get out the perfect taste
23		(2.5)	(2.5)
24	Jon:	ja det er kreativt [det-]	well that sure is creative [this-]
25	Pia:	[viste]	[didn't]
26		ikke at svensker	know the Swedes
27		var så vågal	were so bold
28	Erik:	nei	no
29		(1.4)	(1.4)
30		det er	it's
31		[normalt (.) alle gör så här]	[normal (.) everybody does it like this]
32	Pia:	[ha: haha]	[ha: haha]
33		(1.4)	(1.4)
34	Pia:	hua	hua
35		(1.2)	(1.2)
36	Hans:	ikke ??drill?? svenskene heller	also don't ??make fun of?? the Swedes
37	Erik:	ha ha ha	ha ha ha
38	Anne:	ha ha	ha ha
39		(1.2)	(1.2)
40	Hans:	Erik	Erik

At this moment in time, Erik is already renowned / infamous within the group for his food combinations. Jon's question in line 10 indicates that it would be unusual to put *brunost* / brown cheese on top of other food items on Erik's plate. Erik aligns with this stance in line 13 and 17 when he explains that he is going to have it "on the side", and that there is "no danger" in what he is doing, conveying that there is no need for the others to worry. However, in 20 and 22 he also maintains that one has to try to find the perfect taste combination, defending his general tendency to combine food items in unusual ways. Jon acknowledges this by conceding that it is "creative" (line 24). This could be heard as a positive evaluation but in this context "creative" could also be seen as a euphemism for "weird" or "deviant" (cf. the discussion of the relationship between creativity and normativity in Pitzl, this volume). This is the interpretation Erik seems to orient to in line 31 when he claims that his practice is "normal". It is noteworthy that when Jon chooses to characterise the food combination as "creative" it has not as of yet been described as a Swedish practice, it is still about Erik's food practices, which might also be one reason why the meaning-shifter "creative" is used instead of other adjectives that could be interpreted as a more unambiguous critique.

In lines 25–27, Pia, who has been laughing throughout the entire exchange, turns Erik's questionable assortment and combination of foods into something prototypically Swedish rather than something that specifically concerns Erik. Erik replies that his behaviour is "normal" and that "everybody does it" (line 30), which makes Pia laugh. In line 36, Hans interjects with an imperative, "ikke drill svenskene heller". In both Norwegian and Swedish *drille/drilla* means 'to exercise' though it also has an old-fashioned meaning of 'making fun of' which would seem more appropriate in this particular context, meaning that Hans is literally saying something like 'do not tease/mock the Swedes'.

The representation of a connection between food habits and cultures is often strong (Karrebæk 2012, 2016), and here it has the effect of setting Erik off from the others in the group by identifying his food habits as an outcome of him being a Swede. Hans sides with Erik (as a Swede) but also invokes Erik's name somewhat reproachfully in line 40, indicating that he too finds Erik's food combinations somehow inappropriate or deviant – despite Erik's claim that his habits are "normal". In this excerpt, then, the potential of national categories to generate othering becomes apparent once again. The excerpt also shows that the very practice of othering has become established as an acceptable and *normal* form of behaviour within the group: a form of othering that could be considered "mock-othering" (similar to Labov's [1972] mock styles).

Finally, it is worth noticing how the use of a generalised category, once again (cf. Jon's implicit critique of Hans' readings of the technical drawings in Excerpt 2), seems to be a way for participants to provide a comment on another group member's unusual practice without making it personal. This is arguably what Pia does in this excerpt, while Jon delivers his comments on-record, questioning Erik directly. Finally, Hans once again enters his performative mode and turns the whole affair into another case of "the others" (the Norwegians) teasing the Swedes, activating the latter category as subalterns, and positioning himself, as a member of this category, as a "victim".

4.2.4 Subverting the hierarchy

The next excerpt exemplifies how national categories can also be used to subvert the hierarchies that have been established within the team. Excerpt 4 below is taken from the team's second internal meeting held 15 days into their collaboration (*Meeting rooms 2* in Figure 2). At this meeting, Luisa, the Spanish project planning leader, is also present. She has been part of the team from the very beginning, but she has been working from the central office most of the time rather than in the construction site offices. This means that she has had relatively few interactions with the other team members up until now. Luisa proposes that the meeting rooms in the site office should be given specific names, arguing that it will be easier to identify and book them in the online calendar this way. After a couple of turns where no one actually suggests names for the meeting rooms, Hans suggests calling them "Sweden" and "Norway" (interestingly using the English names for the two countries).

Excerpt 4: Møterom 2 / *Meeting rooms 2*

1	Hans:	[det store heter Sweden og]		[the big one is called Sweden and]
2	Pia:	[ha]		[ha]
3	Hans:	??dette heter?? Nor [way]		??this one is called?? Nor [way]
4	Luisa:	ha	[ha ha] okei ja	ha [ha ha] okay yes
5	Anne:		[ha ha]	[ha ha]
6		(0.6)		(0.6)
7	Luisa:	[det er greit det]		[that's fine]
8	Pia:	[ha ha ha] ha ha		[ha ha ha] ha ha
9	Jon:	nei (.) ha ha		no (.) ha ha
10		det er ha ha ha		it is ha ha ha
11		((everybody laughs))		
12	Anne:	??det er ikke greit det??		??it is not fine??
13	Jon:	Kamilla har du et forslag (0.4)		Kamilla do you have a suggestion (0.4)
14		hva skal vi kalle møterommene		what should we call the meeting rooms
15		(0.2)		(0.2)
16		eller er det helt uavhengig [??av??]		or is that totally independent [??of??]
17	Luisa:		[stor] og lite	[big] and small

In this excerpt, Hans is challenging the locally established hierarchy with Norway and Norwegians placed metaphorically above Sweden and Swedes (cf. Excerpts 1–3) by proposing names for the small and big meeting rooms according to the size of Norway and Sweden. This proposal would entail that the big meeting room would be called Sweden, as Sweden is bigger than Norway, geographically speaking. As noted above, he refers to the two countries by using their English names. If this code-switch is meant to function as a contextualisation cue (Gumperz 1982), it is hard to predict what the intended meaning might be, but it could perhaps help project his proposal as a joke – another playful stab at the Norwegian-Swedish relation.

Five days earlier, Hans had made the exact same suggestion in a meeting with Pia (*Meeting rooms 1* in Figure 2). However, Pia did not take up this suggestion as anything but a joke which is also what seems to be the outcome this time. Indeed, Pia and Anne laugh and seem to treat Hans' proposal as a joke (lines 2 and 5). So does Luisa, but she also, in contrast to Pia and Anne, *accepts* Hans' suggestion, although with some hesitation (lines 4 and 7). Luisa's acceptance causes Jon to remark, laughingly, that the suggestion is indeed *not* acceptable (lines 9–10); a conclusion that Anne also takes up in line 12. This prompts laughter from all of the other team members, which we take to display alignment with Jon's stance towards the proposal as a laughable, a ridiculous idea that ought to be rejected. In effect, this sequence then reaffirms – or restores – the order that has already been established within the group concerning the relationship between Swedes and Norwegians, and, by implication, Norway and Sweden.

Subsequently, Jon asks Kamilla, possibly positioning her as a *Danish* observer who might be perceived as a third "neutral" Scandinavian part, what she thinks they should call the rooms. However, before she gets a chance to answer, Luisa quickly interjects that they could simply call them "small" and "big" (line 17). Luisa's effort to quickly provide an alternative solution may be related to her earlier acceptance of Hans' suggestion. Being Spanish, Luisa has no personal stake in the Scandinavian naming competition (her national background is virtually "erased" in the context of the construction site where she is simply classed as a "foreign" worker), but it seems clear that she orients to Jon's rejection. Playing the Scandinavian stereotype game of mutual othering is clearly tricky, and in this situation, Luisa transgresses against the norm that has been built up so far: Swedes cannot be granted the upper-hand in the Swedish-Norwegian relationship. This example also illustrates, then, how this norm over a relatively short period of time seems to have sedimented amongst the members who have been exposed to each other the most.

4.2.5 When stereotypes sting

Excerpts 1 through 4, which are all taken from the beginning of the team collaboration, show that the national stereotypes of Swedes and Norwegians are used for multiple purposes though clearly embedded in specific interpretive frames that allow participants to play on dichotomies related to "national identities" and social hierarchies. The indexical fields being produced around the labels "Swedes" and "Norwegians" are highly complex and often ambiguous, allowing the participants to use the labels and their associated stereotypical meanings as resources for pursuing a range of interactional and interpersonal goals. In the excerpts presented so far, the key is playful and good-humoured, and an interactional norm for playful othering has emerged along with a hierarchical relationship between Swedes and Norwegians. Still, the othering that this stereotypical relation allows for may also be used for conflictual rather than humorous ends.

In the following excerpt, which is taken from a progress meeting approximately half a year into the project, the Swedish stereotype is used in a very different way. Unlike the examples we have seen from the beginning of the project, this excerpt illustrates a situation where the use of a Swedish stereotype is *not* acceptable to the involved participants. At this point in the process, the contractor has had to do some restructuring which has led to staff changes. Pia and Nils have been let go for different reasons, and some of the carpenters are also being moved to other sites and replaced by leased workers who are more flexible and cheaper in terms of up- and down-sizing the production. The night before the conversation in Excerpt 5 takes place, the team has had a meeting with the managers from the contractor's headquarters, and this meeting is what they are discussing in the excerpt below. Hans and Linus, both Swedish foremen, are recounting to the rest of the team their interaction with one of the Norwegian managers, Anders, from the meeting the previous evening. In this account, Hans and Linus have made reasonable suggestions, but were met with a negative response from Anders, as Hans describes in the excerpt. Johan, whom they also mention, is the project manager of the construction project and though he is not part of daily management, he is the one responsible for overseeing the project and the team.

Excerpt 5: Typisk svensk / *Typical Swedish*

1	Hans:	og så slenger han utt	and then he just exclaims
2		sig bare så her (0.3) ah (.)	he just says (0.3) ah (.)
3		??Hans är ju sånn här??	??Hans is just like that??
4		(0.3) typisk svensk ??sa han??	(0.3) typical Swedish ??he said??
5		(0.6) helt på fullt alvor	(0.6) in complete and utter earnest
6	Linus:	ar først han [sa nei] xxx	yea first he [said no] xxx
7	Hans:	[sittet]	[sat]
8		(0.2)	(0.2)
9	Linus:	[ja]	[yes]
10	Hans:	[ja]	[yes]
11	Linus:	mhm	mhm

12	Anne:	hmhm	hmhm
13		(0.4)	(0.4)
14	Hans:	[ar fa-]	[yea ac-]
15	Jon:	[typi]sk svensk (.)	[typi]cal Swedish (.)
16		hva ligger han i det	what does he mean by that
17	Hans:	ja: det ligger han i at (0.5)	yeah: he means that (0.5)
18		vi skal bare h- opp (1.6) inn penger	we just want h- about (1.6) get money
19		(0.3) det var bare penger	(0.3) it was all about money
20	Anne:	hah	hah
21	Jon:	og det er ikke Johan	and that is not Johan
22		(0.7)	(0.7)
23	Linus:	ja [m-]	yes [m-]
24	Hans:	[net]top [det var] liså-	[ex]actly [that was] lik-
25	Linus:	[nettop]	[exactly]
26	Hans:	[det var det som vi [också liksom] svara]	[that's what we also [kind of] replied]
27	Jon:	[ha ha ha ha]	[ha ha ha ha]
28	Linus:	[precis]	[exactly]
29	Hans:	mm	mm
30		altså det var ju sånn jævla	I mean it was a bloody
31		slag i kjeften på oss to	sucker punch for the two of us
32		när vi sitter här	when we sit here

Hans clearly shows that he is upset about being described as "typical Swedish" (line 4), and he and Linus agree that the manager was being "sordid". In line 16, Jon asks for Hans' interpretation of what Anders meant by "typical Swedish", and Hans suggests that it meant they were only thinking about making money (lines 17–19), implying that Swedes are greedy or very profit-oriented, which may latch onto the idea that Swedes are highly industrious businesspeople. Interestingly, the idea that they "are only in it for the money" runs directly counter to the self-perception of the company, which is a family-owned business with a strong social responsibility profile. Based on this ethnographic context, Anne's "hah" in line 20 can be heard as an expression of contempt at this proposal, displaying affiliation with Hans and Linus' experience of having been treated unfairly.

As in the other excerpts where stereotypes of Norwegians and Swedes are used, Hans and Linus arguably feel othered by Anders. In contrast to the other excerpts, we hear Hans' tone as being quite severe in this excerpt, and he seems truly upset, which would indicate that he does not understand the othering to be meant in jest, but rather in earnest (mirroring Labov's observations on insults sometimes being interpreted as personal rather than ritual). According to Hans' account, Anders implied that Swedes, unlike Norwegians, only care about making money, and this was perceived as an explicit reproach. In response, Jon sides with Hans and Linus by suggesting that their leader Johan is in fact also "only thinking about money". By trying to defuse the stereotypes in this way, and by questioning the implicit indexical value of the stereotype of "the Swede", Jon is seemingly trying to "repair" some of the interpersonal damage done by Anders. He also clearly shows that while he may happily participate in inter-Scandinavian banter (as exemplified by Excerpts 1–4), he does not – in this instance – see the Swedes as actual "others". In short, the wider circulating stereotype that allows for Norwegian-Swedish othering is in this excerpt being interpreted as malign criticism rather than humorous banter, and this breaks with the interactional norm for stereotyping that the team has created and relied upon. However, the stereotyping reported in this excerpt allows the team to strengthen their norm by rejecting the legitimacy of Anders' malign stereotyping.

5 Discussion and concluding remarks

In the analysis above, we have demonstrated how the members of the management team deploy national stereotypes as interactional resources that allow them to categorise individuals and groups and subsequently position themselves and others *vis-à-vis* these groups. The distinction between "Swedes" and "Norwegians" is a highly productive trope in creating differentiation within the team and providing a frame for their ongoing negotiation of interpersonal relationships through mutual othering. In many ways, then, the excerpts we have analysed represent almost textbook-like empirical evidence of how stereotypes can be used to segment and organize "the social world into social categories or groups" (Hewstone & Giles 1986: 11) based on generalizations and categorical judgements, serving individual as well as collective functions (Tajfel 1981). At the same time, our analysis also brings out how the stereotypes are used as part of different interactional endeavours, including the construction of interpersonal relationships and the delivery of personal remarks in a non-personalised way (cf. Excerpt 2 about misreading technical drawings and Excerpt 3 about odd food habits).

In sum, the analyses we have presented have shown that the stereotypes serve a variety of interactional functions within the group, with the local meaning of the stereotypes being built up over time. Thus, we have demonstrated how a more or less casual comment about "bloody Swedes" at the very first meeting of the management group (Excerpt 1) is picked up and turned into an opportunity to engage in banter based on perceived differences between Swedes and Norwegians. Once established, this particular way of deploying the stereotypes then repeatedly resurfaces in the interaction, incrementally establishing an interactional norm for humour-mediated discussions within the group. It is noteworthy how more and more team members begin to contribute actively to the process of stereotyping over time, and how it crops up in different contexts, often presenting social gambits for the group. For example, the stereotypes surface in discussions about (1) who has the best solutions to technical problems, (2) how the meeting rooms should be named, and (3) what constitutes "normal" and "abnormal" (or "creative") eating habits. In all these cases, the stereotypes are used as resources that essentially produce othering, distinguishing "Swedes" (and potentially other foreigners) from "Norwegians". At the same time, the two categories are imbued with different and fluctuating meanings to support arguments about one group's superiority over the other: country size may be used as an argument for naming rights, food items may turn into a discussion of the group members' respective normalcy and deviance, and so forth.

Crucially, though, the participants treat the process of social differentiation inherent in this discursive practice as an unproblematic part of a good-humoured ritual which seems to create a sense of shared group identity. The locally developed discursive norm for stereotype meaning and use is highlighted in Excerpt 5 where Hans provides an account of another sort of stereotyping: a critical situation where being classified and stereotyped as a Swede by a Norwegian colleague is not acceptable due to Hans and Linus experiencing this stereotype use as negative and non-humorous othering. The use of stereotypes acquires meaning with reference to locally established norms, and if another normative framework is perceived to be in play, the interactional meanings of the stereotypes are likely to change.

The study at hand has also demonstrated how emerging, local norms are far from the only norms that play into the group's stereotype use. The participants' ability – even from the early beginnings of the collaboration – to use stereotypes as an interactional resource implies that the participants must to some extent be drawing on similar ideas about how the stereotypes in question can be used (a point which was also evident in the opening vignette). In other words, the stereotypes and *their principles of use* are available to the participants from the outset as "reflexive models of meaningful, expected and appropriate conduct" (Piippo, this volume), i.e. as norms.

So, to conclude, stereotypes may be, and often are, normative packages that define how group insiders and outsiders alike should expect a member of a particular group to be, think and act. Yet, these normative packages may be reconfigured in local settings as they are enacted as part of emerging discursive and interactional norms. In this way, a new indexical field is created where the stereotypes' meaning potential is partly derived from the stable normative packages and partly from the emerging local norms. This position between stable and emerging norms contributes to making the interactional deployment of stereotypes a double-edged sword. In the analysis presented here, we have explored some quite risky gambits in the deployment of national stereotypes, which were not guaranteed to succeed, but which gradually came to be established as "the done thing" within the group. This way of deploying national stereotypes may not have succeeded in other contexts; in fact, it seems quite obvious that deploying national stereotypes in this way will only work as a means of building in-group solidarity as long as the participants share normative frameworks that allow them to evaluate such behaviour positively.[5]

If, as Durkheim would have it, norms are the building blocks of society, we have demonstrated how a group of people with very little prior knowledge of each other have adopted and adapted a subset of such generic building blocks to fashion their own local community. The excerpts we have analysed may be seen as snapshots of moments where the normative "glue" that enables human sociality is being (re-)produced. This process is communicative at its core, and one that has always had a central position in sociolinguistics and related disciplines. Studying norms is a study of "the micro" and "the macro", the individual and the structural, the "constructures" (Blommaert 2018) of social life. Studying norms from a sociolinguistic perspective entails a deeper understanding of how phenomena such as stereotyping, discrimination, social cohesion, differentiation along with many others are born out of and feed into daily life in all its complexity. By examining norms and exploring how they come into being, we not only gain a fuller understanding of the role of language in social life, but also a better basis for applying our insights and raising general awareness about norms and their effects in interaction.

Transcription conventions

Left column	Transcript of recording
Right column	English paraphrase
Identifier	Jon:
Timed pause	(0.2)
Micro pause	(.)
Overlap markers top	[normal (.) everybody does it like this]
Overlap markers bottom	[ha: haha]
Transcriber uncertainty	??he said??
Unintelligible	xxx
Prolonged sound	haha:::
Comments	((provided in double parentheses))

---

[5] An interesting observation that might merit more analytical attention in the future is the fact that the use of national stereotyping is introduced by two of the team's most established members in terms of rank and tenure, namely the project leader, Jon, and the experienced and respected foreman, Hans.

References

Agha, Asif. 2003. The social life of cultural value. *Language & Communication* 23 (3–4). 231–273.
Agha, Asif. 2007. *Language and social relations*. Cambridge: Cambridge University Press.
Alexander, Michelle G., Marilynn B. Brewer & Robert W. Livingston. 2005. Putting stereotype content in context: Image theory and interethnic stereotypes. *Personality and Social Psychology Bulletin* 31 (6). 781–794.
Allport, Gordon W. 1979. *The nature of prejudice*. New York: Basic Books.
Augoustinos, Martha & Iain Walker. 1995. *Social cognition: An integrated introduction*. London: Sage.
Blommaert, Jan. 2010. *The sociolinguistics of globalization*. Cambridge: Cambridge University Press.
Blommaert, Jan. 2018. *Durkheim and the Internet: On sociolinguistics and the sociological imagination*. London: Bloomsbury.
Caffi, Claudia. 2006. Pragmatic presupposition. In Keith Brown (ed.), *Encyclopedia of language and linguistics, vol. 4*, 2nd edn. 17–25. Oxford: Elsevier.
Carr, E. Summerson and Michael Lempert. 2016. *Scale: Discourse and dimensions of social life*. Oakland: University of California Press.
Cicourel, Aaron V. 1987. The interpenetration of communicative contexts: Examples from medical encounters. *Social Psychology Quarterly* 50. 217–226.
Copland, Fiona & Angela Creese. 2015. *Linguistic ethnography: Collecting, analysing and presenting data*. London: Sage.
Day, Dennis. 2008. In a bigger, messo, context. *Journal of Pragmatics* 40. 979–996.
Delfino, Jennifer B. 2016. Fighting words? Joning as conflict talk and identity performance among African American preadolescents. *Journal of Sociolinguistics* 20 (5). 631–653.
Eckert, Penelope. 2008. Variation and the indexical field. *Journal of Sociolinguistics* 12 (4). 453–476.
Fabricius, Anne H. & Janus Mortensen. 2013. Language ideology and the notion of 'construct resource': A case study of modern RP. In Tore Kristiansen and Stefan Grondelaers (eds.), *Language (de)standardisation in Late Modern Europe: Experimental studies*, 375–401. Oslo: Novus.
Gumperz, John J. 1982. *Discourse strategies*. Cambridge: Cambridge University Press.
Hewstone, Miles & Howard Giles. 1986. Social groups and social stereotypes in intergroup communication: A review and model of intergroup communication breakdown. In William B. Gudykunst (ed.), *Intergroup communication*, 10–26. London: Edward Arnold.
Hultgren, Anna Kristina. 2011. 'Building rapport' with customers across the world: The global diffusion of a call centre speech style. *Journal of Sociolinguistics* 15 (1). 36–64.
Hymes, Dell H. 1974. *Foundations in sociolinguistics: An ethnographic approach*. Philadelphia, PA: University of Pennsylvania Press.
Jaffe, Alexandra. 2016. Indexicality, stance and fields in sociolinguistics. In Nikolas Coupland (ed.), *Sociolinguistics: Theoretical debates*, 86–112. Cambridge: Cambridge University Press.
Jaspers, Jürgen & Sarah Van Hoof. 2019. Style and stylisation. In Karen Tusting (ed.), *The Routledge handbook of linguistic ethnography*. London: Routledge.

Jenkins, Richard. 1994. Rethinking ethnicity: Identity, categorization, and power. *Ethnic and Racial Studies* 17 (2). 197–223.

Jørgensen, J. Normann. 2008. Polylingual languaging around and among children and adolescents. *International Journal of Multilingualism* 5 (3). 161–176.

Karrebæk, Martha Sif. 2012. "What's in Your Lunch Box Today?": Health, respectability, and ethnicity in the primary classroom. *Journal of Linguistic Anthropology* 22 (1). 1–22.

Karrebæk, Martha Sif. 2016. Rye bread for lunch, lasagne for breakfast: Enregisterment, classrooms, and national food norms in superdiversity. In Karel Arnaut, Martha Sif Karrebæk, Massimiliano Spotti & Jan Blommaert (eds.), *Engaging superdiversity: Recombining spaces, times and language practices*, 90–120. Bristol: Multilingual Matters.

Kraft, Kamilla. 2017. Constructing migrant workers: Multilingualism and communication in the transnational construction site. Oslo: University of Oslo PhD dissertation.

Labov, William. 1972. Rules for ritual insults. In David Sudnow (ed.), *Studies in social interaction,* 120–169. New York: Free Press.

MacWhinney, Brian. 2000. *The CHILDES project: Tools for analyzing talk*. 3rd edn. Mahwah, N.J: Lawrence Erlbaum Associates.

Meyerhoff, Miriam & Nancy Niedzielski. 2003. The globalisation of vernacular variation. *Journal of Sociolinguistics* 7(4). 534–555.

Moerman, Michael. 1988. *Talking culture: Ethnography and conversation analysis*. Philadelphia: University of Pennsylvania Press.

Mortensen, Janus & Nikolas Coupland. 2018. Style and styling. In Jan-Ola Östman and Jef Verschueren (eds.), *Handbook of Pragmatics*, 201–220. Amsterdam: John Benjamins Publishing Company.

Piippo, Irina. 2012. Viewing norms dialogically: An action-oriented approach to sociolinguistic metatheory. Helsinki: University of Helsinki PhD Dissertation.

Rampton, Ben, Janet Maybin & Celia Roberts. 2015. Theory and method in linguistic ethnography. In Julia Snell, Sara Shaw & Fiona Copland (eds.), *Linguistic ethnography: Interdisciplinary explorations*, 14–50. London: Palgrave.

Said, Edward W. 2003 [1978]. *Orientalism*. London: Penguin Classics.

Silverstein, Michael. 2003. Indexical order and the dialectics of sociolinguistic life. *Language & Communication* 23. 193–229.

Tajfel, Henri. 1981. *Human groups and social categories: Studies in social psychology*. Cambridge: Cambridge University Press.

Marie-Luise Pitzl
6 Multilingual creativity and emerging norms in interaction: Towards a methodology for micro-diachronic analysis

1 Introduction

The theoretical discussion of norms often remains in the background in linguistic research, and it is particularly rare to find empirical studies that explore the emergence of linguistic and social norms in interaction. Along with other chapters in the present volume, this is the gap that the present chapter seeks to address. The chapter theorizes linguistic norms from the perspective of creativity, focusing on the question of how norms can be studied as a sociolinguistic phenomenon, especially in linguistically and culturally diverse, fleeting social contexts. Taking English as a Lingua Franca (ELF) interactions as a case in point, the chapter builds on recent work on Transient International Groups (TIGs) (Pitzl 2018c) and Transient Multilingual Communities (TMCs) (Mortensen 2017). It examines one long speech event among European exchange students in VOICE (Vienna-Oxford International Corpus of English) and describes multilingual creativity and emerging norms in this transient ELF context. A central aim of the analysis is to suggest principles and tools for a micro-diachronic approach to spoken interaction in order to empirically trace and visualize initial stages of situational norm development.

2 Creativity, (linguistic) norms and English as a lingua franca (ELF)

While creativity may seem an odd or surprising choice of phenomenon for a discussion of sociolinguistic norms, this is only so at first glance. Upon closer inspection, the link between creativity and norms is in fact a very close one because creativity is in many ways the very opposite of normativity. Paradoxically, any discussion or definition of creativity has to engage with the notion of norms to some extent, since creativity involves some form of divergence from what is considered normal. From

---

Acknowledgements: The research in this chapter was supported by the Austrian Science Fund (FWF): V747-G (Elise-Richter Grant 'English as a lingua franca in Transient International Groups').

the perspective of linguistic creativity research, we might tentatively define norms as analytic constructs concerning subsets of identifiable/observable regularities of linguistic behavior against which creative behavior can be identified. Although norms are, of course, proposed as relevant with regard to (more or less specified) contexts of language use and/or communities and groups of language users, they can be seen as analytic constructs in the sense that they are postulated (and relied upon) by researchers. Most norms concerning language use tend to be proposed on the basis of regularities observable in 3rd person data (e.g. corpora, recorded conversations), but of course the relevance or existence of a particular norm can also be argued for on the basis of elicited participant perspectives (i.e. 2nd person data such as interviews) or introspection (i.e. 1st person data, although exclusive reliance on introspection is less common today than it was several decades ago).

Regularities that can be posited as norms exist simultaneously on all levels of language use, e.g. at the level of grammar, derivational morphology, lexis or literal vs. figurative language use.[1] Yet, creativity research (as most other research in linguistics) often tends to focus on one linguistic level or phenomenon at a time. In consequence, certain (sets of) norms tend to be in the foreground in a study, while other norms remain in the background, as it is impossible to focus on *all* linguistic norms relevant to a context of language use at the same time. Depending on the level of language investigated, some norms may be considered regular and systematic (and might be referred to as *rules*), other norms may be more obscure and less systematic (and might be referred to as *conventions*).

2.1 Norm-following and norm-transcending creativity: A synchronic glimpse at potential change

Many scholars implicitly or explicitly distinguish two kinds or types of creativity. While different creativity researchers use different labels for these, I have suggested grouping these by making a distinction between norm-following and norm-developing (Pitzl 2012) or, more recently, *norm-following* and *norm-transcending* creativity (Pitzl 2018a). Both types of creativity bring about individual realizations of a normative system. While norm-following creative realizations stay within the boundaries of the system, instances of norm-transcending creativity go beyond these boundaries. Crucially, the same expression(s) – like *chin chin* or *na zdrowie* (see below) – can in fact be norm-following and norm-transcending

---

[1] A more detailed discussion with references for these various approaches to creativity can be found in Pitzl (2013).

at the same time, but at different linguistic levels (see Pitzl 2012: 34–37, 2018a: 33–37). Having transcended a norm, norm-transcending creativity may prompt modifications in the normative system itself and thus have the potential to trigger linguistic change. Crucially, instances of norm-transcending creativity do not automatically lead to change; they only have the potential to do so.

Relating this distinction between norm-following and norm-transcending creativity to Taylor's (2012: 245–246) distinction between creativity and innovation, Larsen-Freeman (2016) discusses what she calls the nonteleological character of language, and of ELF in particular. In doing so, she argues convincingly that "as long as there are speakers who use ELF meaningfully through interactions with other ELF users, new properties will emerge, and in contrast to a putative endstate grammar, no endpoint will be reached" (Larsen-Freeman 2016: 140). While she points out that "both creations and innovations are norm-referenced" (Larsen-Freeman 2016: 142) and in this sense "'backward-looking'" (Larsen-Freeman 2016: 142), she elaborates that

> [t]here is no 'target' towards which ELF is evolving. It is ever labile. Any potentially system-changing innovation, then, would be in support of regularizing, expressiveness, social positioning, communicative efficiency, or motivated by other pragmatic factors. ELF speakers might accommodate to other ELF users in the moment, but these would essentially be local, contingent, and situated adaptations, often interactively co-constructed, in fulfillment of ELF's functional purpose, and therefore only potentially candidates for language change. (Larsen-Freeman 2016: 142)

It would seem that this is an apt description not only of ELF, but of language use in many contexts, especially in situations where groups of speakers are linguistically and regio-culturally diverse, prototypically multilingual, largely unacquainted and may interact only for a relatively short amount of time. Yet, this does not mean that these groups of speakers may not develop temporary norms that become characteristic for their group. Such (new) linguistic group norms will be influenced by pre-existing norms of individual speakers, of sub-groups of speakers or of the context of situation for example (cf. Hymes' 1974 norms of interaction) and many other factors. The influence that particular pre-existing norms have in a given situation or group, however, is largely unpredictable and difficult to observe. In terms of creativity and language change, the initial phase of norm emergence is most interesting, since it confronts us with the "actuation riddle" (Weinreich, Labov, & Herzog 1968: 186), namely "the problem of explaining why and how linguistic change actually comes about" (Mortensen & Hazel 2017: 271). Yet, this phase is also most difficult to capture empirically.

2.2 Normative systems, multilingual creativity and the dynamic nature of norms

Before we turn to the investigation of norm emergence, a comment about what can be denoted by a *normative system* is necessary (see also Baird, Baker, & Kitazawa 2014). As noted above, it is quite common for (socio)linguists to regard different levels of language (such as grammar, lexis, morphology, pronunciation or idioms) as normative systems that are organized by more or less regular and more or less transparent rules and conventions. It is also quite common, however, to conceive of entire *languages and *varieties as such normative systems.[2] In this sense, metapragmatically transcending the boundaries of a *language by means of code-switching, code-mixing or translanguaging can arguably be seen as creative in many – though not in all – contexts.

Following this conceptualization, this chapter examines *multilingual creativity* as instances where interactants perceptibly transcend *language boundaries in spoken interaction. At the same time, it rejects the assumption that translanguaging practices or code-mixing are always creative. If extensive code-mixing is – or becomes – the common mode of communication for a particular group or community, then "transcending [*]language boundaries might arguably not be seen as very creative for this group" (Pitzl 2018b: 235; cf. Jenkins 2015; Cogo 2016; also see Auer's 1999 distinction between code-switching vs. language mixing and fused lects and Gafaranga & Torras' 2001 notion of the bilingual medium). Two factors are crucial to note in this respect.

The first is that there is *never only one normative linguistic system* that applies to a communicative situation, but always several ones. In consequence, the same stretch of language can be creative in a norm-following way as well as in a norm-transcending way. This point is illustrated by many instances of multilingual creativity described below. Thus, occurrences of words like *chin chin*, *proost*, *na zdrowie* and *skål* in an interaction in which speakers primarily converse in *English can be seen as instances of norm-transcending creativity at the level of *language choice, especially if they are initially metapragmatically flagged as crossing *language boundaries by speakers themselves. Yet, as instances of intra-sentential (or maybe better intra-turn or intra-utterance) code-switches, the lexical elements are smoothly integrated into *English sentence structures. They are thus norm-following on the level of syntax. I would argue that it is this simultaneously norm-following and

---

[2] Following the convention established in Pitzl (2018a, 2018c), all instances that refer to individual *languages or *varieties (as well as the terms *language/s and *variety/ies themselves) are marked with an asterisk to emphasize their non-boundedness and non-homogeneity.

norm-transcending nature that actually makes these – and many other – instances of linguistic creativity intelligible and thus effective and functional.

A second aspect is that when we refer to normative systems, we do so at a certain point in time. This is obvious when historical linguists talk about large-scale diachronic developments, but it also applies to all synchronic language use in communities and groups. Norms are not norms once and for all; they get adapted and change over time (cf. discussion in Harder, this volume; see also Fabricius, this volume). These changes are usually triggered, I propose, by instances of creativity. So, when is something creative? And how long does it take for a feature of language to become normal and un-creative in a group of speakers? And how does this process – from creative to un-creative/normal – actually manifest itself in spoken interaction?

These questions map out a research undertaking that goes beyond the scope of this chapter. Yet, in order to begin to investigate these questions systematically, we need research contexts, conceptual frameworks and methodological tools that allow us to do so. My contention is that conceptual frameworks need to highlight the transient dimension of many present-day interactions, especially in multilingual contexts (Section 3), while methodologies need to provide tools that enable scholars to adopt a diachronic take on synchronic data in order to trace how initial creativity may actuate situational norm emergence (Section 4).

3 Transient language contact, multilingual resources and accommodation

Before I turn in more detail to the methodological aspects of micro-diachronic data analysis in Section 4, I would like to contextualize the approach in this chapter by relating it to recent work on *Transient International Groups (TIGs)* (Pitzl 2018c) and *Transient Multilingual Communities (TMCs)* (Mortensen 2017). Work on TIGs and TMCs shares a common interest in the study of multilingual contexts in which participants do not share a common first language (L1) and/or regio-cultural background, are (fairly) newly acquainted, and potentially only interact for a short amount of time. Such contexts tend to be low on a *scale of semiotic sedimentation* with regard to linguistic, but also social norms (Mortensen 2017: 274–276). What makes them interesting, but also challenging for research is that not only norms but also "the norm center will not be given", but "a matter to be explored" (Mortensen 2017: 274) and jointly developed in interaction.

Work on Transient International Groups (Pitzl 2016, 2018a, 2018c) is highly compatible with work on TMCs, but puts a stronger emphasis on the *group dimen-*

sion of multilingual encounters. Among other things, it proposes schematic visual representations of group constellations with the intention of heightening our awareness of different kinds of diversity in multilingual groups (see Figure 1a, 1b, 1c). Since TIGs can be "somewhere on a scale or cline from *highly diverse* to *bilateral*" (Pitzl 2018c: 31, italics in original) such visual representations – as schematic and approximate as they may currently be – can help scholars perceive a difference between a TIG that is more or less symmetrically bilateral (Figure 1a), asymmetrically bilateral (Figure 1b) or rather diverse (Figure 1c and below).

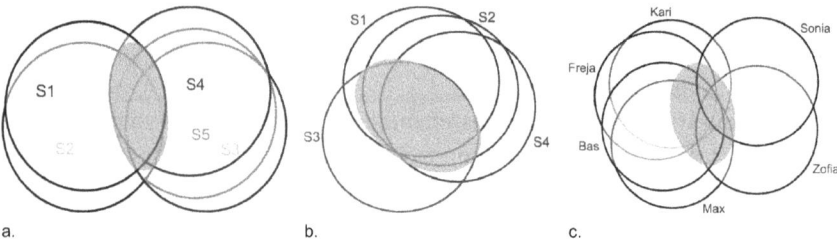

Figure 1: Schematic representation of Multilingual Resource Pool of a symmetric-bilateral (a), an asymmetric-bilateral (b) and a diverse (c) TIG.[3]

These visualizations draw on the basic proposition that multilingual interactants' *Individual Multilingual Repertoires* (IMRs) will form a (shared) *Multilingual Resource Pool* (MRP) in any given situation, when these speakers interact. They are informed by a language contact perspective that sees each individual TIG – and hence many ELF or other lingua franca encounters – as sites of transient language contact (see Pitzl 2016: 296–299, 2018a: 192–199 for a more detailed discussion).

Since TIG constellations differ, speakers' IMRs overlap to a greater or lesser degree in the central area of a group's MRP in Figures 1a to 1c, i.e. the pool of multilingual resources that interactants share to begin with is smaller or larger. If the MRP of a TIG is diverse (see Figure 1c), many different *languages and distinct multilingual repertoires are in contact. Even if a lingua franca TIG is only bilateral, it involves more complex language contact than many local/regional diglossic situations typically examined in bilingualism research in which primarily

---

3 Figures 1a, 1b and 1c represent TIGs in different speech events from VOICE. Figure 1c represents the six main interactants of the diverse TIG in LEcon560 analyzed in this chapter. Figure 1a represents the bilateral business TIG of PBmtg3 (analyzed in Pitzl 2021). Figure 1b represents the asymmetric-bilateral TIG in LEcon329, LEcon547 and LEcon548 (analyzed in Pitzl 2018c). The abbreviations S1, S2, etc. indicate individual speakers.

two languages are in contact and contrastively perceived as "we code" and "they code" by speakers (Auer 1999: 311). Crucially, transient language contact in TIGs/ TMCs includes not only speakers' L1s, their *Englishes (if *English is their lingua franca) and any other *languages they might know, but also all "bits and pieces" (cf. Canagarajah 2018: 36) of additional *languages that they might have picked up somewhere informally without ever having explicitly learned the *language. All these factors will have an impact on how multi-/translingual norms are negotiated in a TIG and will influence which instances of (multilingual) creativity are most successful in the sense of being taken up through processes of convergence. Transient language contact in situational MRPs thus clearly involves more than a contact of what Mauranen (2012: 29–30) calls similects.

A phenomenon that has the potential to help us relate creativity and norm development in interaction is accommodation. In ELF research, accommodation – especially *convergence* – has been emphasized as a relevant concept for many years (see Jenkins's 2000 early work on pronunciation) and has retained prominence (see e.g. Cogo & Dewey 2006; Cogo 2009; Seidlhofer 2009; Mauranen 2012: 48–52). Originating from social psychology, communication accommodation theory (CAT) (e.g. Giles, Coupland, & Coupland 1991) has been influential in sociolinguistics, as it seeks to account for "how speakers adjust their language use in interaction to both manage social distance and regulate comprehension" (Gasiorek, Giles, & Soliz 2015: 3). Accommodative processes have been investigated in a wide range of situations, studying how interactants converge, i.e. make their "communication styles [. . .] more similar", or diverge in order to make their "communication styles [. . .] more different or deviant from the communicative desires and/or norms of others" (Gasiorek, Giles, & Soliz 2015: 2).

While convergence can, on the one hand, be seen as a general socio-psychological concept that influences speakers' communicative behavior, it can, on the other hand, be applied as a category in the descriptive analysis of data. In the latter case, descriptive studies can indicate specific points in an interaction where speakers can be seen to converge or diverge to their interlocutor(s) with regard to a specific linguistic phenomenon. Being closely related – but certainly not limited – to conversational phenomena like other-repetition (see e.g. Lichtkoppler 2007: 46; Seidlhofer 2011: 101; Mauranen 2012: 219), convergence has been shown to be a recurring feature in many ELF interactions. However, current research methods for describing interaction only provide episodic evidence of how speakers converge linguistically during relatively short phases of conversation (i.e. a few turns or utterances in a conversational excerpt). Also CAT scholars themselves emphasize the need for more longitudinal research and for studies that explore accommodation in multiparty interactions (Pitts & Harwood 2015: 90–91).

Since we have established that *creativity* has to do with departing from a – more or less explicit or perceptible – norm or convention, norm-transcending creativity (including code-switching as an instance of multilingual creativity) might be linked to *accommodation* by being considered a special type of *divergence*. The conceptual relationship of these two concepts – creativity and accommodation – is certainly complex and warrants further theoretical engagement that goes beyond the scope of this chapter. For the present discussion of norm development, my tentative suggestion is that local norm development in specific TIGs/TMCs is likely to involve individual instances of creativity (as a type of *divergence*) that *may* be followed by instances or phases of *convergence*. If our interest is in describing how linguistic (and possibly also social) norms are developed by multilingual speakers in interaction in transient contexts, it would seem important to investigate empirically *whether and how* instances of creativity are actually succeeded by convergence, for example through conversational phenomena like other-repetition, echoing or mirroring. To do this, it is necessary to develop analytical approaches that allow us to move beyond the analysis of single extracts of conversations.

4 A micro-diachronic approach to synchronic spoken interaction

In order to systematically explore the questions concerning multilingual creativity and norm development raised in the previous sections, this chapter relies on what I call a *micro-diachronic approach to spoken interaction* (which will be introduced in more detail below). This approach was first suggested in Pitzl (2018c), where initial premises are discussed. The analysis in this chapter builds on and expands the initial tool set in an attempt to further systematize the approach (see also Pitzl 2021). The study at hand focuses on code-switching and the use of non-*English elements in an ELF context and explores how these gradually morph from being instances of multilingual creativity to becoming more normal practices in a TIG.

In general terms, the proposed micro-diachronic approach draws on and is informed by conversation analytic, interactional sociolinguistic, discourse analytic and discursive pragmatic methods that are combined with corpus linguistic tools (such as specific searches triggered by qualitative observations or the reliance on annotation already available in corpus transcripts). What makes the approach micro-diachronic is that detailed qualitative data analysis, manual and (semi-)automatic annotation of a linguistic phenomenon in spoken interaction are combined with the close-meshed structural annotation of time segments and/or utterance sequences. This combination of *content and structural annotation*

makes it possible to supplement traditional methods of data analysis, such as the discussion of data extracts (see Section 4.3.1) or concordance lines with novel tools and visualizations. These include
a. holistic portraits and overviews
    i.   of speaker participation (see Figure 2)
    ii. of the observed phenomenon/phenomena (see Figures 4 and 5)
b. micro-diachronic charts
    i.   of speaker participation (see Figure 3)
    ii. of the observed phenomena (see Figures 6–8).

Especially the latter (*micro-diachronic charts*) make it possible to explore the real-time development of communication (including creativity and norms) in spoken interaction. Yet, the use of *holistic tools*, i.e. tools that look at the entire duration of a transcribed TIG interaction, rather than only at short portions, is equally important, since these quantitative overviews allow the researcher to get a sense of the investigated phenomenon/phenomena and of the interaction in their entirety. They are, for example, useful in characterizing a TIG with regard to how actively individual speakers do (or do not) verbally participate – in the interaction in general (Section 4.2) and with regard to a particular linguistic phenomenon (see Section 4.3.2). The full analytic potential of the methodology is achieved through the combination of micro-diachronic and holistic tools with established methods like the discussion of data extracts and examples. Admittedly, this is at present a rather elaborate affair, since the new methodological tools need to be introduced alongside the findings obtained through them.

Although both holistic and micro-diachronic charts operate with numbers – and thus involve some quantification of analyzed phenomena – it is important to stress that the micro-diachronic methodology is *highly qualitative* at its core. Its aim is *not* to provide readers with frequencies in a traditional sense in order to check whether or not they are statistically significant, but to use holistic and micro-diachronic charts to contextualize and sequentialize in-depth discussions of language use in interaction.

In terms of practicalities, the analysis in this chapter is carried out using qualitative data analysis (QDA) software (MAXQDA). Micro-diachronic and holistic charts were created making use of electronic spreadsheets containing overviews, coding and annotation reports exported from the QDA software. In the following, methodology and findings are discussed conjointly rather than separately, as this seems most conducive for showing the research potential of the proposed tools, not just for the study of (multilingual) creativity, but also for the study of TIGs and TMCs, sociolinguistic norm development, creativity and accommodation more generally.

4.1 Ethnographic contextualization of the data: A casual conversation among exchange students

The interaction investigated in the following is one long speech event (LEcon560) among students that was recorded and transcribed for VOICE (Vienna-Oxford International Corpus of English). The conversation takes place during an informal gathering at a pub, where students from various European countries (and some local Austrian students) get to know each other at the beginning of the non-Austrians' semester abroad in Vienna. As specified in the event description (see VOICE 2013, LEcon560), although some students have met briefly before, some meet for the first time during this speech event. So although the speech event does not constitute T_0, i.e. the first meeting for all interactants (cf. Pitzl 2018c: 34–35), it was chosen because it offers a detailed glimpse at the kind of informal interactions that are bound to happen in many initial phases of study abroad experiences (cf. e.g. Kalocsai 2014).

The recording of LEcon560 lasts for almost two and a half hours (142 minutes). Of these, 125 minutes were transcribed in detail. Short gaps are indicated in the transcript (cf. Figure 3) because portions of the recording were unintelligible, primarily due to the high level of background noise in the pub and/or multiple parallel conversations.

Transcription format and transcription practices, i.e. what is/is not transcribed and how features of spoken language are rendered in mark-up, follow the standards developed for ELF interactions in the VOICE project (VOICE Project 2007; VOICE 2013; see also Pitzl 2018a: 86–89). As is common practice in VOICE, non-*English elements are indicated by means of L1 (first language), LN (other-language) or, rarely, LQ (unclear if L1 or LN) tags in the transcript. In addition, the mark-up of L1/LN/LQ tags also specifies the *language switched to (if known) and provides translations { } into *English where possible (see e.g. Breiteneder et al. 2006: 182).[4] One reason for choosing this particular speech event is that it includes an unusually high number – and thus density – of non-*English elements (i.e. L1/LN/LQ tags), as discussed below.

---

4 As discussed elsewhere (Pitzl 2021: 100–102), the transcribed non-*English L1/LN/LQ elements in VOICE do not necessarily constitute the full extent of code-switching and multilingual practices in recorded interactions, as for example longer portions of speech in *languages other than *English are generally not transcribed in the corpus. There is no gap that is due to 'non-*English' speech in LEcon560, but use of *languages other than *English is mentioned in some contextual notes indicating untranscribed parallel conversations. *Languages mentioned in these contextual notes are *German (5 cases), *Spanish (3), and *Polish (1), *Danish (1) and *Norwegian (1).

4.2 TIG characterization and interaction profile

In contrast to the bilateral TIGs in Figures 1a and 1b, the group of students in LEcon560 can be characterized as *a diverse TIG* (see Figure 1c). As specified in the metadata provided in VOICE, the speech event involves a total of ten speakers. Of these, one is the researcher (who records the interaction) and one is a non-participant, who only joins the conversation for a few seconds. Both researcher and non-participant utter only a few words and are not active participants throughout the conversation. Upon closer inspection, the same is true for two other speakers (both L1 *German) who also say very little (with 9 and 16 utterances, respectively).

This leaves *six speakers* who are the *main participants* interacting in LEcon560. These six constitute a diverse TIG, in the sense that they come from six different countries (Poland, Spain, Norway, Denmark, the Netherlands and Austria) and have six different L1 backgrounds: *Polish (VOICE ID = P683, f), *Spanish/*Catalan (P684, f), *Norwegian (P685, f), *Danish (P686, f), *Dutch (P687, m), and *German (P689, m). In spite of this diverse constellation, parts of the speakers' *English(es) repertoires will be shared, i.e. located in the central overlapping area of the situational MRP. Although knowledge of *German cannot be taken for granted by the students, there is ample evidence in the data that most speakers also share some knowledge of *German (in addition to *English). Yet, which bits of pieces of (other) *languages are – or are not – shared by (all or some) speakers is initially largely invisible, to the interactants and to the researcher. Importantly, whether visible or not, what is shared initially (i.e. at T_0) is gradually expanded by speakers through interaction (cf. Pitzl 2018c: 35).

With six main interactants, LEcon560 is not just a speech event in a diverse TIG but also an *unmoderated, highly interactive multiparty conversation* in a leisure context. According to the metadata in VOICE, the 125 minutes transcribed contain 21,867 words. These 21,867 words correspond to 3,038 utterances in the transcript. Utterances here are not turns at talk in a conversation analytic (CA) sense (cf. Pitzl 2018a: 87). Some solely contain backchannels, laughter, single words or word fragment(s). They are thus not necessarily bids for the floor and also include all words rendered as overlapping speech. Putting the number of words and utterances in relation, an average utterance in LEcon560 contains 7.2 words. With regard to the pace and degree of interactivity of the conversation, we arrive at an average of 175 words and 24.3 utterances per minute (again, including all overlapping speech and backchanneling). It therefore seems safe to say that LEcon560 is indeed a highly interactive and fast-paced conversation.

Why is such interactivity and participation profiling relevant? Because the degree of active speaker participation and interactivity in interaction allows the researcher to get a sense of the abundance (or lack) of opportunities for productive accommodation. Since accommodation in speech production (both convergence as well as divergence) requires for interactants to adjust their language use *to each other*, a highly interactive conversation will abound in opportunities for participants to actually do so. Whether or not they make use of these opportunities is a different matter, to be answered by data analysis.[5]

Having established the degree of interactivity, we can look at how much the six core participants of the student TIG in LEcon560 actually participate. Starting with a holistic view, Figure 2 provides the number of utterances with corresponding percentages for each speaker in the speech event as a whole.

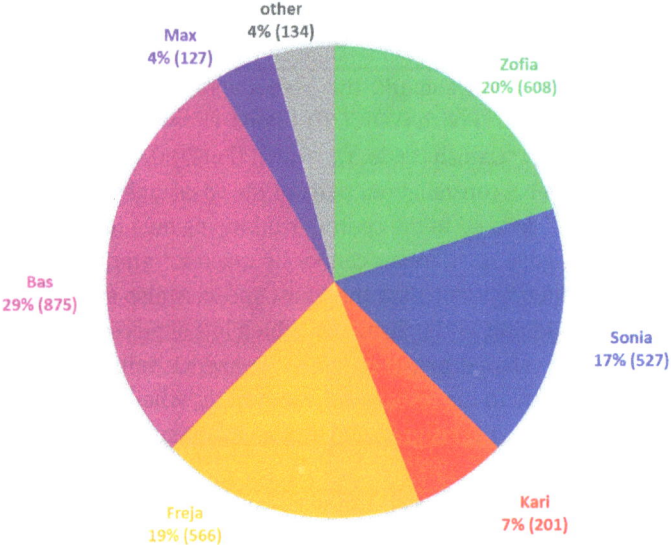

Figure 2: Number of utterances per speaker (VOICE, LEcon560; n=3,038): Holistic view.

While Bas (VOICE ID = P687; names are pseudonyms) participates most actively in terms of verbal output and contributes close to one third (29 %) of all utterances, three other speakers, i.e. Zofia (P683), Sonia (P684) and Freja (P686), also contribute between 17 % and 20 % of all utterances each. In comparison, Kari (P685) and Max (P689) speak less (7 % and 4 % of utterances). These are interesting observations with regard to the investigation of potential norm development.

---

[5] Of course, I do not wish to imply that productive accommodation in interaction is the only kind of accommodation. Speakers can also accommodate receptively, as shown by e.g. Cogo and Dewey (2012: 103–106), or they can orient to "imagined" norms or stereotypes (see Kraft and Mortensen, this volume), both of which are also possible in less interactive speech events.

Although active verbal participation might not be the only indicator of speakers' potential influence on norm development, it constitutes a good point of reference, especially when put in relation to a particular linguistic phenomenon (see Figure 4 below).[6]

As is common in unmoderated multiparty conversations, we need to note that the six main speakers in the student TIG do not all interact with all others all the time. This fact cannot be inferred from the overview in Figure 2 but becomes visible to some extent when speaker contributions are displayed micro-diachronically (Figure 3).

Making use of structural coding, Figure 3 displays how many utterances each speaker contributes in each three-minute segment throughout the conversation. With regard to methodology, the kind and length of structural segmentation is the choice of the researcher. In addition to (or instead of) time segments, a conversation can be rendered micro-diachronically using for example utterance segments (see Figures 6–8; see also Pitzl 2021). The micro-diachronic view in Figure 3 illustrates that, although there are six main speakers, the transcript increasingly represents dyadic and triadic phases of interaction that are interspersed with stretches where four or more speakers interact. Dyads and triads can be seen in Figure 3, for example, when

- Bas mainly interacts with Freja in minutes 21 to 26 and minutes 57 to 62
- Freja mainly interacts with Kari in minutes 39 to 47
- Bas, Sonia and Zofia interact with each other in minutes 81 to 104 and again minutes 114 to 119
- and Bas interacts with Sonia in minutes 105 to 113

Such conversational dyads and triads are actually quite common when bigger groups (i.e. more than three or four speakers) are allowed to organize interaction and conversational topics freely (i.e. when there are no external norms imposed upon interaction by means of, for example, a meeting agenda, a chair person, a teacher or the interactive constraints of an institutional setting).

The micro-diachronic chart also illustrates the limitations of even detailed transcription of such highly interactive unstructured multiparty contexts. During the dyads and triads represented in the transcript, other speakers are likely to also have interacted with other participants (or with other people in the pub, for example when getting up to buy a drink at the bar). Although VOICE transcripts

---

6 The 134 (4 %) utterances allocated to "other" include utterances by the four other speakers as well as all utterances attributed to groups of speakers (SS) or unidentified male or female speakers (SX-f, SX-m). For the six main speakers, uncertain utterances (e.g. P683-X) have been counted for the respective speaker (e.g. P683, Bas).

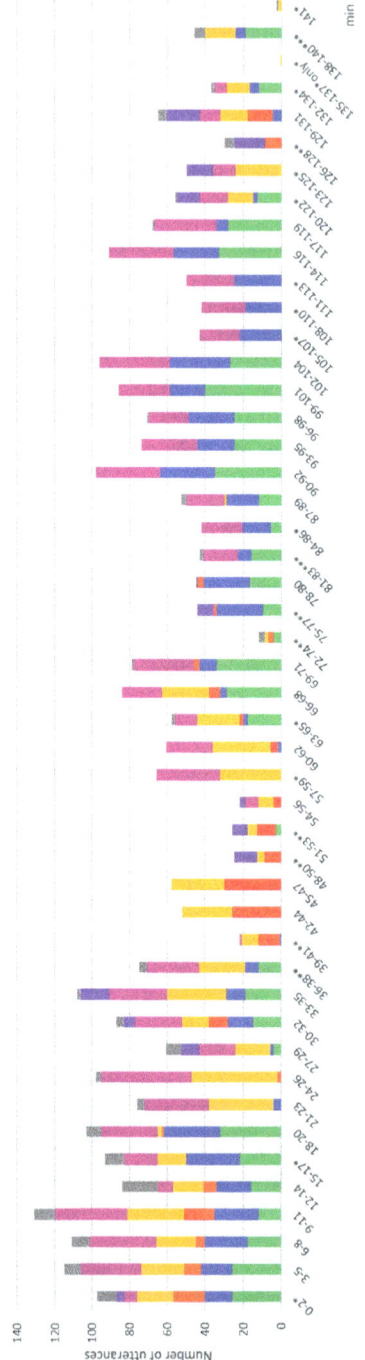

Figure 3: Number of utterances per speaker (VOICE, LEcon560; n=3,038): Micro-diachronic view (3-minute segments).[7]

---

[7] Each * symbol in a track indicates a gap in the transcript.

indicate quite frequently that such *parallel conversations* took place, for corpus building it has usually been feasible to transcribe only one of these conversational strands. In future data collection and transcription to be conducted specifically for the investigation of TIGs/TMCs, it would be desirable to attempt to record and transcribe these parallel conversational strands – although this opens up a range of questions as to how such parallel strands are to be most suitably represented in transcripts.

More importantly, with regard to the issue of describing initial stages of norm development, the dyads and triads in Figure 3 indicate that in unmoderated multiparty conversations, new norms might first emerge in sub-groups (e.g. dyads or triads) and only gradually travel to the group as a whole: If one (or more) instance(s) of norm-transcending creativity occurs in a dyad or triad and is subsequently followed by instances or phases of convergence in this dyad or triad (for instance, through other-repetition, echoing or mirroring linguistic structures or linguistic behavior), this will not yet create an emerging norm for the entire TIG. In order for this to happen, the new pattern will need to be passed on, recycled and expanded in interaction with other speakers (i.e. speakers who were not part of the first original dyad or triad). This, in turn, will involve further instances of creativity and convergence (see Section 4.3.3).

4.3 Exploring the phenomenon: Multilingual creativity

Having provided some ethnographic, holistic and micro-diachronic information on speaker participation and degree of interactivity, we now turn to the phenomenon at hand: multilingual creativity and the potential of norm emergence concerning non-*English use. Section 4.3.1 discusses a short data extract in which some students teach each other to toast in different *languages. Having made use of this established method of data presentation, the subsequent sections introduce new tools. Section 4.3.2 offers an overview of the non-*English elements in the entire interaction. Section 4.3.3. offers a micro-diachronic view of the phenomenon, discussing how this approach helps us trace how initially creative code-switches may gradually become established trans- or multilingual practices in a TIG.

4.3.1 Introducing multilingual cheers: The conversational view

In the minute preceding the exchange in Extract 1, Bas (m, L1 *Dutch) returns to the table, just having bought drinks at the bar, and is asked by Sonia (f, L1s *Spanish/*Catalan) whether he remembered to bring *nachos* (utterances 574,

577). Bas admits that he forgot, which triggers laughter from the group (utterances 580–582). When everyone seems to have their drink in front of them, Sonia says *chin chin* (utterance 584). Although *chin chin* – as well as *nachos* – defy a traditional categorization of "belonging" to just one particular *language (both could be seen as *Spanish or as loanwords that have become part of the *English lexicon), Sonia's use of *chin chin* appears to be an instance of multilingual creativity since she explicitly frames *chin chin* as Spanish (utterance 586), which triggers the following sequence:

Extract 1: Multilingual cheers (VOICE, LEcon560; speaker IDs replaced by pseudonyms)

584	Sonia:	<L1spa> **chin chin** </L1spa> (.)
585	Zofia:	cheers (.) {parallel conversation between Bas and Freja starts}
586	Sonia:	in spanish it's <L1spa> **chin chin** {cheers} </L1spa> (.)
587	Zofia:	er in polish <L1pol> **na zdrowie** {cheers} </L1pol> (.)
588	Sonia:	<LNpol> **na zdrowie** {cheers} </LNpol> (.)
589	Zofia:	<L1pol> **na zdrowie** {cheers} </L1pol> (.)
590	Sonia:	<LNpol> **na zdrowie** {cheers} </LNpol> =
		{parallel conversation between Freja and Bas ends and parallel conversation between Zofia and Sonia starts; they continue to talk about saying cheers in different languages}
591	Freja:	= how do you say e:r cheers in e:r holland (1) dutch (.)
592	Bas:	er all (.) all ALL sorts of ways actually <1> but </1>
593	Freja:	<1> all </1> right =
594	Bas:	= most people say <L1dut> **proost** {cheers} </L1dut> (.)
595	Freja:	right (.)
596	Bas:	like in danish it's <LNger> **prost?** {cheers} </LNger> (.) yeah in (.) i- <LNger> **pr- prost** {cheers} </LNger> is in: er is in denmark? (.)
597	Freja:	o:h no (.) that's <L1dan> **skål** {cheers} </L1dan> (.)
598	Bas:	a:h <LNdan> **skål** {cheers} </LNdan> yah
599	Sonia-x:	<LNdan> **skål?** {cheers} </LNdan> (.)
600	Bas:	yah (2) {Franz joins the group}
601	Franz:	<L1ger> ist hier noch frei? {is this seat still available} </L1ger>
		{parallel conversation between Zofia and Sonia ends} (1)

At the beginning of Extract 1, Zofia (f, L1 *Polish) reciprocates Sonia's toast by saying *cheers* (utterance 585). She thus converges on the level of content, which demonstrates that she has understood the meaning of Sonia's *chin chin*. At the same time, Zofia does not converge in terms of lexical choice, but replies with what we might say is the more conventional or typical *English toast, namely *cheers*. Although the use of *cheers* is a perfectly appropriate response, it prompts Sonia to repeat her toast and frame it explicitly as non-*English and thus flag it as multilingual: *in spanish it's chin chin* (utterance 586). At this point, Zofia converges on the level of *language choice – or maybe better, on the level of the translanguaging or multilingual mode adopted – in the sense that she also moves away from *English *cheers*. Yet, she simultaneously also diverges from Sonia's use of *Spanish* and supplies her own L1, using an almost identical syntactic structure as Sonia before her: *in polish na zdrowie* (utterance 587). This is followed by three instances of next-turn verbatim other-repetition, an interactive conversational strategy that "could be seen as ultimate convergence" (Seidlhofer 2011: 101). Both speakers thereby reinforce and/or practice *na zdrowie*, with Sonia showing interest in learning a phrase from Zofia's L1, a practice that is – or rather becomes – fairly prominent in this student group. Through the instances of next-turn verbatim repetition, I would argue *na zdrowie* gradually becomes less foreign to Sonia, less divergent in the conversation and thus a more normal part of language use in this TIG – or rather, at this point, for Sonia and Zofia.

As can be seen, the exchange between Zofia and Sonia happens in a dyadic fashion and a parallel conversation between Bas (m, L1 *Dutch) and Freja (f, L1 *Danish) ensues. Bas and Freja continue the topic of multilingual cheers, mirroring the multilingual creativity of Zofia and Sonia by introducing their own L1 elements for saying cheers. In doing so, they might not only be mirroring Zofia and Sonia, but might also converge towards a more wide-spread sociopragmatic routine of multilingual cheers in TIGs/TMCs – but we cannot be sure of this. In Freja and Bas's conversational dyad (utterances 591–598), Freja explicitly asks Bas for information on how to say *cheers* in his L1 Dutch, which Bas supplies and Freja confirms with *right* (utterance 595). Instead of simply asking about "Danish", Bas then voices a guess (presumably partly based on his L1 *Dutch and his knowledge of *German), which ends up sounding like the *German word for toasting *prost* (utterance 596). Freja then provides the appropriate *Danish form *skål*. Like in Zofia and Sonia's dyad, this is met with immediate verbatim other-repetition from Bas and one other speaker (presumably Sonia, hence "Sonia-x" in the transcript, listening in and joining Freja and Bas's conversation again).

It is obvious that a lot is going on in this short sequence of less than 20 utterances. Not only is there a high density of non-*English elements (in speakers' L1s as well as LNs), of code-switching as multilingual creativity and of subsequent convergence, which happens especially – but not exclusively – in the form of next-turn verbatim other-repetition. There are many instances when speakers explicitly refer to their own or others' *languages or countries (*spanish, polish, holland, dutch, danish, denmark*). These instances of explicit reference (Pitzl 2018c) provide key clues for the speakers (cf. Cogo and Dewey 2006: 68–69) and flag these non-*English elements (cf. Hynninen et al. 2017) as multilingual. The fact that the group of interactants is a diverse TIG (rather than bilateral) is reflected in the number of *languages that are indexed through the switches as well as through the instances of explicit reference in this short episode: Four speakers switch to four different *languages (five, if you count the accidental *German *prost*).

All four interactants in Extract 1 are clearly involved in expanding their individual multilingual repertoires (IMRs), even if learning to say *cheers* in different languages is admittedly a rather mundane affair, not unique to this group of multilingual speakers. But even if fairly banal, through this conversational activity the speakers expand the shared multilingual resource pool (MRP) and the potential for shared multilingual practices of the group – which has the potential for norm development, especially in the context of a ritualized and recurring activity such as toasting. Yet, it would be premature to claim or posit the emergence of a new norm concerning multilingual cheers in this TIG based on just this one short conversational exchange. For this to become possible, I suggest that we need to supplement the preceding discussion and presentation of transcribed data with additional ways of data presentation and visualization. This will allow us to get a sense of the bigger picture of the interaction in the TIG by means of holistic (Section 4.3.2) as well as micro-diachronic (Section 4.3.3) views.

4.3.2 Non-*English elements in the student TIG: A holistic overview

Moving from this individual episode of multilingual cheers to the more general perspective of the whole speech event, the first key point to make is that the use of elements in *languages other than *English is a very prominent feature of LEcon560. Making use of the L1/LN/LQ tags annotated in VOICE transcripts, we can establish that, out of the 3,038 utterances in LEcon560, 219 (i.e. 7.21 %) contain at least one L1/LN/LQ tag. Of these 219 utterances, 21 include two L1/LN/LQ tags and one contains three. This leads to a total of 241 L1/LN/LQ tags indicated in LEcon560, each of which contain one or more non-*English word(s).[8]

This number is noticeably higher than in other speech events in VOICE. For comparison, the entire corpus contains 3,601 L1/LN/LQ tags, which means that a remarkable 6.7 % of all L1/LN/LQ tags in VOICE occur in the student TIG in LEcon560. This finding is even more remarkable, if we consider that the number of non-*English elements in VOICE is considerably higher than, for example, in ELFA (Corpus of English as a lingua franca in academic settings). Hynninen, Pietikäinen and Vechinnikova (2017: 101) report "651 code-switches occurring in 82

---

[8] As useful as the mark-up of non-*English speech is for the analysis of code-switching and multilingual practices, marking the use of different *languages in transcripts also has its downsides, as it is, of course, not unproblematic conceptually and runs the risk of reinforcing the perceived boundedness of individual *languages (see Cogo 2018: 364; Pitzl 2021).

speech events" when "search[ing] the ELFA corpus for all the elements tagged as <FOREIGN>". So, the 241 L1/LN/LQ tags in LEcon560 correspond to more than two thirds (37.1 %) of all so-called foreign elements in ELFA, a corpus that is equal to VOICE in size (namely one million words of spoken ELF). Although such differences between VOICE and ELFA could in principle be partly due to differences in corpus design concerning data selection and/or transcription (cf. Pitzl 2021), LEcon560 also stands out in comparison to the rest of VOICE. This indicates that the use of non-*English elements in the examined student TIG is not limited to Extract 1, but something that must go widely beyond the *cheers* episode in the transcript.

More interesting than simply looking at global numbers of L1/LN/LQ tags, however, is investigating how much individual speakers in the TIG make use of non-*English elements and which *languages they "switch" to. Figure 4 provides a holistic overview of the distribution of all utterances with L1/LN/LQ tags (n=219) among the six main participants of LEcon560. Comparing this with the distribution of utterances in general (see Figure 2 above), it can be attested that the two charts look fairly similar. There are some shifts where pie segments for non-*English elements (Figure 4) increase or decrease in comparison to the total number of utterances (Figure 2), yet, these shifts are fairly small.

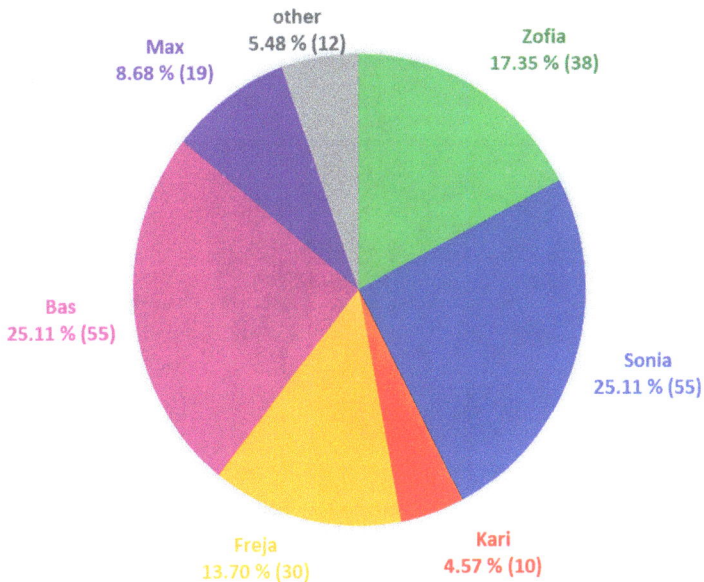

Figure 4: Utterances with non-*English elements per speaker (VOICE, LEcon560; n=219): Holistic view.

What such a holistic overview of the examined phenomenon in an interaction provides is the insight that all main speakers contribute to the occurrence of the phenomenon (here: the use of non-*English elements) and they do so more or less to the same extent as they verbally contribute to the interaction in general. That is to say, roughly speaking, those who speak less contribute fewer non-*English elements; those who speak more also contribute more "switches". The high number of multilingual elements in LEcon560 is not the result of only one or two speakers. Should it become possible to identify a newly emerging norm with regard to multilingual practices in this TIG, these are likely to be the result of interaction (as evidenced by Extract 1), not the result of individual patterns of use by just one or two speakers.

In addition to considering the active involvement of speakers, it might often be useful to get a sense of certain categories or subtypes of the phenomenon explored in a study. With regard to multilingual creativity and non-*English elements, it is interesting, for example, to look at which *languages are actually used by the participants in the course of LEcon560.

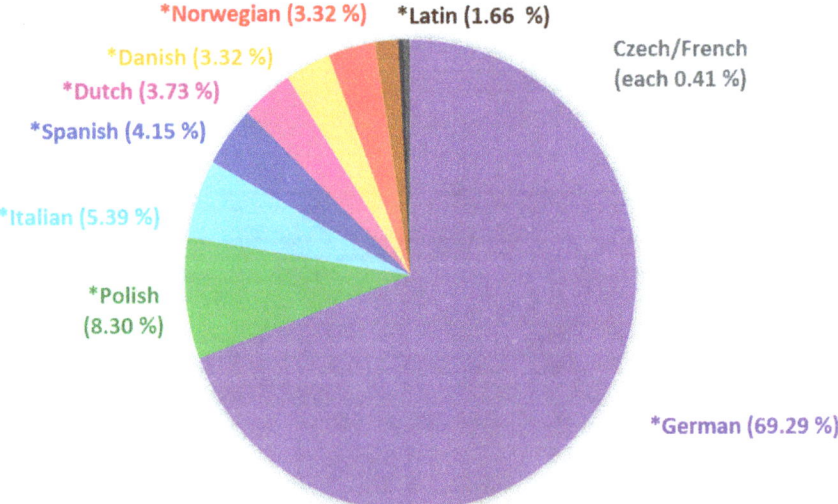

Figure 5: *Languages switched into (VOICE, LEcon560; n=241): Holistic view.

As can be seen in Figure 5, almost two thirds (69.29 %) of all L1/LN/LQ tags (n=241) in LEcon560 are occurrences of *German, while the remaining third (30.71 %) comprises a range of other *languages, even beyond participants' L1s. The prominence of *German elements may seem surprising in light of the multilingual *cheers* episode in Extract 1, which contains no intentional use of *German (only Bas's accidental *German *prost*). It is, however, not uncommon for non-*English elements to be prompted by the locality (i.e. the local/regional setting) in which an interaction takes place (see e.g. Pölzl & Seidlhofer 2006, Hynninen et al. 2017: 110–112, Pitzl 2018c: 44–53). A further aspect that contributes to the frequent use of *German elements is a general interest in language learning and a high level of metalinguistic awareness evidenced by participants in different phases of the conversation (see below). In general, the number of LN elements (n=188) is much higher in LEcon560 than the number of L1 elements (n=53) in this conversation, which might be interpreted as a further indicator of participants' interest in learning about (and using elements) from *languages other than *English and their L1 (i.e. LN).

In light of the frequent use of *German (LN *German n=144; L1 *German n=25), the multilingual *cheers* episode is not particularly typical for the multilingual elements used in the speech event. Crucially, this does not make Extract 1 insignificant or irrelevant. In terms of multilingual creativity, the initial uses of *chin chin, na zdrowie, proost* and *skål* (that diverge from *English but are also not *German) and the subsequent converging (other-)repetitions might actually be quite salient for the TIG participants. Although the frequency of these other *language elements is lower than *German, they tend to be used by several speakers (two, three or more participants). Yet, the holistic view of Figure 5 does not actually provide a portrait of what happens sequentially *throughout* the conversation. This is, however, the most crucial perspective for the study of norm development. In order to incorporate this dimension, the next section adopts a micro-diachronic view of the phenomenon.

4.3.3 From code-switching and multilingual creativity to multilingual practices and the initial emergence of translingual norms? – A micro-diachronic view of interaction

Building on and complementing the ethnographic contextualization (Section 4.1.), the TIG characterization and interaction profile (Section 4.2.), the conversational (Section 4.3.1) and the holistic view (Section 4.3.2), this section explores the phenomenon with the help of micro-diachronic visualizations. Starting with a general micro-diachronic portrait, Figure 6 displays the number of utterances containing L1/LN/LQ tags (n=219) throughout LEcon560.

In Figure 6, the interaction has been segmented according to sequences of 100 utterances. What can be seen in this view is that non-*English elements are used intermittently in the student TIG: While some of the 100-utterance segments contain zero or very few (i.e. one to four) utterances with non-*English elements,

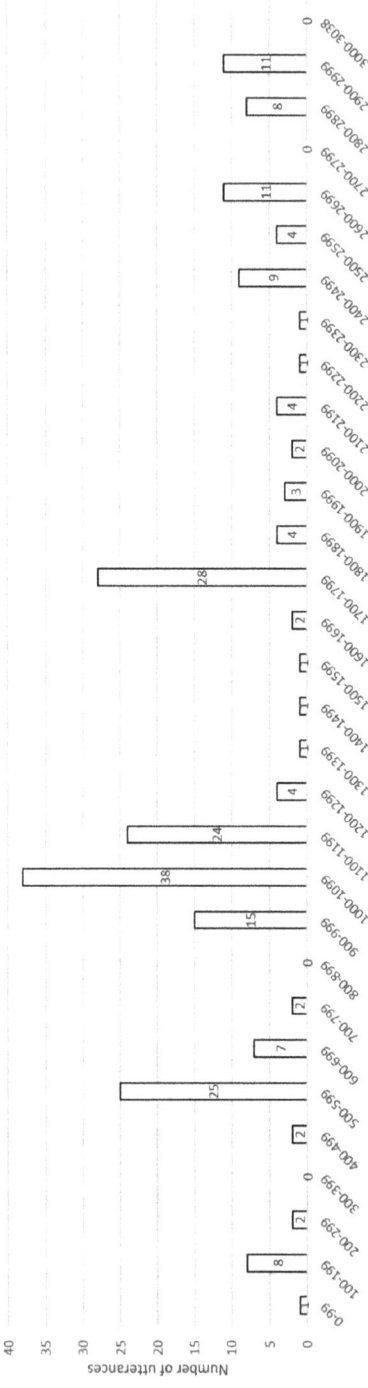

Figure 6: Utterances with non-*English elements (LEcon560; n=219): Micro-diachronic view (utterance segments).

six of them contain between seven and eleven utterances with at least one L1/LN/LQ tag. This is already indicative of the fact that using non-*English elements is quite common in this TIG. Most noticeable, however, are those five segments that contain an even more substantial number. Ranging from 15 utterances to 38 (out of 100) utterances, there are clearly some phases of the interaction (especially between utterances 900 and 1199) in which non-*English elements play a prominent role. Yet, as might be expected, this is a recurring and intermittent – rather than a continuous – phenomenon in the student TIG. In other words, the use of other *languages is clearly not everything these students do. Hence, the processes involved are clearly not a matter of a simple gradual increase in frequency.

Since I have emphasized that the proposed methodology is qualitative (rather than quantitative) at its core, it is interesting to examine in more detail which non-*English elements are actually used during which phases of the conversation. This will be insightful and essential concerning the potential for norm development in the group. Figures 7 and 8 thus provide more detailed micro-diachronic views with information on the use of different *languages (Figure 7) and a loose categorization of the functional purposes (Figure 8) that these non-*English elements fulfill.

In addition to displaying the general prominence of *German elements, Figure 7 shows that most segments with a high number of non-*English elements contain elements from several *languages (in particular *German, *Polish, *Spanish, *Dutch, *Danish and *Norwegian). The exception to this is the segment from utterance 1700 to 1799, where all L1/LN tags indicate *German (more on this below). The clustering of elements from several *languages in the same segment mirrors the pattern of the exchange shown in Extract 1, suggesting that the sort of multilingual creativity displayed in the extract constitutes a more general phenomenon in the data.

As pointed out above, the emergence of a multilingual norm can only be proposed very tentatively on the basis of Extract 1 alone. However, once we supplement conversational and holistic views with micro-diachronic views of the interaction, we can demonstrate that multilingual cheering actually goes beyond Extract 1 (584–601). As shown in Figure 8, instances of speakers saying cheers in different *languages do not only happen in Seg 5,[9] but also (alongside other types of "switches") in Seg 9, Seg 10 and Seg 11 (and once in Seg 29). In total, there are 38 instances of "cheers" in *languages other than *English, which take place in 35 utterances throughout LEcon560. The conversational patterns in utterances 995

---

[9] I refer to utterance segments here by using the initial one or two numbers, i.e. utterance 500-599 is Seg 5, utterance 1100-1199 is Seg 11.

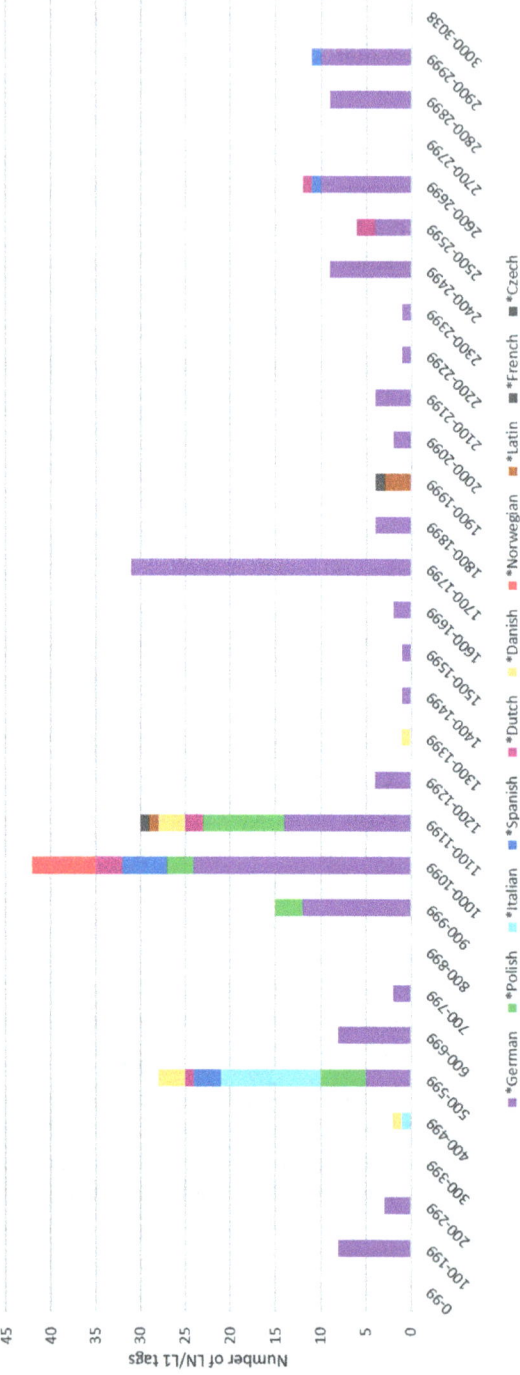

Figure 7: *Languages of non-*English elements (VOICE, LEcon560; n=241): Micro-diachronic view.

to 1023 and 1156 to 1175 mirror, build upon and develop the theme of multilingual cheers in the group. Thus, other speakers learn *na zdrowie* and *chin chin* and Kari from Norway introduces *Norwegian *skål* (1013–1023). Verbatim other-repetition or what Mauranen (2012: 223–226) refers to as "echoing as relational practice" (cf. Holmes & Marra 2004) can be observed with close density in these phases. Speakers accommodate and converge to each other, adopting and repeating the proposed multilingual elements.

Alongside the recurring use of multilingual cheers, Figure 8 also shows that LEcon560 contains a high number of non-*English elements that I have loosely grouped using the label "Language learning" (n=98). Throughout the conversation, the participants repeatedly talk about different *languages and, in doing so, introduce and repeat non-*English words in order to make comparisons, enquire about or teach each other words from their L1s and other *languages. In particular, Seg 10 and 11 (but also Seg 17) show a high density of LN/L1 tags used in this way. After the second cheers episode (995–1023), Bas, Freja and Max discuss how grammatical gender is expressed in the *German determiner and inflectional system (1024–1053), which leads Bas and Max to compare meaning relations between *German *maedchen, magd* and *Dutch *maagd* (1064–1085). This triggers a comparison of *German *jungfrau* (1092–1105; 1117), *Danish *jomfru* (1108–1116) and even *Polish *dziewica* (1129), as Bas (L1 *Dutch) and Max's (L1 *German) conversational thread is joined by Freja (L1 *Danish) and Zofia (L1 *Polish). Just a few utterances later, after having talked about the Latin origin of *Polish *kolumna* (1139–1155), the third cheers episode occurs, which leads Bas to compare *Polish *na zdrowie* with *Czech *na zdravie* (1175).

In Seg 17, which in contrast to Seg 10 and 11 exclusively contains *German elements (cf. Figure 7), the language learning orientation is topicalized as Zofia and Bas discuss (sometimes with Sonia) various labels that appear on their mobile phones after having intentionally changed the phone's language settings to *German. In this passage (1702–1775), Bas and Zofia use words like *zufaelliger titel, menue, kontakte, mitteilungen, adressbuch, telefonbuch, einstellungen, anrufliste, kalender, kamera, dateimanager* in high density without flagging them. This indicates that – at this stage of the conversation – they have become aware that, in addition to *English, they share a fair amount of *German in the central area of their MRP and presumably also that they have in common a general interest in learning (about) *languages.

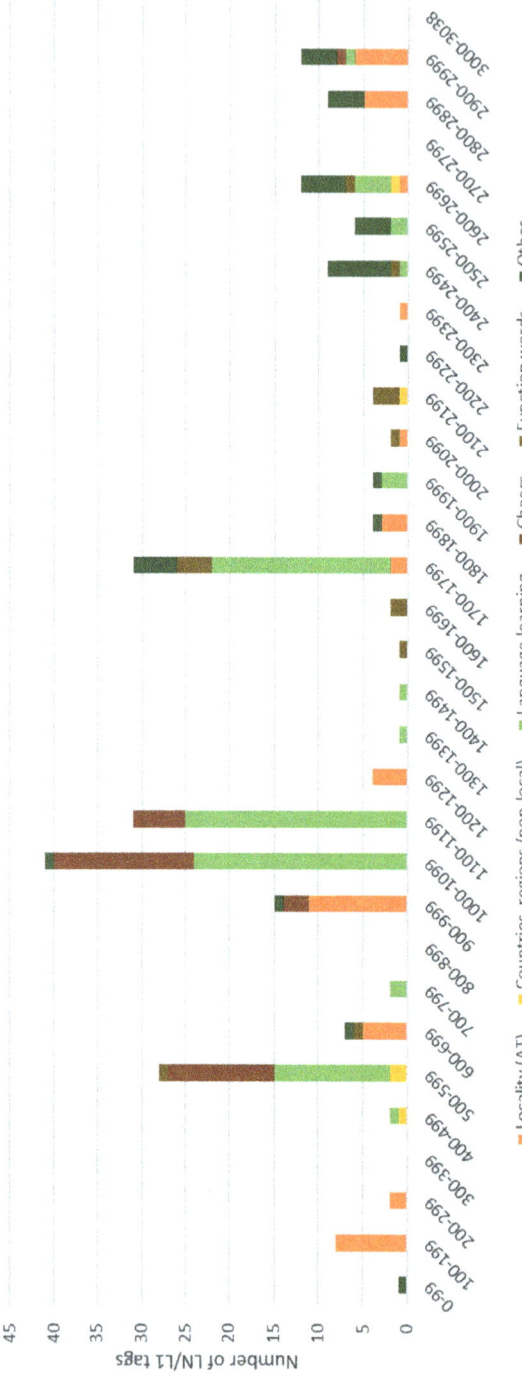

Figure 8: Functional purposes of non-*English elements (LEcon560; n=241): Micro-diachronic view.

5 Discussion and concluding remarks

Building on recent work on transient international groups, I have suggested in this chapter that norm emergence is likely to involve instances of norm-transcending creativity as well as (subsequent) phases of convergence. In order to systematically investigate both processes (i.e. creativity and convergence) beyond short data extracts, the chapter proposed and applied a micro-diachronic approach to the analysis of spoken interaction. It examined the use of non-*English elements in a diverse TIG of exchange students (LEcon560 in VOICE). In doing so, holistic and micro-diachronic techniques for analyzing and visualizing interactive spoken data were introduced and it was exemplified how these techniques can be used to complement established research practices (like the discussion of excerpts of conversational transcripts).

The micro-diachronic analysis of non-*English elements and multilingual creativity in LEcon560 demonstrated that accommodative processes like convergence do not only happen at an immediate next-turn/next-utterance level, but also more longitudinally as an interaction unfolds and the MRP of a TIG gradually expands. Instances of multilingual cheers that are first observable in Extract 1 (=Seg 5 in Figure 8) were shown to align with subsequent episodes of multilingual cheering (Seg 9–10 and Seg 11 in Figure 8), which gradually makes the use of non-*English words for saying "cheers" less creative and more normal or common in this TIG.

Having ethnographically and longitudinally engaged with an Erasmus student Community of Practice (CoP) in Hungary, Kalocsai (2014: 110–133) discusses and explores the "shared negotiable resources" of her group. Having spent a whole semester with her Erasmus CoP, Kalocsai (2014: 123) describes that eventually,

> when the students were to say "happy birthday", "cheers" and "enjoy your meal", they typically did it in more than one language. First they used the Hungarian form, and then repeated the form in other languages as appropriate. For instance, if the students were having a small dinner party, any *one student may have said "cheers" in four or five languages, depending on how many L1 speakers of different languages were present*. However, if the students were at their weekly European Club Evening (where most of the Erasmus Family were present), it was "right" to perform the above rituals only in the organizers' L1. Thus, if it was an Italian evening, those students acted appropriately who said *Salute* "cheers", even if in their immediate environment there were no Italian speakers. In a situation like this I was once told, "Say 'Salute!' It's an Italian evening!" (Kalocsai 2014: 123, my italics)

The student TIG examined in this chapter is not identical to Kalocsai's student CoP, but clearly shows some similarities in terms of socio-demographic and contextual parameters. The "norms and practices" that Kalocsai (2014: 103) describes are the result of students having spent a whole semester abroad in which they had time to develop their own local multilingual ways of performing certain activities. The diverse student TIG examined in this chapter is clearly not a CoP (yet) – and we do not know whether the speakers involved ever met again after LEcon560.

The point of investigating TIGs/TMCs (and not only CoPs) and of applying micro-diachronic tools for data analysis is to make possible a systematic representation of the most initial stages of such local norm development in heterogenous multilingual situations. Longitudinal studies like Kalocsai's (2014) often rely heavily on interviews and observational data and are extremely valuable in being able to narrate how matters evolve throughout a longer period of time (e.g. an exchange term). But we have not really begun to fully explore the possibilities of showing – in terms of concrete linguistic description on the basis of 3rd person evidence – how such situational norms may begin to emerge in spoken interaction.

Throughout the chapter, I have intentionally used the phrase non-*English elements on many occasions, rather than referring to them as multilingual practices. By adopting this terminology, I wish to highlight that non-*English elements are likely to be made up of (a) initial individual instances of multilingual creativity that may be followed by (b) instances/phases of convergence (such as verbatim other- and self-repetition) in interaction. This may (or may not), eventually, lead to (c) particular kinds of multilingual practices that become specific for a group. Although such multilingual practices are likely to sediment (cf. Mortensen 2017) as more stable or tangible norms (that could be reported by participants in interviews, for example) only over longer periods of time (i.e. weeks or months), situational multilingual practices might emerge also in short-lived TIGs/TMCs in the course of single interactions. Such situational multilingual practices are emergent, not yet sedimented norms that are locally and interactionally established in interaction by participants.

Micro-diachronic portraits of interaction make it possible to make visible how interactants converge and tacitly agree on such local practices, but also help us understand how and why these are not generalizable across (E)LF contexts and situations. While a bilateral TIG of business professionals may jointly establish the use of L1 side sequences as their predominant multilingual etiquette (cf. Pitzl 2021), the diverse student TIG studied in this chapter might be developing an emergent situational norm for multilingual cheering, for mutual language teaching/learning and for relying on (local) *German expressions without the need to check comprehension or flag them as *German. Future descriptions and micro-diachronic portraits of TIG/TMC interactions are therefore needed in order to deepen our understanding of interactional norm development and of the influence that different contextual factors have on these.

Transcription conventions

?	Words spoken with rising intonation are followed by a question mark.
(.)	Every brief pause in speech (up to a good half second) is marked with a full stop in parentheses.
=	Indicates that a speaker continues, completes or supports another speaker's turn immediately (i.e. without a pause).
o:h no	Lengthened sounds are marked with a colon.
(1)	Longer pauses are timed to the nearest second and marked with the number of seconds in parentheses, e.g. (1) = 1 second.
<1> </1>, <2> </2>	Whenever two or more utterances happen at the same time, the overlaps are marked with numbered tags.
<L1spa> **chin chin** </L1spa>	Utterances in a participant's first language (L1) are put between tags indicating the speaker's L1.
<LNpol> **na zdrowie** </LNpol>	Utterances in languages which are neither English nor the speaker's first language are marked LN with the language indicated.
{parallel conversation}	Contextual information is added between curly brackets { } if it is relevant to the understanding of the interaction.

These conventions represent a subset of the VOICE transcription conventions (VOICE Project 2007).

References

Auer, Peter. 1999. From codeswitching via language mixing to fused lects: Toward a dynamic typology of bilingual speech. *The International Journal of Bilingualism* 3 (4). 309–332.

Baird, Robert, Will Baker & Mariko Kitazawa. 2014. The complexity of ELF. *Journal of English as a Lingua Franca* 3 (1). 171–196.

Breiteneder, Angelika, Marie-Luise Pitzl, Stefan Majewski & Theresa Klimpfinger. 2006. VOICE recording – methodological challenges in the compilation of a corpus of spoken ELF. *Nordic Journal of English Studies* 5 (2). 161–188.

Canagarajah, Suresh. 2018. Translingual practice as spatial repertoires: Expanding the paradigm beyond structuralist orientations. *Applied Linguistics* 39 (1). 31–54.

Cogo, Alessia. 2009. Accommodating difference in ELF conversations: A study of pragmatic strategies. In Anna Mauranen & Elina Ranta (eds.), *English as a lingua franca: Studies and findings*, 254–273. Newcastle upon Tyne: Cambridge Scholars Publishing.

Cogo, Alessia. 2016. "They all take the risk and make the effort": Intercultural accommodation and multilingualism in a BELF community of practice. In Lucilla Lopriore & Enrico Grazzi (eds.), *Intercultural Communication. New Perspectives from ELF*, 365–383. Rome: Roma Tre Press.

Cogo, Alessia. 2018. ELF and multilingualism. In Jennifer Jenkins, Will Baker and Martin Dewey (eds.), *The Routledge handbook of English as a lingua franca*, 357–368. London: Routledge.

Cogo, Alessia & Martin Dewey. 2006. Efficiency in ELF communication: From pragmatic motives to lexico-grammatical innovation. *Nordic Journal of English Studies* 5 (2). 59–93.

Cogo, Alessia & Martin Dewey. 2012. *Analyzing English as a lingua franca: A corpus-driven investigation*. London: Continuum.

Gafaranga, Joseph & Maria-Carme Torras. 2001. Language versus medium in the study of bilingual conversation. *The International Journal of Bilingualism* 5 (2). 195–219.

Gasiorek, Jessica, Howard Giles & Jordan Soliz. 2015. Accommodating new vistas. *Language & Communication* 41 (1). 1–5.

Giles, Howard, Justine Coupland & Nikolas Coupland. 1991. Accommodation theory: Communication, context, and consequence. In Howard Giles, Justine Coupland & Nikolas Coupland (eds.), *Contexts of accommodation: Developments in applied sociolinguistics*, 1–68. Cambridge: Cambridge University Press.

Holmes, Janet & Meredith Marra. 2004. Relational practice in the workplace: Women's talk or gendered discourse? *Language in Society* 33 (3). 377–398.

Hymes, Dell H. 1974. *Foundations in sociolinguistics: An ethnographic approach*. Philadelphia: University of Pennsylvania Press.

Hynninen, Niina, Kaisa S. Pietikäinen & Svetlana Vetchinnikova. 2017. Multilingualism in English as a lingua franca: Flagging as an indicator of perceived acceptability and intelligibility. In Arja Nurmi, Tanja Rütten & Päivi Pahta (eds.), *Challenging the myth of monolingual corpora*, 95–126. Leiden, Boston: Brill/Rodopi.

Jenkins, Jennifer. 2000. *The phonology of English as an international language*. Oxford: Oxford University Press.

Jenkins, Jennifer. 2015. Repositioning English and multilingualism in English as a lingua franca. *Englishes in Practice* 2 (3). 49–85.

Kalocsai, Karolina. 2014. *Communities of practice and English as a lingua franca: A study of erasmus students in a Central European context*. Berlin: De Gruyter Mouton.

Larsen-Freeman, Diane. 2016. Complexity theory and ELF: A matter of nonteleology. In Marie-Luise Pitzl & Ruth Osimk-Teasdale (eds.), *English as a lingua franca: Perspectives and prospects. Contributions in honour of Barbara Seidlhofer*, 139–145. Boston: De Gruyter Mouton.

Lichtkoppler, Julia. 2007. "Male. Male." – "Male?" – "The sex is male." The role of repetition in English as a lingua franca conversations. *Vienna English Working PaperS* 16 (1). 39–65.

Mauranen, Anna. 2012. *Exploring ELF. Academic English shaped by non-native speakers*. Cambridge: Cambridge University Press.

Mortensen, Janus. 2017. Transient multilingual communities as a field of investigation: Challenges and opportunities. *Journal of Linguistic Anthropology* 27 (3). 271–288.

Mortensen, Janus & Spencer Hazel. 2017. Lending bureaucracy voice: Negotiating English in institutional encounters. In Markku Filppula, Juhani Klemola, Anna Mauranen & Svetlana Vetchinnikova (eds.), *Changing English: Global and local perspectives*, 255–276. Berlin: De Gruyter Mouton.

Pitts, Margaret J. & Jake Harwood. 2015. Communication accommodation competence: The nature and nurture of accommodative resources across the lifespan. *Language & Communication* 41. 89–99.

Pitzl, Marie-Luise. 2012. Creativity meets convention: Idiom variation and re-metaphorization in ELF. *Journal of English as a Lingua Franca* 1 (1). 27–55.

Pitzl, Marie-Luise. 2013. Creativity in language use. In Jan-Ola Östman and Jef Verschueren (eds.), *Handbook of Pragmatics. 2013 Installment*, 1–28. Amsterdam: Benjamins.

Pitzl, Marie-Luise. 2016. World Englishes and creative idioms in English as a lingua franca. *World Englishes* 35 (2). 293–309.
Pitzl, Marie-Luise. 2018a. *Creativity in English as a lingua franca: Idiom and metaphor*. Boston: Mouton de Gruyter.
Pitzl, Marie-Luise. 2018b. Creativity, idioms and metaphorical language in ELF. In Jennifer Jenkins, Will Baker & Martin Dewey (eds.), *The Routledge handbook of English as a lingua franca*, 233–243. London: Routledge.
Pitzl, Marie-Luise. 2018c. Transient International Groups (TIGs): Exploring the group and development dimension of ELF. *Journal of English as a Lingua Franca* 7 (1). 25–58.
Pitzl, Marie-Luise. 2021. Tracing the emergence of situational multilingual practices in a BELF meeting: Micro-diachronic analysis and implications of corpus design. In Kumiko Murata (ed.), *ELF research methods and approaches to data and analyses: Theoretical and methodological underpinnings*, 97–125. London: Routledge.
Pölzl, Ulrike & Barbara Seidlhofer. 2006. In and on their own terms: The "habitat factor" in English as a lingua franca interactions. *International Journal of the Sociology of Language* 177. 151–176.
Seidlhofer, Barbara. 2009. Accommodation and the idiom principle in English as a lingua franca. *Intercultural Pragmatics* 6 (2). 195–215.
Seidlhofer, Barbara. 2011. *Understanding English as a lingua franca*. Oxford: Oxford University Press.
Taylor, John R. 2012. *The mental corpus: How language is represented in the mind*. Oxford: Oxford University Press.
VERBI software. 2019. *MAXQDA 2018*. Berlin: VERBI software.
VOICE Project. 2007. *VOICE transcription conventions* [2.1]. http://www.univie.ac.at/voice/voice.php?page=transcription_general_information (13 February 2019).
VOICE. 2013. *The Vienna-Oxford International Corpus of English* (version 2.0 XML). Director: Barbara Seidlhofer; Researchers: Angelika Breiteneder, Theresa Klimpfinger, Stefan Majewski, Ruth Osimk-Teasdale, Marie-Luise Pitzl, Michael Radeka.
Weinreich, Uriel, William Labov & Marvin I. Herzog. 1968. Empirical foundations for a theory of language change. In Winfred Lehmann & Yakov Malkiel (eds.), *Directions for historical linguistics: A symposium*, 95–195. Austin: University of Texas Press.

Anne Fabricius
7 What's in a sociolinguistic norm? The case of change in prevocalic /r/ in Received Pronunciation

1 Introduction

The present volume gives an opportunity for dialogue on the topic of norms between different research traditions within sociolinguistics and related disciplines, and the chance to reflect on the concept of norms in light of differing epistemologies and phenomenologies within these disciplines. As I demonstrate in this chapter, studies of language variation and change are acutely attuned to *observing* language practice, *documenting* variable language practice as a statistical phenomenon, and *collecting* evidence of changing practice as well as changing perceptions and evaluations of practice. All of this based on the assumption that it is in the ongoing flow and gradual sedimentation of language production and perception that we find sociolinguistic norms. In the understanding developed in this chapter, sociolinguistic norms are expectations, construals, and understandings, grounded in *constructs* and *construct resources* – socially constructed, historically contingent, and socially managed artifacts of language production and perception.

The chapter is organized as follows. In section two, I reflect on theoretical definitions of the concept of *norm* within quantitative Labovian sociolinguistics, examining theoretical assumptions and claims contained in some of the key early sources for sociolinguistic theory. I will also refer to *enregisterment* and *indexicality* (Agha 2007; Silverstein 2003, 2016; Johnstone 2011; Eckert 2008), terms which originated from within linguistic anthropology, and which have been utilized by sociolinguists to link the quantitative study of language form-in-social-space to the process of meaning-making in the social realm. In section three I turn specifically to defining the notions *construct resource* and *construct-RP* (Received Pronunciation) in particular, asking how the latter has changed over time. In section

Acknowledgements: I would like to acknowledge the generous responses and critical contributions of Marie-Louise Pitzl, Jose Mompean, Jürgen Jaspers, Peter Harder, Janus Mortensen, Kamilla Kraft, Nikolas Coupland and the participants at the seminar *Norms and the Study of Language in Social Life* at the University of Copenhagen on 1st and 2nd March 2019. All of them have had a hand in improving and refining my observations and arguments as presented in this chapter, and any remaining shortcomings are solely my own.

https://doi.org/10.1515/9781501511882-007

four, I will hone in on one *construct resource* in British English, the tapped/trilled prevocalic /r/, which I will contextualize historically, using earlier studies of older recordings of RP speakers. One underlying assumption for quantitative sociolinguistics has long been that significant patterns of language use (most commonly in phonological and grammatical variables, but also in discourse variables; see e.g. Pichler 2016) are best revealed through analysis of large-scale data sets. In this optic, individual instances tell us less than the pictures that statistical trends over suitably-defined populations can reveal. Following this tradition, the examples cited in this part of the analysis below are based on larger-scale data sets and quantitative trends identified there.

In section five, I exemplify the trilled/tapped /r/'s current ambiguous status, using contemporary performance speech data from Geoffrey Cox, Attorney-General of the UK from July 2018 to 13th February 2020. In this way, we can begin to understand the present norms surrounding this speech feature in a concrete performance against a backdrop of studies of its historical status (Fabricius 2017; Mackenzie 2017). This qualitative focus on a single instance of data moves beyond the initial broader quantitative perspective, and shows how a combination of different types of data and methods can help to isolate and contextualize norm-based *constructs* and *construct resources* (Fabricius & Mortensen 2013; Mortensen 2014), thus illustrating and illuminating variation and change in sociolinguistic norms.

To demonstrate the *construct resource* relationship – like the linguistic sign itself, a construct resource is essentially a relationship – in section six, I present social media evidence of semiotic equivocation about the indexicality that trilled and tapped /r/ can carry as part of a speech style. Recipients' reactions range from approval and excitement to ridicule and explicit rejection of the trilled and tapped /r/ as simply outdated. The meaning generated is ambiguous and multiplex, because the interpretive norm related to this particular construct resource lies in suspension semiotically, between older and newer indexical fields. In short, the two analyses in the chapter demonstrate that the production norm of pre-vocalic /r/ in native-RP has changed statistically (section four), and if a speaker chooses to "ignore" or "play with" this change and perform a type of "linguistic time-travelling" (section five) using, among other things, tapped and trilled /r/'s as a construct resource, this is *a meaning-generating move*. This very neatly shows that the two sides of the *construct resource* (attested quantitative patterns of use and an associated scope of indexical meanings) do not develop in lockstep with each other over time. The range of audience responses positions tapped/trilled /r/ as a historical "drag" (cf. Silverstein 2016), a persistent historical construct resource that now harks to the past, as its meanings have been reconfiguring over time. The theoretical claim here is that the construct resource, as a distillation of a particular speech production and its relation to a semiotic field, is well placed to identify a norm of expectation, an interpretive norm, a way of understanding that is normative, in the sense that it is socially conventionalized and habituated, and yet malleable over time. Finally, in section seven I draw conclusions for the chapter.

2 What's in a norm? The view from language variation and change

Norms featured in Labov's very earliest definition of the speech community, as the following quote shows:

> The speech community is not defined by any marked agreement in the use of language elements, so much as by participation in a set of shared norms; these norms may be observed in overt types of evaluative behavior, and by the uniformity of abstract patterns of variation which are invariant with respect to particular levels of usage. (Labov 1972: 120–1)

This quote is often used and critiqued in discussions of the *speech community* (e.g. Patrick 2008; Rampton 2010; Jacquemet 2018), which constitutes the sociolinguistic locus of norms in a population in a geographical setting. Speech community remained for many years a central concept in the discipline, one which urban sociolinguistics inherited directly from the (ultimately Neogrammarian) dialectological tradition, which held up non-mobile communities as central to the dialectological and historical linguistic enterprise (Patrick 2008). This was seen in community delimitations and divisions by means of isoglosses for individual features (as in the famous case of the North German/Dutch *Rhenish Fan*, for instance).

The concept of the *sociolinguistic variable* was introduced as a statistically-modelled quantitative linguistic pattern (either categorical or constrained, changing or stable) with a systematic social anchoring. For most mainstream work within Language Variation and Change (LVC), the quantitative details of variable linguistic practice remain central to the analysis. These details give access to the phonological or grammatical framing of the linguistic content of an abstract norm of speech behavior, a *production norm*, typically encompassing adjustments in quantitative levels of production in uniform directions, so-called style-shifts. These frequency shifts crucially hinge on a speaker's evaluations of the speech context (and personal linguistic monitoring). In this optic, community norms can be plotted through quantitative investigation of dialectological practice in context.

Labov's concern in transferring dialectology to the urban space was to uncover these uniform normative patterns of language use, as well as subconscious style-shifting and conscious overt evaluation in the context of sociolinguistic interviews. These interviews could reveal the sociolinguistic status of features that could be mapped to the larger urban population. One of Labov's key findings was that when pressed to pay more conscious attention to matters of fine-grained pronunciation (such as in citation of minimal pairs or reading passages), the population of Lower East Side New Yorkers all behaved in similar ways and in the same directions, changing their speech according to similar patterns, even though the details of rates of production varied (Labov 1966). This could then be taken to indicate the existence of a speech community based on shared evaluative norms.

Labov (1966, republished in 2006) refers more specifically to *norms of correctness* (concerning post-vocalic /r/ in New York, for instance). These norms could be demonstrated (Labov 2006: 298–299) by means of subjective reaction tests, which made them distinct from *norms of covert prestige* (and accent solidarity), which the subjective reaction tests could not demonstrate. The *social stratification* of language in New York that Labov was describing was a thoroughgoing class-delimited social order, whereby class groups acted in concert with respect to the ranges of variation produced in their community. Thus, we find the abstract example of increasing rates of post-vocalic /r/ (from different baselines) in careful as opposed to casual speech for all three department stores, reflecting different social statuses in the class order of the city at large, in the New York Department store study (Labov 1966), a pattern that has since been replicated multiple times (Fowler 1986; Mather 2011).

In addition, different levels of awareness (and perhaps overt "normativeness") attach to sociolinguistic variables, as per the distinction between *indicators*, *markers* and *stereotypes* (Labov 2001: 196), positioned along a scale of social salience and awareness. *Indicators* are changes from below which are incipient and not available to conscious evaluation; *markers* and *stereotypes* are overtly recognizable, subject to social stratification and style-shifting, and in the case of stereotypes, subject to overt commentary (a case I return to below). The LVC literature contains many examples of sociolinguistic variables, many from English-speaking contexts, but also from other languages such as French, Spanish, Danish or Beijing Chinese. Crucially, indicators, markers and stereotypes will be features of a speech community's grammar, not an individual's grammar. The Northern Cities Vowel Shift in the northern US for example, encompassing a series of interlinked chain-shifting vocalic variables, is a pattern which generalizes across vast swathes of the US population, with local variations if the pattern has arrived through diffusion rather than generational transmission (for example in St. Louis, Missouri; Friedman 2014).

Downes was another early sociolinguistic theorist who also used an explicit definition of norms when he wrote (1984: 214):

> A language change involves a change in norms... We have said that the norms we are referring to are norms of pronunciation at which speakers aim in producing the variants of a variable feature; and an interpretation of the variants in terms of their social meaning. The norm is also what makes it possible to say that centralization [on Martha's Vineyard: AHF, ed.] encodes local identity. So, a norm has two sides.

Citing Williams (1968), a work coming from a more general social science background, Downes (1984:215) defined norms as "intersubjective group standards":

> Williams (1968) writes "A norm... is not a statistical average of actual behavior but rather a cultural (shared) definition of desirable behavior". So when we are talking about a norm in relation to a sociolinguistic variable, we are not talking about the actual frequencies speakers produce, but rather the intersubjective group standard, or the rule, that guides or motivates the act of its production.

This is consistent with Labov's emphasis on "uniformity of abstract patterns of variation" (Labov 1972: 120–1). Downes continues (1984: 215):

> norms are legitimated by *values* and *beliefs*. Behind every norm is a value... Within the community where the rule is known, it creates intelligible action and governs mutual expectation in interaction. Such norms or rules make *possible* a social life which is constituted by actions, because they *constitute* the very actions themselves. (emphasis in original)

We are approaching here the concept of norms as socially-constituted expectations. In Labov's three-volume magnum opus, *Principles of Linguistic Change* (Labov 1994, 2001, 2010) the term "norm" permeates volume two, where social factors in linguistic variation and change are primary. Norms are mentioned in the discussion of topics such as the acquisition of local sociolinguistic norms by newcomers to a community (referring to Payne's 1980 study of Philadelphia), different gender patterns in adherence to and divergence from norms, and uniformity within a community regarding evaluative speech norms. Overt and covert norms are distinguished in the book in terms that reflect Trudgill's (1972) definitions of overt and covert prestige. Labov hypothesizes that covert norms "balance" overt norms in that "every overtly stigmatized feature[1] has prestige in the social

---

[1] *Feature* here is a structurally-defined variable linguistic feature, part of the grammar or the phonology (my note, AF).

contexts where it is normally used, and ... every prestige feature will be awarded an equal and opposite stigma in those opposing contexts" (Labov 2001: 196). One individual's concept of a stigmatized pronunciation might thus be another's "prestige" (or maybe just non-stigmatized) feature. This is exemplified in Fabricius (2000), where I discuss the evaluative status of t-glottalling in modern RP in the late twentieth century as being "between stigma and prestige" when used in certain (pre-consonantal) phonological environments, but not others (pre-vocalic, pre-pause), where it remained stigmatized and speakers shifted away from it in read-aloud speech contexts. This normative multiplicity and ambiguity can go further: the same listener can simultaneously regard one and the same feature as stigmatized or prestigious, depending on the context in which it is produced, and by whom. Traditional RP spoken by the Queen is expected; from the mouth of a schoolchild it can be parodic (Rampton 2006).

In more recent years, we have also seen an increasing focus in LVC studies on the importance of studies of perception (Chevrot et al. 2018; Walker et al. 2018; Drager 2015; Campbell-Kibler 2012). This work employs experimental methods, taking inspiration from psycholinguistics, and utilizing findings from production studies to great effect. The cross-fertilization of sociolinguistics and cognitive linguistics in the study of linguistic heterogeneity is thus well underway.

From a perceptual perspective, then, we might roughly gloss a concept of *perception norms* as listener expectations and construals that can be revealed through studies of perception and attitudinal reactions (see e.g. Bailey 2018, which demonstrates non-social perceptual factors in the changing perception and production of [ŋg] in British Northern English). These expectations and construals will be generationally sensitive, we would expect, given the role that perceptual re-analysis of variation at many levels has been shown to play in community language change over time (Sneller et al. 2019; Harrington et al. 2008).

Honing in on micro-cases of perception, as exemplified by overt commentary on stereotypes of language variation, we sometimes find examples of explicit metalinguistic talk that encapsulate some ingredients of a language change on the move. In Fabricius and Mortensen (2013) and Mortensen and Fabricius (2014), we termed these *construct resources*. This was a term we coined to parallel the discourse of *linguistic resources* which was circulating in social constructionist accounts of language at the time (e.g. Quist 2008). In Fabricius and Mortensen (2013: 375–6), we defined construct resources as:

> ... ideological postulates about language variation and social meaning, which emerge historically and circulate in society. The notion of the construct resource is posited as an isolatable (and at the same time relational) unit at the linguistic form/social meaning interface, above the level of the individual linguistic sign.

These construals can sometimes crystallize as gems of citable language or naming practice. In the UK, for instance, *talking posh*, or, on a more specifically phonetic level, *rolling your r's, dropping your t's, dropping your g's, dropping your aitches*, for instance, have long circulated as construct resources. These are metalinguistic labels that enable specific links to be established between language form and indexical associations. Construals of language can be built out of many ingredients and sometimes depend on very fine-grained phonetic details (tongue placement in the production of /s/ for instance, discussed in Levon et al. 2017). When clusters of construct resources pattern together, this will be part of the constitution of a *construct,* or an *enregistered variety*, a type of variety-specific construct or ideology, a sum total or perhaps a common denominator of many construct resources. It is striking, for example, that many construct resources that have crystallized around non-standard accents in England consistently carry a similar "deficit" perspective: a non-standard accent speaker has long been said to be *dropping g's, dropping t's, dropping aitches*.

These construct resources can be identified through a qualitative examination of various speech phenomena: interactional moves, uptake in conversation, explicit metalinguistic labelling, and overt performances using phonetic detail (such as the pronunciation of the word *posh* in the data example discussed in Fabricius & Mortensen 2013: 390). Not all language features undergoing variation and change will necessarily be in conscious community awareness at any one time (indicators will not be, markers and stereotypes will be, by definition). Those that are above the level of consciousness can be particularly susceptible to distillation as construct resources, and some such resources can be very robust historically. *Dropping the h* as a negative stereotype for /h/-deletion initially in lexical words, for instance, was recorded in England in the Victorian era (Mugglestone 2003).

This means that patterns of performance across contexts will be guided by adherence to or deviation from intersubjective group standards, or norms, which themselves will provide a template of understanding for listeners "in the know". Here we can make a direct link between norms of behavior and norms of perception. In the understanding developed here, then, norms construct expectations, and work as *construals* (as the term is used in psychology and within sociolinguistics, in Levon 2018), i.e. interpretative mechanisms that enable sociolinguistic constructs and construct resources to be understood. Norms are predicated on these socially constructed, historically contingent, and socially managed artifacts of production and perception.

This idea of norms as folk-based mechanisms that make up the sociolinguistic life of language performance is reinforced further by work in linguistic anthropology, a field which has deeply influenced variationism in recent years. This move has shifted Labovian-type dialectologically focused LVC studies away from a "first-wave" emphasis on sociolinguistic correlations as mirrors of large scale etic social structures (such as socioeconomic class and gender) towards so-called "second" and "third wave" studies (Eckert 2018) that have emerged in the last twenty years. Third wave variationist sociolinguistics works with the idea that speech communities develop normative *registers* (following Agha 2003, 2007) or *constructs* (as I would term them), systematized norms of language-in-context that are underpinned in a community by speech perceptions and indexical fields of associations between form and meaning (Eckert 2018). This is also implied in the idea that language forms point to a type of speaker or *persona* (Coupland 2001), the claim that, over and above carrying propositional meaning or constituting speech acts, language forms can be used (more or less agentively) by speakers to index identities-in-the-moment relating to place, class, age, ethnicity, or stance, or some other factor. In Eckert's terms, members of the community as listeners work with habituated and emergent construals of language within an indexical field (Eckert 2018). Silverstein (e.g. 2003) has had a strong influence here: he has always insisted on regarding orders of indexicality and the process of indexical semiosis as central to the study of language. Indeed, his definition of language change itself places this front and centre. This contrasts with Labov's sociologically-founded embeddedness in social structure, which is evident especially in his identification of the "leaders of linguistic change" in Philadelphia (Labov 2001). Silverstein writes (2016: 63):

> Language change is a movement of a sociological structure of repertoires of enregisterment – with or without explicitly standardized ones – distributed over a language community, always changing but always imminent in the variance of *parole* in which people perform their context-relevant identities via indexical semiosis.

One concomitant of this description of the movement of norms is going to be relevant in our discussion of the data below. Silverstein (2016: 60) writes:

> Where sociolinguistic variability turns into a movement of a language's norms, in every case we find register shibboleths – in essence, Labovian markers becoming stereotypes – that anchor an ethnometapragmatically identifiable aspect of social identity ... the co-occurrence of which with particular forms linked in enregisterment is the way that "drags" and "pulls" manifest in the economy of change as languages – unstable and always changing structures of interlocked registers – move along in time within the population of their users.

This description of "structures of interlocked registers" I find particularly fruitful from my own perspective as a long-term observer of modern RP, an empirically-observable sociolinguistic vernacular (native RP) and at the same time one of the enregistered large scale linguistic constructs of the English-speaking world *par excellence*. In the data example discussed below, I present the case of tapped and trilled /r/s, a case of what Silverstein would probably call a "drag" – in the sense of an outdated piece of linguistic variation, one that is no longer productive, not currently transmitted, not at all showing community incrementation in young cohorts following the direction of an active change. Nonetheless, it is still present in the sociolinguistic landscape as an identifiable *construct resource* (Fabricius & Mortensen 2013) or *register shibboleth* (Silverstein 2016), a relic, a receding pronunciation feature with a semiotic value, a piece of the phonetic past dragging its heels, and one that is noticeably and markedly different from other variants (prevocalic alveolar approximant /r/ and labial /r/; Foulkes & Docherty 2000) that are pulling the language into the future.

3 Construct-RP

Having established some parameters in the definition of norms within LVC studies, we turn now to consider RP.[2] As a prominent feature of the UK sociolinguistic landscape, it has been studied from many angles over many years (in the work of phoneticians such as Daniel Jones, A.C. Gimson and John Wells and sociolinguistically, in publications such as Fabricius 2000, 2002a, 2002b, 2005, 2007, 2017, 2018, 2019, Hannisdal 2006 and Fabricius & Mortensen 2013). In what follows, I will treat RP (as I always have done) as a sociolinguistic phenomenon from the point of view of language variation and change. In my PhD thesis work, (Fabricius 2000, see also 2002a, 2005) a crucial theoretical distinction between elite vernacular sociolect and standard language *construct* was made using a binary distinction between the terms *native-RP* and *construct-RP*. This distinction was used to dissolve a systematic inbuilt ambiguity in the accent label RP (which is present in any essentializing accent label such as *Cockney, Scouse*). It makes an explicit distinction between RP as "a vernacular" (phonetic features as part of a first language of socialization) and RP as an abstract, more-or-less explicitly codified and enregistered folk-linguistic model (which can however also be someone's vernacular). Construct-RP, the abstract notion of RP's linguistic form and status is just as much a property of the speech community (at whatever scale) as the vernacular form, native-RP.

Agha (2003; 2007) introduced the concept of the enregistered RP voice – what I would call construct-RP – in his presentation of the term *enregisterment*. He claims that *(construct) RP* became enregistered as a folk concept over the span

---

[2] This section also draws on work published in Fabricius (2018).

of the nineteenth century, meaning that it became a recognized set of phonetic patterns. This process is described for example in macro-sociolinguistic and micro-phonetic terms in Mugglestone's (2003) *Talking proper*. The enregistered/construct RP came to embody a certain type of voice, in folk terms, suited to a certain setting, resonant of a certain type of person or persona (see for example Agha's characterological figure *Mr Round;* Agha 2003, 2007). As a spoken register, RP was immediately available to the BBC in the 1920s (Schwyter 2016) as a normative model. However, as Schwyter shows, the corporation's own Advisory Committee on Spoken English actually had major difficulties in reaching agreement on specific pronunciation norms throughout its lifespan (which ran from 1926 to 1939). This may to some extent cast doubt on the claim that the enregistered RP voice at that time really was a shared sociolinguistic construct; Schwyter's data suggests it was mostly on the level of non-systematic lexical variations in pronunciation that disputes occurred. In any case, Agha's concept of the *enregistered voice* was indeed part of what I intended the term *construct-RP* to cover in Fabricius (2000, 2002a, 2005), but *construct-RP* was also defined to include codified manuals and dictionaries of the accent as explicit models. These are called *text-artifacts* in Agha's anthropological perspective: they themselves also function as further vehicles of enregisterment processes (see further Fabricius 2018).

As Agha (2007) describes it, the process of systematization/codification of the accent and its characterization as "received" or "authorized" by an external authority is part of a general linguistic-anthropological mechanism that produces a standard accent ideal that is, importantly, *external to any one speaker*. This sense of distance between ideal and speaker eventually makes it easier for claims to be made that "no one speaks RP any longer", if RP is solely understood as a construct model that comes up short against the forces of linguistic variation and change and no longer matches the language people are surrounded by.

If the term *standard language/variety* is reserved for such a socially-generated and historically sustained mental *construct*, it can be kept distinct from the concept of an *elite* (or even *establishment*) *sociolect*. This latter term can then be reserved to refer to linguistic patterns evidenced in the first language of socialization (i.e. the *vernacular* in that particular sense, not in its other sense of a "non-standard variety") of a social group occupying a particular socio-economic niche within a socially stratified society. The term *elite sociolect* is of course also an idealization, since no group contains completely homogeneous or identical speakers, enabling the identification of one single sociolect shared by all. This has of course been a cardinal point for much Labovian variationist work: that the variable grammar/phonology that was being sought was the property of the community, not the individual, and that any individual will evidence patterns which can best be understood as manifestations of a more abstract group pattern.

So, given the idea that there is a *construct RP* (or perhaps, in everyday terms, as Mugglestone puts it, an idea of *talking posh*) out there, a community-achieved set of indexical values associated with *sounds-in-a-system*, a *register*, to use Agha's term, the evolution of this construct will be, as Silverstein (2016) points out, a chartable ongoing historical process, an envelope of indexical variation shifting in socio-space/time. It will be sociologically-structured, contingent upon social processes and sedimentations, with the possibilities of emergent meanings playing in the ebb and flow of the tide, as it were. *Construct-RP* will shift alongside shifts in *native-RP*, the ongoing generational renewal of the elite sociolect, but potentially at different paces and in different ways, with different *drags* and *pulls* at work.

One feature of a "traditionalist" or "conservative" speech construct (such as the traditional understanding of RP) is that it will include relic features for longer than they are instantiated in daily discourse for the majority of speakers of that variety. Old-fashioned voices have a role, not just as reminders of the past, but as frames against which newer voices can be contrasted, presumably to signify conservative values in the same way as innovations can express progressive values. In Fabricius and Mortensen (2013: 380), we wrote about it in this way:

> The established (and Establishment) enregisterment of RP makes it a very clear case of a style 'steeped in history'. . . a style that to this day carries heavy ideological weight . . . a style that most speakers who are familiar with the sociolinguistic landscape of the UK will be aware of. . . a style they will be able to use as an interpretive frame. . .

Alongside this, there is also the possibility of a macro-level process that Coupland has dubbed *sociolinguistic change*. He defines it thus: "sociolinguistic change is broadly defined as *consequential change over time in language-society relations* [emphasis in original]" (Coupland 2016: 433). This concept gives a broader perspective to the relationships of constructs and vernacular varieties. It allows for the recognition of changes in specific juxtapositions of expectations or norms, changes as to what counts as contemporary indexical connections between linguistic form, indexical meaning and a sense of place or context. In essence, what is possible and validated as a linguistic form in one type of speech setting does not remain constant over time. One instance of this, as Coupland (2014) has pointed out, would be a reconfiguring of a particular sociolinguistic landscape (such as broadcast media) and its expectations as to what forms of speech are most appropriate, recognized or acknowledged in that setting. News-reading, for instance, and chat show formats have both shown evidence of sociolinguistic change in the past forty to fifty years in many places globally, not just in the United Kingdom. As section five will show, traditional RP speech features in a political speech in 2018 do not automatically elicit approval or deference: positive and negative reactions combine in the explicit responses recorded here.

4 Analysis 1: Trilled and tapped /r/ in RP

The phonetic feature I will focus on in this section is the realization of prevocalic /r/ as a production norm over time. Note that RP, being a non-rhotic variety, does not exhibit variation in *post*-vocalic /r/ (the /r/ in *card* and *car*) when followed by another consonant (e.g. card) or a pause (e.g. car).[3] Yet it did exhibit variation here, according to Mugglestone (2003), at the beginning of the 1800s, where realization of post-vocalic /r/ was a disappearing feature. There is plenty of documented commentary on the loss of post-vocalic /r/ as it made its way from stigmatized "vulgar" innovation to acceptable language norm in the first half of the nineteenth century (Mugglestone 2003: 86–89). The character of change in prevocalic /r/ has been less frequently studied (Foulkes & Docherty 2000; Fabricius 2017), but its change has been no less dramatic. As I will show below, taps and trills have generationally "lost out" in English in England over the course of the twentieth century, being usurped by alveolar and (more recently) labial /ɹ/'s which dominate younger speakers' productions.

In a specific sociolinguistic study of change in prevocalic /r/ realization across a set of fourteen RP speakers born between 1880 and 1920, and recorded between 1939 and 1977 (Fabricius 2017), I examined the changing rates of occurrence of a set of different phonetic variants in four different phonetic environments: word-initial, as in the word *real*; word-medial, for example in *history*, or *very*; linking r, where orthographic r is pronounced in a non-rhotic variety across a word boundary followed by a vowel, as in *there appeared*; and within a consonant cluster, as in *broad, three, greatly*. Note that these slightly different phonological contexts can also be subsumed under the category *prevocalic /r/ in syllable onsets*, either word-initially (*real*) or in clusters (*three*) or intervocalic /r/ word-internally (*history*) or across word boundaries (*there is*). In the last two contexts, the /r/ can be considered prevocalic if we stipulate that it is the vowel after, not the vowel before which is triggering the r-ful realization.[4]

The data recordings came from a variety of speech settings, genres, and types of TV or radio programme, some of which consisted of interviewed personal reminiscences, while others were from documentary features. In all, just under four hours of recordings were analyzed, yielding 2,511 tokens of prevocalic /r/. The

---

[3] Note, however, that linking /r/ (e.g. *bar* followed by a vowel) remains inherently variable in RP (e.g. Mompean & Gómez 2011; Pavlík 2016).
[4] We could also define /r/ here as pre-nuclear as opposed to post-nuclear /r/ in car /+pause/, card. This works for some cases but not all, however. /r/ is pre-nuclear in *history*, but apparently not in *very* where, in common with cases of linking /r/, arguments can be made in favour of ambisyllabicity. I thank Jose Mompean for this observation.

data were analyzed auditorily and explored for patterns of co-variation between speaker profile, linguistic characteristics and date of recording. Significant patterns of reduction in rates of trilled and tapped /r/ were found according to both date of birth of the speaker, and date of the actual recording.

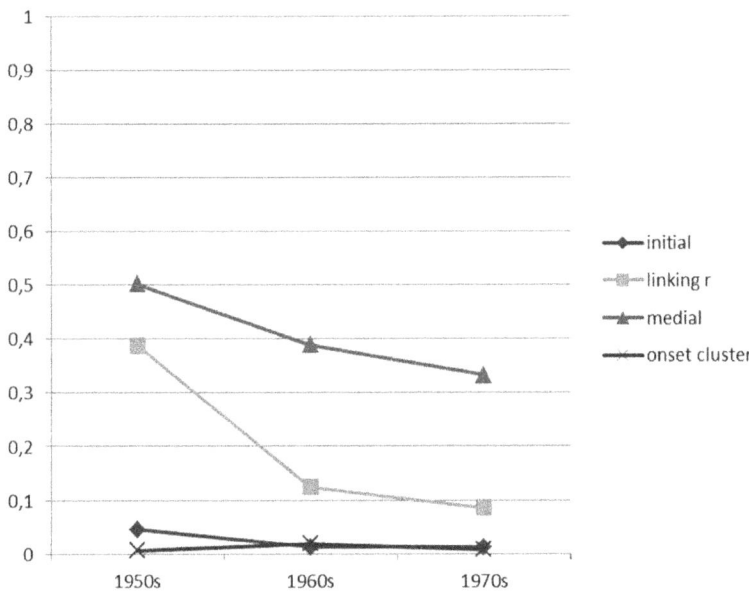

Figure 1: Trilled and tapped /r/ according to date of recording. Reproduced with permission from Fabricius (2017: 54).

Figure 1 shows these results according to year of recording. Over the three decades 1950s to 1970s, the highest initial rates and greatest falls occur in linking /r/ (e.g. *after all*) and medial/intervocalic /r/ (e.g. in *barrow* and similar words) as changing phonetic production norms. Rates of tapping and trilling in other environments (consonant clusters and initial /r/) are negligible in the earlier and later recordings in the corpus.

The results of the 2017 study also show that tapped and trilled variants of /r/ (analyzed together as "taps") seemed to have a different social and linguistic profile to "labialized" variants, which were found primarily in the speech of three of the fourteen individuals. This suggests that these /r/ variants could have filled different indexical niches at that time. We can note Wells' (1982: 282) description of the labiodental approximant as being "often regarded as an upper-class affectation", although he also felt it was almost as frequent among other types of speakers (see also Foulkes & Docherty 2000). Trilled and tapped /r/ in the corpus occurred in all 343 times, with only 10 of those instances being actual trills. The chapter also points out (Fabricius 2017: 50) the fact that five of these instances of trills were in one monologue (a dramatic radio documentary on the life of Vincent van Gogh, narrated by the poet laureate Cecil Day Lewis), which hints suggestively at a historical "performative status" of trilled /r/, which we will discuss further in the contemporary data example presented below.

Further evidence of the historical status of norms for tapped /r/ comes from MacKenzie's (2017) research using a real-time corpus of TV presentation speech by Sir David Attenborough, an RP speaker born in 1926. Mackenzie carried out a comparison of recordings from 1956–61 (alternating between voice-over narration and speaking to camera) with recordings from 2006 (*Planet Earth*), which consist only of voice-over narration. Her analysis of 1,628 tokens of intervocalic and linking /r/ using mixed effects logistic regression showed no significant change in overall rates of tapped /r/ (suggesting real-time stability in the speaker's adult production). When the word-internal intervocalic and linking /r/ environments were separated however, a significant drop in word-internal tapping was found, alongside an increase in tapping in linking /r/ environments. What this amounted to in post-hoc testing was that the environmental difference (intervocalic (medial) versus linking /r/) which was significant in the 1950s was no longer significant in the 2000s. This is interesting in comparison with the data example presented below (Analysis 2) where the main environments for taps and trills are precisely the same.⁵

This picture is moreover further complicated by an overall word frequency effect that Mackenzie finds in her data, to the effect that very frequent linking /r/ collocations (such as *there are, for a*) become over time more likely to be treated similarly to other intervocalic environments such as *very*. Mackenzie therefore concludes that "it is thus possible that after having had decades of experience pronouncing high-frequency two-word collocations, Attenborough has come to mentally store them as something more like individual words", a case of "change in production stemming from increased experience with one's language over time" (2017: 8).⁶ So in this one case, we see something that is more likely to be the result of speaker-internal reorganization of an individual grammar, rather than a historical response to a changing sociolinguistic landscape. As Mackenzie notes, "although Attenborough must be hearing fewer [ɾ]'s in the 2000s than

---

5 Note however that the small sample size in the present chapter prohibits a statistical comparison within the data, so the conclusions drawn here are exemplificatory and illustrative rather than statistically-founded.
6 This suggests, following footnote 4 above, that the ambisyllabicity that these environments share may be what is leading them to be analyzed similarly by the speaker.

he did in the 1950s, his pronunciation in his nature documentaries has not kept pace" (2017: 8). Indeed, it seems his (small c-) conservative stylistic norm has its own value as his linguistic trademark; otherwise, he would possibly have been encouraged to change it. Overall, then, we see that prevocalic /r/ has historically been "on the move", with evidence of a landscape of changing production norms, and the potential therefore for changing indexical embeddings over time. The latter are explored in more depth below.

5 Analysis 2: *Rolling r's* as a *construct resource* in 2018

In this section, I use a single piece of performative data to illustrate a contemporary pattern of norms of usage and evaluation of the alveolar trill and alveolar tap realizations of prevocalic /r/. Tapped and trilled prevocalic /r/s are found in the performative register speech of Geoffrey Cox, born in 1960. Cox was educated at the independent King's College Taunton, and studied Law and Classics at Downing College, Cambridge. Cox is a QC, a Queen's Counsel, and has been a practicing barrister since the early 1990s. He became Attorney-General of the United Kingdom in July 2018. The data I consider here comes from his Conservative Party Conference speech on 3rd October 2018,[7] some three months after entering the Cabinet. The speech gained considerable attention in the press, not least because it immediately preceded the conference speech of the then Prime Minister, Theresa May, and thus had a large audience. One most remarkable, and remarked-upon, feature of the speech was Cox's delivery, and especially his use of tapped and trilled /r/ (against a backdrop of alveolar approximant /r/) eighteen times during a twelve-minute speech. This was immediately responded to in real time on social media, as I will also demonstrate below.

The following transcript shows the distribution of taps and trills as bolded words. All other prevocalic /r/s were alveolar approximants, of the type most frequent in present-day RP speech in general; the newer labial /r/ is not part of Cox's repertoire, at least as it is manifested here.

> Well ah Ladies and gentlemen it's good to see so many of you here to listen to the attorney general it ah it shows what a respect our party has for the rule of law ladies and gentlemen I have been asked to come as the newest member of the cabinet to tell you a little bit about why it was that I joined the cabinet

---

[7] https://www.youtube.com/watch?v=4_SpicQhGtU (Accessed 21 July 2020).

which seems a strange thing to ask someone to speak about cause if you're asked to do a job for your country I don't think you should refuse the request, do you? No. At eleven pm on the twenty ninth of march twenty nineteen we will leave the European Union and soon thereafter in an extraordin**ary (medial tap)** moment in our history, the EU institutions will no longer have linking the right to make laws **for our (linking tap)** country, and that power will belong exclusively to the **sovereign (medial trill)** parliament of Great Britain and Northern Ireland. Ladies and gentlemen, that is a precious prize. Like millions of others I voted to leave the European Union, not because I didn't wish to continue our special and close friendship and collaboration with our friends there but because the political and democratic price of ever closer union was just too high. I was fifteen true I was once fifteen. I was fifteen at the time of the first referendum. My generation did not get to vote: we waited forty-one years to do so and now some want another referendum after two and the Labour Party are poised waiting to see which way the wind blows, but this government and this prime minister will not be deflected from the solemn obligation that is imposed upon her government, when five hundred and forty four members of parliament voted to devolve the decision to leave to the British people and once they had given their decision, four hundred and ninety eight members of parliament voted to give notice under article fifty of our intention to do so. She will deliver the prize that millions voted for and fulfill the largest democratic mandate that any vote has ever **returned (initial trill)** ever returned in our history and that is why that is why I accepted her request to join this government as its attorney general. Because it will take a dogged determined single-minded clarity and firmness of purpose to translate that decision into reality and it was clear to me then and even more so now that the prime minister will not flinch from her duty and the central mission that the people of this country have set us, to take control of our borders as Sajid Javid has announced, to resume full **sovereign (medial trill)** rights **over our (linking tap)** laws, as we will **assuredly (medial tap)** do under our proposals, to cease the obligation to support the future budgets of the EU by huge annual payments. But in the **real** world **(initial trill)** in the real world nothing so valuable is ever gained without sacrifice and compromise and as Dominic Raab in his excellent speech here said: in a negotiation pragmatism is inevitable and necessary. Since the seventeenth **century (medial tap)** the special genius of the British peoples has been the flexibility to find **compromises (medial cluster trill)** and constitutional arrangements that may not possess ideological or theoretical purity but which work and we have asked we have asked that the European Union commit to that same flexibility to preserve the economic benefits of smooth and fluent trade across our borders while doing justice to the **desire of (linking tap)** the British people for self-government and to maintain both the integrity of the United Kingdom and of the EU legal order. We know that on both sides there are men and women who possess the vision and the good will to see how essential it is that acceptable arrangements are found. You know as a lawyer I have negotiated many agreements over the years and as Dominic said I know that the nature of a negotiation is with apologies to the Rolling Stones that you can't always get what you want. But we, but we have to be grown up about it and we have now **reached (initial trill)** the critical moment when I am convinced we must resolve

> to put aside our **differences (medial tap)** and unite behind the prime minister to ensure that the decision of the twenty-third to ensure that the decision of the twenty-third of June twenty sixteen is not set at naught by those who would have us remain in the European Union. That would indeed have catastrophic consequences for the democracy of our country we here who argue that this great democratic mandate must be given effect are the optimists. The whole premise and principle of Brexit is based on hope, not fear. We need not fear. We need not fear self-government we believe that a nation like the United Kingdom will soon be able to gather her strength and in close and amicable association with her friends step out again into the world as a free independent and sovereign partner to the other democracies. To build a future of opportunity, the seeds of which have been sown here this week **for all (linking tap)** the generations of her people. **Three (cluster tap)** hundred thousand new homes a year by the mid twenty twenties giving the opportunity of home ownership to the young. An education system that **encourages (medial tap)** aspiration and the skills to achieve it, already **delivering (medial tap)** for the nearly two million more children who are now in good **or outstanding (linking tap)** schools and an economy that rewards hard work and enterprise, helping businesses to cut employment (*sic*) to the lowest levels we have seen since the nineteen seventies, giving the security of a regular wage to over three point three more million people million people in work and so let us say with Milton methinks I see in my mind a noble and puissant nation, rousing herself like a strong man after sleep and shaking her invincible locks methinks I see her as an eagle muing her mighty youth and kindling her undazzled eyes at the full midday beam. Ladies and gentlemen let us seize that prize. Thank you.

This transcript gives us a qualitative picture of the words Cox is uttering with these highly unusual pronunciations (seen from the perspective of 2018 at least). To get another perspective, in purely quantitative phonetic terms, we can look at the occurrences of taps and trills against a background of other variants of the variable prevocalic /r/. As noted in the section above, four phonetic environment possibilities for pre-vocalic /r/ are present in any sample of spoken English: word-initial, word-medial, linking /r/ and within a consonant cluster (disregarding for now the phonetic makeup of the cluster). Considering these tap and trill variants as rates within a percentage framework shows us their purely quantitative frequency. Figure 2 below shows the four phonetic environments scaled against alveolar approximants and other possibilities (affricated realisations in /tr/ and /dr/ in the consonant cluster environment, for instance).

As we can see in Figure 2, in no phonetic environment are taps and trills in the majority. They remain a "flavoring" rather than major dominant variants, but in word-initial environments, for instance, trills constitute 13% of tokens, so just over one in eight realizations is actually this highly-unusual feature for modern day Southern English, the trill. The other environment where taps feature strongly is the linking /r/ environment, where they represent just under 42%, nearly half

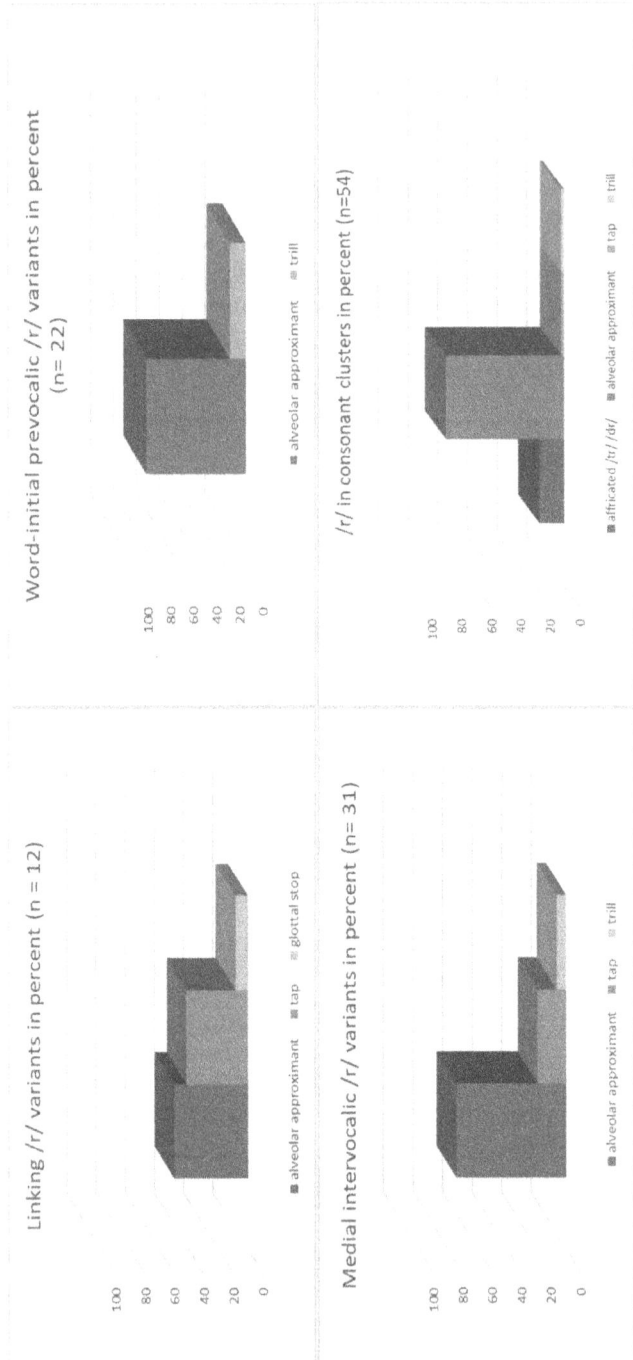

Figure 2: Rates of variance in prevocalic /r/, in four phonetic environments. Speaker: Geoffrey Cox, Conservative Party Conference Speech, Birmingham, 3rd October 2018.

of all tokens. Word-medially, taps are also noticeably frequent: 19.3%, or just under one in five, while trills in this environment occur at 6%. If we compare these results to Figure 1, it is noticeable that Cox's rates of tapping in linking /r/ correspond nicely to the 1950's decade of recording, where linking /r/'s in that sample were tapped at around 40%. Given that Cox himself was born in 1960, this is indeed an anachronistic personal use of tapped /r/, against the backdrop of speech produced by adults in the period up to ten years before he was even born.

There is also much to say about the lexical content of this speech, and indeed the individual words that are presented containing trills and taps; *sovereign*, for instance, occurs twice, both times with a medial trill. In discourse analytical terms, Cox can be said to be "doing being an establishment Brexiteer Attorney General" in a very precise and historically-aware way that includes explicit phonetic performance of highly meaningful rhotic realisations, playing on old-fashioned speech norms to produce old-fashioned (and 'lordly') political stances. His text explicitly evokes the historical significance of the Brexit referendum, the chance to vote on European Union membership that his generation waited for, for more than forty years. He cites the loss of sovereignty that membership of the EU, as he claims, had eroded. Exit from the European Union is framed as regaining British strength, sovereignty and power to step out independently. It is framed as a message of hope and "a precious prize", a trope he refers to more than once. He quotes the esteemed English poet of the seventeenth century, Milton, at length. This is a speech conjuring up renewed political power waiting to be unleashed as a "mighty force" once Britain leaves the European Union. His harkening back to older forms of spoken (and written-to-be-spoken, in the case of the Milton poem) English embellishes, reinforces and helps to carry this highly historically-aware political discourse. The indexicality of trilled and tapped /r/ phonetically links the past explicitly to the present.

6 (Social) media reception

How then was this performance received? What norms of interpretation came into play in its reception? As the British press reported the same day, the speech was considered somewhat of a sensation by conference delegates, and to some extent also by the wider British public. Much commentary on it focused on the nature of the delivery and a characterization of Cox's voice. The following is a representative sample collected by Buzzfeed and the BBC, further reporting from the *Mirror* and the *Guardian*, and an interview with Cox in the *Times* three days later. It should be noted that many of the comments reflect local British knowledge and cultural references that will not necessarily be explained further here (and that readers may or may not be familiar with). The evocation of this knowledge that the respondents make merely serves to illustrate the firm embedding of this sort of semiotic work in a long historical trajectory of observation of and commentary on local speech styles, and this style in particular.

(1) ... And frankly, this guy absolutely nailed it. No one really listened to what he was saying – they just let his thunderous declarations wash over them like a warm bath. (https://www.buzzfeed.com/alanwhite/people-are-really-losing-it-over-the-stentorian-oratory-of)

(2) (H)onestly has Brexit ever sounded more noble. (Alan White @aljwhite)

(3) Watching Geoffrey Cox talking about Brexit feels surprisingly like watching Brian Blessed delivering one of the great Shakespearean monologues. (Gordon Rayner @gordonrayner)

(4) Geoffrey Cox hasn't even finished speaking yet and he's already been compared to: * Gandalf * Mufasa * Brian Blessed * Picard * Simon Callow * Tom Baker * An Evil Richard Burgon. (Mikey Smith @mikeysmith)

(5) Geoffrey Cox's voice is just amazing. Like Vincent Price in Thriller. (Jessica Elgot @jessicaelgot)

(6) OK, this is a bit bonkers, but Geoffrey Cox is currently giving one of the all time great conference speeches. ((((Dan Hodges)))@DPJHodges)

(7) Why have the Tories not deployed Geoffrey Cox before? He has Boris-like abilities to rouse an audience. Amazing performance. (Gordon Rayner @gordonrayner)

(8) Geoffrey Cox wows Tories with warm-up act for PM . . . As well as clearly delighting Conservative supporters and amusing journalists, his stentorian performance sent tongues wagging about an unlikely leadership bid. (https://www.bbc.com/news/uk-politics-45735831)

(9) ... And to be honest, he didn't need a microphone. Most residents of the Midlands could have popped their heads out of an upstairs window and heard his booming, silken tones wafting on the wind . . . Almost as soon as he took to the stage, he was compared to a string of classical English actors, including Sir Ian McKellen, Brian Blessed and Patrick Stewart. (https://www.mirror.co.uk/news/politics/tory-gandalf-geoffrey-cox-upstages-13353390)

(10) ... But 20 minutes later, in a booming speech peppered with Milton and the Rolling Stones, delighted Tory delegates were cheering to the rafters ... The extraordinary speech, delivered in an oratory style variously compared to Brian Blessed, Tom Baker and Terry Wogan ... The delivery made such an impression, the prime minister ad-libbed a reference to her colleague in her own speech, joking that should she lose her voice like last year, "I could just ask to borrow the voice of Geoffrey Cox". (https://www.theguardian.com/politics/2018/oct/03/attorney-generals-speech-delights-tory-conference-delegates)

(11) ... What we hadn't heard, perhaps since about 1955, was a speech by a cabinet minister who rolls his rs with such relish that he talks about the "rrrrrreal world". Mr Cox's voice, laden with more ripe fruitfulness than a Keats ode, coupled with his confident courtroom thespianism, made everyone watching his performance in Birmingham sit up and start sharing clips on YouTube. (https://www.thetimes.co.uk/article/geoffrey-cox-the-time-for-brexit-squabbling-is-over-mvtkhtlws)

(12) ... What magnificent oratory! Exactly the pick-me-up we all needed at the end of a rather drab party conference. Whoever cast Geoffrey Cox, QC, as Theresa May's warm-up man deserves a pay rise ... Mr Cox, the new attorney-general, given his big chance at the tender age of 58, seemed to have wandered in from rehearsals for *Iolanthe*. In a rich baritone that was part Rumpole, part RSC ham, with a hint of Terry Wogan, he addressed the hall as if they were jurors at the Old Bailey and he was pleading for Mrs May's life. He leant casually on the lectern, puffing his cheeks in regret at his client's predicament, before pulling the lapels of his jacket together as if it were a gown and stiffening his back to show the nobility of the law. (https://www.thetimes.co.uk/article/vim-and-vigour-as-may-comes-out-of-hiding-gdh35cnzk; The Times)

However, the approval was not universal, as the BBC page also points out. The following tweets from Adrian Hilton and Dawn Foster are two examples:

(13) I won't be popular with this: everyone's praising @'Geoffrey_Cox's speech #CPC18, but.. well, it was like watching 1950s Shakespearean ham: too much 'methinks' and clipped Olivier affectation, and not enough inner-authentic method. Styles change.. Sorry. (https://twitter.com/Adrian_Hilton/status/1047506627883139075)

(14) Attorney General Geoffrey Cox sounds exactly like he's telling a horror story on 1940s tv. (Dawn Foster @DawnHFoster)

The Guardian's John Crace, in his *Politics* column also reported it ironically:

(15) Then the attorney general, Geoffrey Cox, chose to use his 10-minute introduction as a pantomime audition. Blackadder channels Brian Blessed. The audience went wild and if the Tory party conference had ended at that point everyone would have gone home delirious. (https://www.theguardian.com/politics/2018/oct/03/too-long-devoid-content-theresa-may-conference-speech-total-success)

These listeners are responding normatively to a combination of the propositional content and the presence of trilled and tapped /r/, because, as we have seen, these variants are unusual against the backdrop of the generational pattern Cox represents. Cox was born in 1960, when such features had been steadily decreasing in frequency across phonetic contexts since the 1950s (Fabricius 2017). Moreover, the equivocation about its reception is interesting to me, with tapped/trilled /r/ as an example of a *construct resource* whose norm-value has become ambiguous. It can convince and seem authoritative, elegant, or noble, or it can seem over-played, outdated and over-the-top. As the commentary shows, trills and taps can be met with approbation (and have been in the past, hence the references to the 1940s and 1950s), or ridicule. Silverstein's moving envelope of enregisterment is fully apparent here, and the unusual /r/'s constitute *register shibboleths* in Silverstein's terms, leading *construct resources* (in my terms) which open out an indexical field of associations: male actors of the past (Vincent Price), roles such as Gandalf, or Dr. Who in the 1970s (Tom Baker), Shakespearian acting (Brian Blessed). Because this last categorization especially runs the risk of "over-acting", comparisons with pantomime and ham acting are also evoked explicitly by listeners/viewers. It is important to note here that it is not the case that any form of conservative RP *per se* in itself is automatically and universally despised. In certain settings RP is still held up as an unquestioned prestige construct. It was described as "immaculate diction" for example, in the report on Prince Charles presenting the weather for BBC Scotland in 2012 (without any tapped or trilled /r/, it should be noted), written up in the Guardian with the by-line "the weather was vile but the diction was immaculate" by Maev Kennedy.[8]

---

8 https://www.theguardian.com/uk/2012/may/10/charles-prince-weather-forecaster-bbc.

7 Conclusion

To conclude, what construct resources and interpretive norms are in evidence here? What makes Cox's speech style work for some listeners as an authoritative voice, as tapped /r/ does for Sir David Attenborough's documentaries? And why does this fall down for other listeners? Is it to do with Cox being younger, and being seen as "borrowing" the voice of the past, time-travelling as was suggested in the Introduction to this chapter? Is it the trill pronunciation in itself which has shifted meaning and become more frequently interpreted as "over the top", as closer to ham acting than genuine authenticity? It seems to me that the British norm for performative speech of this kind has indeed shifted irrevocably. While the tapped/trilled /r/ does work as part of a performance style for some listeners, no longer can Cox's stentorian voice with its tapped and trilled prevocalic /r/s (importantly, alongside strongly positive and historically-aware views on Brexit), automatically resonate as the voice of political authority. This shift has probably been underway since the 1960s, when the first post-World War II generation came of age. Typical of that period's "breaks with the past" are early episodes of *That Was The Week That Was*, with their mocking of Conservative politicians using stylized U(pper-class)-RP (Wells 1982) voices.[9] Note that Cox's performance still can carry serious authoritative meaning for some people – it can still be received with great enthusiasm, by conservative-minded and pro-Brexit members of the Conservative Party especially, perhaps – but for others the style is dated, and somewhat laughable, and staged, reminiscent of pantomime and over-acting: "Styles change.. sorry" (cf. example 13).

Earlier community production norms for these tapped and trilled forms are no longer being transmitted as part of a productive native elite sociolect, and probably have not been since World War Two. Taps and trills, while present in recordings from elderly speakers (born as late as 1920) up until the 1970s (Fabricius 2017), are entirely absent from the sociolinguistic interview data I collected with speakers born from 1966 onwards, in 1997/8 and 2008 (Fabricius 2000, 2019).[10] The phonetic forms do however still participate in an active construct resource, and they can act as shibboleths for a particular type of speaking. The perception of them in use is variable, harkening back to a revered past, or conjuring up a particular type of overdone performance. Geoffrey Cox's choice to use them in

---
9 https://www.youtube.com/watch?v=INxp98-2i6A from 24 minutes in: "The Silent Men of Westminster".
10 This fifty-year gap in our knowledge of the history of RP generational change is now currently being filled through the DIACSEN project coordinated by Jose Mompean, University of Murcia.

his conference speech thus brings back another era, the 1940s or 1950s, for many listeners, just as Brexit ideology itself can do when it is framed as a resurrection of past British glory. There have been occasions in the House of Commons since October 2018 when Cox has performed the same style: for example, on January 15, 2019, just before Theresa May's Brexit deal was defeated for the first time in the Commons in the "First Meaningful Vote" held that day. Listeners' variable perceptions of these forms in 2018–2019, in all their metalinguistic complexity, show Silverstein's moving envelope of enregisterment (Silverstein 2016) at work. The construct resource is always under construction.

To return to our theoretical starting point: LVC studies are concerned with observing evidence of changing linguistic practice and paying attention to changing perceptions and evaluations of that practice. It is in the sedimentation of linguistic production and sociolinguistically-directed perception that we find norms. Sociolinguistic norms are therefore expectations, construals, and understandings, grounded in constructs and construct resources– socially constructed, historically contingent, and socially managed artifacts of production and perception. The data brought to LVC studies nowadays are varied, comprising a combination of large-scale corpus collections, illustrative case studies (as here), perceptual experiments, attitudinal surveys, ethnographic data and explicit metalinguistic commentary. The methods, likewise are multi-faceted, quantitative as well as qualitative. The small-scale case of Cox's Conference speech is an illustrative vignette within the larger quantitative scenario shown above.

From an LVC point of view, then, it has been demonstrated that linguistic norms of production and perception change by transmission and diffusion processes. Likewise, construct resources will always change, just as language variable forms will change, but these two will not always be in complete lockstep. Sociolinguistic norms are in evidence when they engender reactions to *pulls* (into the future) and *drags* (from the past). Silverstein's metaphor of the moving envelope of constructs in language: "unstable and always changing structures of interlocked registers" (Silverstein 2016: 60) gives us a dynamic view, of which we can capture multiple snapshots. I think this especially contributes to an important underlying conceptualization of what language actually is, and how crucial semiosis and indexicality are in that conceptualization. Construct resources (such as the combination of trilled /r/ and tapped /r/ with their different indexical values) are normative floating signifiers upon the flow of language over time. One cannot step into the same sociolinguistic river twice, because history will be continually adding to and judging the weight of evidence in the light of what has gone before. Cox as the over-theatrical attorney-general became by mid-2019 a well-established trope in, for instance, the *Guardian* newspaper. He was indeed asked to take part in Nick Robinson's *Political Thinking* BBC podcast as a "lover of poetry" as well as Attorney-General.[11]

To paraphrase Aitchison (2006), LVC studies that combine these macro and micro levels can ultimately demonstrate that language change is neither progress nor decay, but simply the ongoing linguistic and semiotic transformation of construct resources and the norms they underpin in various complex and especially fascinating ways. Language change is the evolution of an arbitrary and indexically-rich code in a historically contingent and sociologically complex context. One small, bounded and contextualized speech event, such as a Conservative Party Conference address in 2018, is just a small snapshot. But this particular precisely-loaded phonetic performance of the past in a politically-charged atmosphere provides us with an indexically-rich window on a much larger sociolinguistic landscape, showing the demise and semiotic realignment of traditional native-RP and construct-RP norms.

References

Agha, Asif. 2003. The social life of cultural value. *Language & Communication* 23 (3–4). 231–273. https://doi.org/10.1016/S0271-5309(03)00012-0
Agha, Asif. 2007. *Language and social relations*. Cambridge: Cambridge University Press.
Aitchison, Jean. 2006. *Language change: Progress or decay?* 3rd edn. Cambridge: Cambridge University Press.
Bailey, George. 2018. *When sound change isn't led by social change: The case of Northern English (ng)*. Paper presented at the Philological Society meeting on 'Language change in its socio-historical context', University of Sheffield, 16th November 2018. https://personalpages.manchester.ac.uk/staff/george.bailey/research/2018_philsoc_slides.pdf
Campbell-Kibler, K. 2012. Contestation and enregisterment in Ohio's imagined dialects. *Journal of English Linguistics* 40 (3). 281–305. https://doi.org/10.1177/0075424211427911
Chevrot, Jean-Pierre, Katie Drager & Paul Foulkes 2018. Editors' introduction and review: Sociolinguistic variation and cognitive science. *Topics in Cognitive Science* 10 (4). 679–695. https://doi.org/10.1111/tops.12384
Coupland, Nikolas. 2001. Language, situation and the relational self: Theorizing dialect-style in sociolinguistics. In Penelope Eckert & John Rickford (eds.), *Stylistic variation in language*, 185–210. Cambridge: Cambridge University Press.

---

11 https://www.bbc.co.uk/programmes/p075k2tj (Accessed 4th April 2019). Cox was, however, eventually sacked as Attorney-general, early on in Boris Johnson's premiership (https://www.independent.co.uk/news/uk/politics/geoffrey-cox-reshuffle-cabinet-boris-johnson-attorney-general-tory-latest-a9333076.html).

Coupland, Nikolas. 2014. Sociolinguistic change, vernacularization and broadcast British media. In Jannis Androutsopoulos (ed), *Mediatization and Sociolinguistic Change*, 67–96. Berlin: Mouton de Gruyter.

Coupland, Nikolas. 2016. Five Ms for sociolinguistic change. In Nikolas Coupland (ed.), *Sociolinguistics: Theoretical debates*, 433–454. Cambridge: Cambridge University Press.

Downes, William. 1984. *Language and society*. London: Fontana Paperbacks.

Drager, Katie. 2015. *Linguistic variation, identity construction and cognition*. Berlin: Language Science Press.

Eckert, Penelope. 2008. Variation and the indexical field. *Journal of Sociolinguistics* 12 (4). 453–76.

Eckert, Penelope. 2018. *Meaning and linguistic variation: The third wave in sociolinguistics*. Cambridge: Cambridge University Press.

Fabricius, Anne H. 2000. *T-glottalling between stigma and prestige: A sociolinguistic study of Modern RP. Unpublished PhD thesis*. Copenhagen, Denmark: Copenhagen Business School.

Fabricius, Anne H. 2002a. Ongoing change in modern RP. Evidence for the disappearing stigma of t-glottalling. *English World-Wide* 23 (1). 115–136.

Fabricius, Anne H. 2002b. Weak vowels in modern RP: An acoustic study of happY-tensing and KIT/schwa shift. *Language Variation and Change* 14 (2). 211–237. https://doi.org/10.1017/S0954394502142037

Fabricius, Anne H. 2005. Mobility, contact and an accent norm: The case of Received Pronunciation. In Bent Preisler, Anne H. Fabricius, Hartmut Haberland, Susanne Kjærbeck & Karen Risager (eds.), *The consequences of mobility: Linguistic and socio-cultural contact zones*, 120–134. Roskilde, Denmark: Roskilde University.

Fabricius, Anne H. 2007. Variation and change in the TRAP and STRUT vowels of RP: A real time comparison of five acoustic data sets. *Journal of the International Phonetic Association* 37 (3). 293–320. https://doi.org/10.1017/S002510030700312X

Fabricius, Anne H. 2017. Twentieth-century received pronunciation: Prevocalic /r/. In Raymond Hickey (ed.), *Listening to the past: Audio records of accents of English*, 39–65. Cambridge: Cambridge University Press.

Fabricius, Anne H. 2018. Social change, linguistic change and sociolinguistic change in Received Pronunciation. In Natalie Braber & Sandra Jansen (eds.), *Sociolinguistics in England*, 35–66. London: Palgrave Macmillan. https://doi.org/10.1057/978-1-137-56288-3

Fabricius, Anne H. 2019. The anticlockwise checked vowel chain shift in modern RP in the twentieth century: Incrementations and diagonal shifts. In Sasha Calhoun, Paola Escudero, Marija Tabain & Paul Warren (eds.), *Proceedings of the 19th international congress of phonetic sciences, Melbourne, Australia 2019*, 592–596. Canberra, Australia: Australasian Speech Science and Technology Association Inc.

Fabricius, Anne H. & Janus Mortensen. 2013. Language ideology and the notion of "construct resource": A case study of modern RP. In Tore Kristiansen & Stefan Grondelaars (eds.), *Language (de)standardisation in Late Modern Europe: Experimental studies*, 375–402. Oslo: Novus Forlag.

Foulkes, Paul & Gerard J Docherty. 2000. Another chapter in the story of /r/: 'Labiodental' variants in British English. *Journal of Sociolinguistics* 4 (1). 30–59. https://doi.org/10.1111/1467-9481.00102

Fowler, Joy. 1986. The social stratification of (r) in New York City department stores, 24 years after Labov. New York University ms.

Friedman, Lauren. 2014. *The St. Louis corridor: Mixing, competing, and retreating dialects*. Pennsylvania, United States: University of Pennsylvania PhD. http://search.proquest.com/docview/1651240561/abstract/7BDAEB9A21BF4475PQ/1.

Halliday, M. A. K. 1985. *An Introduction to functional grammar*. London: Edward Arnold.

Harrington, Jonathan, Felicity Kleber & Ulrich Reubold. 2008. Compensation for coarticulation, /u/-fronting, and sound change in standard southern British: An acoustic and perceptual study. *The Journal of the Acoustical Society of America* 123 (5). 2825–2835.

Hannisdal, Bente Rebecca. 2006. *Variability and change in Received Pronunciation: A study of six phonological variables in the speech of television newsreaders*. Doctoral thesis, University of Bergen. https://bora.uib.no/handle/1956/2335

Jacquemet, Marco. 2018. Beyond the speech community: On belonging to a multilingual, diasporic, and digital social network. *Language & Communication* 68. 45–56. https://doi.org/10.1016/j.langcom.2018.10.010.

Johnstone, Barbara. 2011. Dialect enregisterment in performance. *Journal of Sociolinguistics* 15 (5). 657–679. https://doi.org/10.1111/j.1467-9841.2011.00512.x

Labov, William. 1972. *Sociolinguistic patterns*. Philadelphia: University of Pennsylvania Press.

Labov, William. 1994. *Principles of linguistic change. Vol. 1: Internal factors*. Malden: Blackwell.

Labov, William. 2001. *Principles of linguistic change. Vol. 2: Social factors*. Malden: Blackwell.

Labov, William. 2006 [1966]. *The social stratification of English in New York City*. Washington: Center for Applied Linguistics. Second edition: Cambridge: Cambridge University Press.

Labov, William. 2010. *Principles of linguistic change. Volume 3: Cognitive and cultural factors*. Chichester: Wiley-Blackwell.

Levon, Erez. 2018. *The systematicity of emergent meaning: Perception, intersubjectivity and language change*. Plenary at NWAV47, New York University. October 2018. https://erezlevon.files.wordpress.com/2019/01/levon_nwavplenary2018.pdf

Levon, Erez, Marie Maegaard and Nicolai Pharao. 2017. Introduction: Tracing the origin of /s/ variation. *Linguistics* 55 (5). 979–992. https://doi.org/10.1515/ling-2017-0016

MacKenzie, Laurel. 2017. Frequency effects over the lifespan: A case study of Attenborough's r's. *Linguistics Vanguard* 3 (1). 1–12. https://doi.org/10.1515/lingvan-2017-0005

Mather, Patrick-André. 2011. The social stratification of /r/ in New York City: Labov's department Store study revisited. *Journal of English Linguistics* 40 (4). 338–356. https://doi.org/10.1177/0075424211431265

Mortensen, Janus & Anne H. Fabricius. 2014. Language ideologies in Danish higher education: Exploring student perspectives. In Anna Kristina Hultgren, Frans Gregersen & Jacob Thøgersen (eds.), *English in Nordic universities: Ideologies and practices*, 193–223. Amsterdam: John Benjamins Publishing Company.

Mugglestone, Lynda. 2003. *Talking proper: The rise of accent as social symbol*. Oxford: Oxford University Press.

Patrick, Peter L. 2008. The speech community. In Jack K. Chambers, Peter Trudgill & Natalie Schilling-Estes (eds.), *The handbook of language variation and change*, 573–597. Oxford: Blackwell Publishing Ltd. https://doi.org/10.1002/9780470756591.ch23

Payne, Arvilla C. 1980. Factors controlling the acquisition of the Philadelphia dialect by out-of-state children. In William Labov (ed.), *Locating language in time and space*, 143–178. New York: Academic Press.

Pichler, Heike (ed.). 2016. *Discourse-pragmatic variation and change in English: New methods and insights*. Cambridge: Cambridge University Press.

Quist, Pia. 2008. Sociolinguistic approaches to multiethnolect: Language variety and stylistic practice. *International Journal of Bilingualism* 12 (1–2). 43–61. https://doi.org/10.1177/1367 0069080120010401

Rampton, Ben. 2006. *Language in late modernity: Interaction in an urban school*. Cambridge: Cambridge University Press.

Rampton, Ben. 2010. Speech community. In Jürgen Jaspers, Jan-Ola Östman & Jef Verschueren, *Handbook of pragmatics highlights 7*, 274–303. Amsterdam: John Benjamins.

Schwyter, Jurg R. 2016. *Dictating to the mob: The history of the BBC advisory committee on spoken English*. Oxford: Oxford University Press.

Silverstein, Michael. 2003. Indexical order and the dialectics of sociolinguistic life. *Language & Communication* 23 (3–4). 193–229. https://doi.org/10.1016/S0271-5309(03)00013-2

Silverstein, Michael. 2016. The "push" of Lautgesetze, the "pull" of enregisterment. In Nikolas Coupland (ed.), *Sociolinguistics: Theoretical debates*, 37–67. Cambridge: Cambridge University Press. https://doi:10.1017/CBO9781107449787.003

Sneller, Betsy, Josef Fruehwald & Charles Yang. 2019. Using the Tolerance Principle to predict phonological change. *Language Variation and Change* 31(1). 1–20. https://doi.org/10.1017/S0954394519000061.

Trudgill, Peter. 1972. Sex, covert prestige and linguistic change in the urban British English of Norwich. *Language in Society* 1 (2), 179–195. https://doi.org/10.1017/S0047404500000488

Walker, Abby, Jennifer Hay, Katie Drager & Kauyumari Sanchez. 2018. Divergence in speech perception. *Linguistics* 56 (1). 257–278. http://dx.doi.org/10.1515/ling-2017-0036

Wells, John C. 1982. *Accents of English (volume 2: The British Isles)*. Cambridge: Cambridge University Press.

Williams. Robin M. 1968. The concept of norms. In D.L. Sills (ed.) *International encyclopedia of the social sciences*. Vol 11. London: Crowell, Collier and Macmillan.

Meredith Marra, Janet Holmes and Bernadette Vine
8 What we share: The impact of norms on successful interaction

1 Introduction: Norms as shared understandings

A sociolinguistic approach to language use is predicated on the existence of "norms", the label we give to the shared understandings upon which we draw when negotiating meaning. As discussed throughout this volume, what exactly is meant by norms is often rather vague. Even within sociolinguistics the term is used in different ways. For example, an agreed understanding of what counts as the standard language (a "sociolinguistic norm") is used as a criterion for delimiting the boundaries of a speech community (cf. Fabricius, this volume), while shared cultural presuppositions ("cultural norms") lie at the heart of Interactional Sociolinguistics, which informs much of the research in our chosen field of workplace discourse analysis. For both areas, norms are foundational but what exactly counts as a norm remains elusive beyond the idea of understandings that are shared by communities at a range of levels of abstraction.

Norms are thus at the core of what we do, yet analysts have not always focused on operationalising these norms. Using an Interactional Sociolinguistics approach, we argue that misunderstandings arise from conflicting norms about appropriate verbal and non-verbal behaviour. Discourse analysts (amongst others) start from the premise that norms are not stable, fixed concepts shared by all members of a society or community or team, but rather dynamic and contextually dependent expectations and conventions which may differentially influence members' practices depending on the extent to which they are shared in relation to a specific interaction. This means recognising norms as multiple, sometimes compatible and sometimes in conflict, but always impacting on our activities.

With this proviso in place, our goal in this chapter is to delve into "what we share" and how this impacts on interaction, specifically in the area of workplace interaction. To this end we take a data-driven approach to consider norms in a range of settings. Our interest is in part driven by the many occasions when a lack of shared understandings *does not* result in communication problems, thereby challenging the assumptions about miscommunication that lie at the heart of Interactional Sociolinguistics. This raises a number of questions, most importantly, *how much* and *what* do we need to share for successful interaction? We thus address a challenging theoretical issue: namely, the relationship between interactional practices which seem to be shared across many communities and the macro-level socio-cultural constraints and local norms which shape these practices. In doing so, we interrogate the operationalisation of the slippery concept of norms, specifically in the workplace context.

2 The Community of Practice (CofP) framework in workplace discourse

Exploring norms necessarily requires consideration of the community to whom the norms apply. The various uses of norms is mirrored in a range of conceptualisations of community. The important distinctions between types of communities have received considerable attention since the 1990s when the Community of Practice (CofP) framework (Lave & Wenger 1991; Wenger 1998) gained popularity as an alternative approach to the more static speech community concept, especially among language and gender researchers (Eckert & McConnell-Ginet 1992; Holmes & Meyerhoff 1999). Many workplace discourse analysts adopted the new approach in order to qualitatively explore the ways in which team members use shared practices to index their community membership (e.g. Holmes & Marra 2002; Holmes & Stubbe 2015; Schnurr 2009; Mullany 2007). Consequently, this is where we start our investigation.

The concept of the "community of practice" has served workplace discourse researchers well in studying the influence of norms developed within established, intact groups. A focus on CofPs has been central to our own body of work on effective workplace talk, represented by analyses of naturally-occurring talk recorded by small teams within larger organisations[1] where the team has fashioned its own particular practices and style of interaction (or "shared repertoire of negotiable resources" which we would argue is a paradigm-specific description of norms), through regular interactions (or "mutual engagement"), and developed its own particular interpretation of the organisation's goals (their "joint negotiated enterprise") (Wenger 1998: 76). To outline the concept and the corresponding access to norms available through this analytic approach, we first offer two illustrative examples. In each case our interpretations are based on the analysis of recorded naturalistic data supplemented by a period of ethnographic observation, participant debriefs and formal interviews.

---

[1] See Holmes & Stubbe (2015), Marra (2008), Vine & Marra (2017) for a description of the adaptable data collection method developed over the lifetime of the project.

The first example is taken from recordings of a well-established group in a large international organisation that fits the criteria of a CofP. The team meets weekly and the members share a very clearly articulated set of goals, i.e. their joint enterprise (Marra 2003; Holmes & Stubbe 2015). They have developed a recognisable shared repertoire of discourse strategies and shared understandings over a considerable time period, both as this specific project team tasked with setting up a new call centre, and in the wider organizational team to which they belong.

Example 1

Context: Meeting of an organisational team tasked with setting up a call centre –
they are considering their advertising. Clara is the manager. Transcription conventions are available at the end of the chapter.

1	Clara:	I think that the testosterone level has been
2		overstated in this photo in this picture . . .
3		the picture overstates the number of men
4		in the call centre
5	Rob:	oh okay
6	Sandy:	there's one gigolo and one pimp
7		and the rest of them are
8	Clara:	[laughs]: call girls:
9	Sandy	call girls
10	Peg:	[laughs]
11	Marl:	and you'll need some more //chunky gold jewellery\
12	Clara:	/and maybe a moustache\\ . . .
13	Marl:	yeah and a shirt that unbuttons (to the waist) . . .
		[general laughter]
14	Clara:	moving right along

This is a typical humorous sequence from this group, instigated by Clara and strongly supported by her second-in-command, and project manager, Sandy. Clara introduces the issue of sexism with a witty description of the predominance of men in the photo that they are debating using for their advertising: "I think that the testosterone level has been overstated in this photo" (lines 1–2). Sandy extends the implications of her use of the word "testosterone" by implying the photo depicts a brothel: "there's one gigolo and one pimp" (line 6). Clara then anticipates his clever analogy (of the call centre to a brothel) by chiming in with "call girls" (line 8). Marlene contributes to the fantasy with suggestions for what the males in the photo should wear, "more chunky gold jewellery" (line 11) and "a shirt that unbuttons (to the waist)" (line 13), overlapping Clara's addition "and maybe a moustache" (line 12). The humour relies on concepts that index not only the brothel, but also a fantastical 1970s-style stereotype where the kind of sexism that the photo represents would still be acceptable, a reality that is very distant to their working situation and which thereby creates an exaggerated contrast with their company call centre. Finally, Clara pulls them back on track with her standard phrase after a humorous distraction, "moving right along" (line 14).

The noteworthy features of this interaction, the shared practices, are those that are quite typical for this team: a great deal of shared laughter, very witty comments co-constructed in a collaborative style as they build on each other's ideas, and an element of competition as each tries to add something clever to the fantasy scenario (see Hay 1996; Salanoa 2020).

The second example also involves humour though it has a rather different flavour. This CofP is an IT project team in a large commercial organization. The team meets weekly and the members share a well-defined set of goals that they have come together to achieve (Marra 2003; Holmes & Stubbe 2015). Like the team in Example 1, they have developed a shared repertoire of discourse strategies and understandings. While Barry is the project manager, Dudley is the more senior manager of the group.

Example 2

Context: Regular meeting of project team; they are discussing a long report.

1	Dudley:	have you read it?
2	Barry:	I have
3	Dudley:	have you already?
4	Barry:	[laughs]
5	Jacob:	and and Callum's read it already
6	Barry:	[laughs]
7	Dudley:	you don't have enough work to do Barry
8	Barry:	I read it I was up till about ( ) no //[laughs]\
9	Jacob:	/[laughs]\\
10	Eric:	well I was up till about midnight last night too
11	Callum:	surfing right?
12	Eric:	no
13	Barry:	[laughs] surfing the net

After asking who has read the very long report (line 1), Dudley expresses incredulity "have you already?" (line 3) when Barry claims he has done so (line 2). Jacob then identifies Callum as having read it too (line 5). Listening to the tone of this exchange, one gets the strong impression that Jacob is "dobbing Callum in" (i.e. calling out his bad behaviour) rather than proposing him for praise, as one might expect since he has completed a task. Dudley's critical comment "you don't have enough work to do Barry" (line 7) supports this interpretation. Those who have read the long report are being held up to ridicule rather than admiration. Barry defensively asserts that he was up late reading it (line 8) only to elicit a competitive comment from Eric "well I was up till about midnight last night too" (line 10). Callum then retorts with the suggestion that rather than reading the report Eric was "surfing right?" (line 11), and ignoring Eric's denial (line 12), Barry joins in to support Callum's accusation and elaborate "surfing the net" (line 13), i.e. whiling away hours on the internet rather than working.

The tone of this interchange is very different from the tone in Example 1. There is an acerbic edge to this very contestive interaction. The participants compete to put each other down and aggressively challenge the truth of each other's claims; and they laugh at, rather than with, each other. Again, this is quite typical for this CofP which is characterised by a very direct and forthright discourse style: they constantly contest each other's claims and arguments, both when they are discussing serious transactional content and when they diverge into humour, as they do here. These are identifiable examples of their shared practices which clearly differ from the first CofP – these represent a distinctive repertoire that has been, and continues to be, negotiated over time.

Gaining this understanding of the different shared practices of each team required a particular methodological approach. Reacting to earlier research on workplace interaction which largely drew on survey or interview data, our methodology has entailed recording material over an extended period of time, and making use of detailed ethnographic information to identify negotiated norms and to support and warrant contextualized interpretations (e.g. Holmes & Stubbe 2015; Vine & Marra 2017). Only with this knowledge can we feel confident in our interpretations of the "emic" understanding of the participants.

Although we have presented only one example (of many) from each community, the different style of interaction provides support for the idea that there are distinct practices in the separate groups. In many cases, as outsiders, we had to rely on our observations and other ethnographic material to understand some of the meanings conveyed; for the participants the meaning does not seem to be an issue – the shared repertoire allows for shortcuts and implicit knowledge (Wenger 1998).

The lens of the CofP captures only one kind of workplace team, namely an established group who interact regularly together and have negotiated ways of talking that are specific to their group. Such intact teams have dominated the literature in workplace discourse analysis for a number of reasons. One is the relative infancy of the field which began to grow and develop in earnest fewer than two decades ago. Within the last ten years a more solid body of work has emerged on which to build. Certain discourse strategies (e.g. directives), discourse activities (e.g. meetings) and certain groups (teams, and most typically CofPs) were taken up for analytic focus first. With maturity, the field is now pushing boundaries and researchers are expanding their interest (see Angouri et al. 2017 and Vine 2018). A related issue which has meant interest has been constrained is access to naturally-occurring data (the chosen data source used by most workplace discourse analysts). Gaining genuine informed consent from workplace participants who willingly participate, often as co-researchers, requires working with a stable and finite group of people. To restrict who might be captured by the recording process and to ensure that consent is given in advance, many researchers choose existing teams with whom contact has been established, goals negotiated and who can be briefed on the research before giving their consent to be included.

These considerations mean that a high proportion of the research to date has taken place in what can be broadly described as "backstage" contexts using Goffman's dramaturgical analogy (Goffman 1959).[2] While research of this kind has many positive results, including nuanced interpretations based on in-depth investigations and well-developed insights, it is also clear that restricting our focus to CofPs offers only part of the story. Increasingly questions are being asked about the application and applicability of the approach to diverse groups (King 2019), and to exploring the embedded nature of communities (Hugman fc; Wilson 2011). Some have labelled teams as CofPs without considering the definitional criteria of joint enterprise, mutual engagement and shared repertoire. Others have recognised the limitations of the usefulness of the model, noting that communities are sometimes intentionally or by circumstance ephemeral and transient, lacking the time and engagement to develop into CofPs.[3]

Recognising this critique, in recent work we have intentionally expanded the scope of workplaces with whom we work to move beyond the traditional established groupings that meet the definitional criteria of a CofP. We have begun to speculate on the norms that govern practices in encounters between (relative or potential) strangers, thereby distinguishing interactions amongst resident staff from interactions with outsiders such as clients, customers or those from other organisations. In these situations the three definitional criteria (joint enterprise, mutual engagement and a repertoire of resources developed over time) may not be met. Yet these kinds of interactions can be the "bread and butter" of working lives. Hence we turn now to data which acts as a contrast with the intact teams that have been the major focus to date, namely ad hoc encounters.

---

[2] Recent exceptions include J. Mortensen and Hazel (2017) on institutional interactions and K. Mortensen and Hazel (2014) on help desk encounters, as well as the monograph on various service encounters by Félix-Brasdefer (2015).
[3] See for example Fletcher (2014) on micro communities of knowledge and the growing body of work on transient communities as represented in this volume by Pitzl, as well as Pitzl (2018) and Lønsmann, Hazel and Haberland (2017).

3 Moving beyond the Community of Practice model

When interactions represent brief, one-off encounters with little expectation of established practices, we have been struck by the importance of the implicit, shared understandings held by the participants in the recordings we have collected. In 2016 we expanded our methodological approach with procedures designed to gain access to interactions between people who may meet on just one occasion, or for one specific activity type (Levinson 1992; Sarangi 2000, 2005). Moving on from the steps we had used for the 30+ workplaces with whom we had collaborated until that point, we adapted our approach for this new setting in order to continue our philosophy of collecting naturally-occurring talk. Working with participants over several months means that intact teams have time to get used to the equipment, and time to get over "tape shyness" (see Holmes & Stubbe 2015). For one-off encounters, we did not have the luxury of this familiarisation period for all interactants – even if the organisational representative was comfortable, the customer or client might only be engaging with them (and us) on one occasion.

To address the methodological challenges, we took inspiration from the "mystery shopper" approach used in market research (Steinman et al. 2012; Zorica, Ivanjko & Spiranec 2014) whereby supermarket or department store employees are evaluated on their performance without being aware of the evaluator's identity. The employees do not know exactly when they will be assessed and the design aims to capture "normal" behaviour. Thus, following initial observations in a wide range of venues and with permission from the workplace participants in selected sites, we audio- and video-recorded interactions between employees and customers, using researchers and research assistants as customers. In practice, our data collectors included younger and older members of our wider team from the Language in the Workplace project, and female and male research assistants with both local accents and international accents to provide the potential for a variety of responses. In each case their instructions were to record their normal engagements in the context – ordering their daily coffee, finding out about exhibits at a museum etc.

The organisational participants knew that their encounters within a certain period might be captured, and they were assured that we would return to them after data collection to ensure they were happy for their interactions to be included in the data set. Interestingly for us as researchers who had spent considerable time in the past navigating consent with others, in these contexts people regularly took the stance that because their interactions were frontstage (to use our terminology) they always acted as if they were being observed, so recording was not a concern to them. The appreciative inquiry approach (Stavros et al. 2015) has guided our selection process for organisations since the mid-1990s when we began our research and continued into this phase. The sites where we recorded were therefore identified beforehand as those where workplace participants interacted effectively. No doubt, knowing that colleagues and customers had positively evaluated their communication contributed to their confidence.

The change to our methods are outlined in Figure 1.

DATA COLLECTION

Established, intact teams	Ad hoc encounters
Make contact with organization and identify mutual benefits	Make contact with organization and identify mutual benefits
Explain research process to all involved	Explain research process to all organizational members
Observe practices and collect ethnographic and background material	Observe practices and collect ethnographic and background material
Collect data: video, audio, interview	Language in the Workplace researchers discreetly video and audio record their interactions with team members. Organizational members check they are happy for data to be included
Debrief with collaborating workplaces	Debrief with collaborating workplaces

Figure 1: Data collection processes.

To date we have used these methods to record data in a number of locations, including cafés, a bookshop, and a museum. The more simple service encounters are the conversations where interaction has been relatively unproblematic, with enough shared understandings between the interactants to facilitate successful achievement of the transactional goals and without reports of relational trouble. The following examples (Examples 3–8) involve customers and service personnel in Wellington cafés. These are low stakes, ad-hoc service encounters between individuals who have little or no existing relationship and limited expectation of further interactions. Their exchanges are typically brief, focussed on service provision, and involve well-established and familiar routines that are observable and recognisable by outsiders (cf. Kuiper & Flindell 2000; Félix-Brasdefer 2015). While minor variations occur, the basic patterns are similar.

The repetitive nature of these encounters is well illustrated in the extracts. Kim identifies as female and Vietnamese, Ben as a Pākehā[4] male, information we provide only in terms of the identities that we predict might have been apparent through phenotype and accent to the café workers with whom they were interacting.

Example 3[5]		Example 4		Example 5	
Michelle:	hello	Clare:	//hi\	Clare:	morning
Kim:	hi um can I have a regular cappuccino take away please with cinnamon?	Kim:	/hey\\ um can I have a regular cappuccino please?	Kim:	hi um a cappuccino take away please
		Clare:	mhm	Clare:	cinnamon?
		Kim:	um with cinnamon on top	Kim:	yep thanks
Michelle:	three eighty thank you	Clare:	three dollars and eighty cents	Clare:	three dollars and eighty cents
				Kim:	oh (card) [gets loyalty card stamped]
Kim:	thank you	Kim:	thank you	Kim:	//awesome\ thanks
Michelle:	thanks			Clare:	/thanks\\
Kim:	awesome thanks				

---

4 Pākehā is a widely-used identification label for non-Māori New Zealanders, most typically those with British/European ancestry.
5 An interesting methodological quandary occurred when Kim reported that she was upset that the café workers did not look at her in the eye when she was ordering, a behaviour she initially perceived as disrespectful to her as an international customer. By looking closely at the wider data set and observing our own encounters across a range of settings we discovered that eye contact regularly occurred only at the end of the transaction regardless of the specific café or the customer. This is a good example of reports of "politeness" not always matching practices.

Example 6		Example 7		Example 8	
Ben:	hi				
Erika:	hello	Michelle:	hi	Adam:	(hi)
Ben:	um can I get a large flat white to go?	Ben:	hi can I get a flat white to go?	Ben:	hi can I get a large flat white to go?
Erika:	yeah sure thing [pause] what's the name?	Michelle:	and what was your name?	Adam:	yeah + and your name?
Ben:	er Ben	Ben:	er Ben	Ben:	er Ben
Erika:	(that's) four eighty thanks	Michelle:	four thirty thank you	Adam:	four eighty thank you
	[pause as payment goes through]		[pause as payment goes through]		[pause as payment goes through]
Erika:	oh	Michelle:	thank you		
Ben:	cool thank you	Ben:	cool cheers	Ben:	cool thank you

These examples illustrate some of the classic components in the transactional exchanges described in the literature on service encounters,[6] and they can be replicated many times from our observations and recorded data. As summarized in this formula, some verbal components are core (in bold) and some optional:

> Greeting(s) + Offer of service + **statement of service required** + request for name + statement of name + **statement of cost** + expression of gratitude
>
> Greeting: e.g. *hi/hello/hey/morning*
> Offer of service: e.g. *what can I get you?*
> **Request for goods/service**: e.g. *a regular cappuccino (please)*
> Request for customer's name: e.g. *and your name?/and what was your name?*
> Statement of name: e.g. *Ben*
> **Statement of cost**: e.g. *three dollars and eighty cents (thanks)*
> Thanks: e.g. *(awesome/great) thanks/thank you*

There is an initial optional opportunity for a greeting by one or both participants. Then the server may verbally enquire what service is required; however, the mere presence and attention of the server may mean that this component is dispensed with. In fact, in our recordings this component is *never* explicitly expressed. The customer states what s/he requires, a core and indispensable component of the interaction. In some cafés the customer's name is required so that it can be called out when the order is filled. In others the servers simply call out the order (e.g. "one cappuccino") and expect customers to self-identify. The second obligatory component in the data (although observations elsewhere suggest this might also

---

[6] For a summary and similar analyses see Félix-Brasdefer (2015). See also Ventola (1987, 2005).

be optional) is the statement of the cost by the server. Finally, one or both participants may end the interaction with "thanks". The core components are obligatory, but the other components are presented here simply as examples, since further components are also possible: e.g. request to obtain or stamp a loyalty card, additional items of food or drink etc.

King (2014) notes that aggregates of people need not be "communities" in order to have shared practices. One option is to consider the concept of a "nexus of practice" (Scollon 2001, 2005; Wong Scollon 2009). In this frame, individuals are linked through a social action, e.g. buying a cup of coffee, or a multiplicity of linked actions, e.g. taking a plane journey (Eckert & McConnell-Ginet 1992: 483; Scollon 2001). In such contexts, shared co-presence (time) and shared knowledge of types of action or the components of activity types (Levinson 1992) are used in order to orient to others, even when interactants are strangers or in previously unfamiliar places. This approach (where the emphasis is placed on the mediated actions) offers a useful tool for interpreting the transactional encounters in which the participants were engaged.

In such encounters, there are many factors that might represent the norms that we are aiming to identify: participants ostensibly share an understanding of the way the transaction is expected to proceed and have access to the routines involved in securing service. While there can be little expectation of locally negotiated practices established over time between the interactants in these fleeting "moments of co-presence" (J. Coupland 2000), it is clear from our recordings that they share implicit understandings of the relevant routines. Knowing these routines does not involve membership of a CofP. These people may never have been in this particular café before, but they know the ropes (or can at least enact the routine appropriately). They share an understanding of the structure of such a transaction, and they acquire the detail by observation in any new context in which they find themselves.

A possible lens for exploring these shared understandings is then the "nexus of practice" model (Scollon 2001). The strength of this model is its foregrounding of shared time and place (Scollon 2001, 2005) which emphasizes co-presence as an analytical vantage point that can tell us about what is expected in a given situation and space. Indeed, Scollon himself used the practice of ordering coffee as his illustrative example throughout his book when proposing the concept (2001) because it is an exemplar of the ways in which overlapping and intersecting practices from the existing habitus (crudely glossed as habits and dispositions) of disparate individuals can come together. Other examples from our observations include supermarket check-out interactions which are typically routine and predictable, purchasing tickets for public transport, attending a concert, going for a swim at a public swimming pool. In each case participants acquire familiarity with the routine by observation and repetition. Hence when first visiting a public swimming pool, for example, it is necessary to observe others to learn the appropriate sequence of actions required: e.g. payment at the entrance, locating the appropriate changing room, stowing possessions in lockers if required, and so on. On public transport in an unfamiliar city, it is necessary to work out who or how to pay for the ride, where to board and exit, as well as rules for engagement (or not) with others *en route*. Our existing habitus gives us enough to start the process, but shared time and space are needed to enact the activity as required.

The relevance of familiarity with the taken-for-granted local, regional, or national norms is highlighted when we visit another locality, region or country. Hence in a suburb of Tokyo the practice of allowing the pool a five minute "rest" each hour during which all swimmers were required to exit the pool caught one of us by surprise. And experience of supermarket check-out processes in New Zealand where some small talk is typically obligatory, even if minimal (see Kuiper & Flindall 2000), contrasts with our experience in Germany where the transaction is more often speedy, focused and the verbal interaction minimal. On Wellington city buses, those exiting typically call out "thank you (driver)", a practice not often observed elsewhere. While we can generally acquire the shared understanding to negotiate meaning with others in a new nexus of practice context fairly quickly, developing awareness of different norms in different contexts is part of the learning process.

Our most recent data collection moved beyond the relative safety of the routine transactions in the café and bookshop and into a museum context where interactions were less formulaic and where there was an inbuilt expectation of difference based on the tourist customers who were a primary clientele for the museum. These "tourists" were drawn from a range of our associates and we found many encounters which were not as transactionally successful as a nexus of practice explanation might suggest. In these cases it seems that the patterns of interaction were much more impacted by contrasting sociocultural norms ("culturally mediated" in Scollon's terms) and the negotiations (from the emic perspective of our researcher participants at least) regularly contained instances of discursive trouble.

There are some parts of the encounters that were relatively standard. Like the café extracts, the opening sequences were reasonably routine.

Example 9		Example 10		Example 11	
		Host:	hello	Samaria:	excuse me
Kalli:	hi there	Min Jee:	hi yeah	Samaria:	hi
Host:	hello				
Kalli:	have you got any new exhibitions on at the moment?	Min Jee:	just got a couple of questions	Samaria:	how do I get to the Māori exhibition?

Using two longer examples from some of these participants we see a more complex pattern emerging:

Example 12

1	Host:	//hi there\
2	Kalli:	/hi there\\ hi have you got um
3		there was a a new um exhibition on I think um was a
4	Host:	[name]?
5	Kalli:	yeah
6	Host:	yeah the [name] one is on level four
7	Kalli:	okay
8	Host:	it's got an entry fee
9	Kalli:	okay
10	Host:	other than that the [name] exhibition is er only
11		[drawls]: a: few weeks old
12	Kalli:	oh //okay\
13	Host:	/it's on\\ level four as well
14	Kalli:	level four okay thank you thanks

This example is a relatively straightforward request for directions, with many tokens indicating that Kalli is understanding what the host is saying to her (lines 7, 9, 12, 14). There is even some evidence that the host shares an understanding of what Kalli might be about to ask when the name of the exhibition is provided to fill Kalli's hesitation as she searches for the right name (the overlapping sequences in lines 3 and 4), an example of collaborative turn completions (e.g. Wagner and Gardner 2004). This prediction and expectation seems to continue when the host provides more than minimal information by making sure that Kalli knows that the exhibition incurs an entrance fee (line 8) and that there is an alternative (lines 10-11) that is only "a few weeks old", suggesting it is also worth a visit because it is new.

In example 13, we again see an extended and elaborated sequence between the host and the visiting tourist.

Example 13

1	Samaria:	excuse me ++ hi [walks closer to Host] so what's on this side?
2	Host F1:	so this is the [exhibit name] here
3	Samaria:	okay
4	Host F1:	yeah
5	Samaria:	[drawls]: mm:
6	Host F1:	and then there's stairs down this side
7		that take you back to level two
8		and the information //centre\
9	Samaria:	/okay\\

10	Host F1:	so you are [pointing on map]
11		you've just come through [exhibit name]
12		and you're here
13	Samaria:	and out there what do you have ou- outside?
14	Host F1:	sunshine //[laughs]\
15	Samaria:	/oh okay\\ so nothing special outside
16	Host F1:	nah it's just a //(little)\ viewing platform yeah
17	Samaria:	/okay\\
18	Samaria:	oh alright and in there you have?
19	Host F1:	so that's [exhibit name] that you've just walked
20		//through in there\ yeah
21	Samaria:	/oh okay\\
22	Host F1:	and then on the other side if you go kind of
23		straight on you'll go into [exhibit name]
24		and if you keep walking through [exhibit name]
25		you've got [exhibit name] there
26	Samaria:	and it should also take me to
27		the [exhibit name] section right?
28	Host F1:	yeah so that is if you keeping going straight over
29		you walk through here
30		through [exhibit name] and [exhibit name] section is here
31	Samaria:	okay awesome thank you //very much\
32	Host F1:	/no problem\\
33	Samaria:	good bye

Samaria begins with the use of an attention getter in the form of "excuse me", a brief pause and then "hi" before asking her question (line 1). Again, the museum host gives an extended answer; although the initial response is brief (line 2), the minimal feedback from Samaria encourages a more extended answer. A repeated pattern then emerges with Samaria asking questions (lines 13, 18, 26-27) and the host answering. This pattern continues until Samaria stops asking questions.

Once again there is an established routine that can be expressed in terms of obligatory and optional steps:

Museum routine
attention getter + greeting(s) + offer of service + **request/statement of information required** + **information provided** + **expression of gratitude**

While this covers the most transactional aspects of the encounter, and allows for dynamic negotiation of relational or people-oriented elements of the conversation, there were occasions when our participants gave us their (emic) perspective which suggested there were interactional troubles that were not so apparent to us as analysts. On these occasions, it was typically a disjunct between sociocultural norms that created miscommunication that may or may not be recognised by the parties. In these situations, our access to the "tourists" and their reflections allowed us to gain further insight.

In the previous example, the host used humour in some of the responses to Samaria. For example, instead of replying that there were no exhibitions outside (perhaps a dispreferred response to give in this context), in line 14 the host quips that outside there is "sunshine", subsequently correcting the humorous response to "nothing special outside" when the humour gets little uptake from Samaria (cf. Bell's (2015) notion of failed humour, arguably arising from lack of understanding of the pragmatics at play). Similarly lack of shared social meaning impacts on the next two tourist encounters involving research associate Ka Keung who identifies as Hong Kong Chinese. These encounters occur at an information desk in a museum.

Example 14

		[One minute wait to be noticed and served at information desk]
		[Ka Keung pointing at information on desk]
1	Ka Keung:	here for students?
2	Host M1:	yes
3	Ka Keung:	[drawls]: er:
4	Host M1:	this is for seniors and students
5	Ka Keung:	okay students as in full time students?
6	Host M1:	er a- a- any students' card
7	Ka Keung:	okay and er seniors sixty years old or?
8	Host M1:	a- as long as you have a students' card it doesn't matter what age
9	Ka Keung:	okay but how about senior? senior //sixty or?\
10	Host M1:	/seniors\\ are over sixty five
11	Ka Keung:	sixty five I see okay thank you

On this occasion, Ka Keung waits for a long time, relying on nonverbal signals as his attention getter and then resorting to the action of pointing and asking a question (line 1). It seems that the host completely misses the illocutionary force of Ka Keung's question, taking at face value his request for information about ticket prices. There are no obvious signals that there is any miscommunication. However, in the light of our ethnographic debrief with Ka Keung, we know that he is checking to see if he himself qualifies as a senior, having recently retired in Hong Kong where retirement age is much lower than in New Zealand. While the host and tourist share some expectations (e.g. information request and delivery routines, the shared focus on the listed prices etc.), this sociocultural assumption about age is not recognised as being an issue.[7]

---

[7] Ka Keung has reflected with us on why this miscommunication might have occurred and he noted that he might be aligning with a Chinese routine for slowly leading up to the important

In the next example, understanding common New Zealand words (of Māori origin) seems to be an expectation that is not shared when Ka Keung visits the museum on another occasion.

Example 15

1	Host M2:	hi there # are you?
2	Ka Keung:	hi I was just wondering do you have any more exhibit of the carving
3	Host M2:	um yeah so all of our Māori um history //Māori\ exhibitions are
4		upstairs [location provided]
5	Ka Keung:	/okay\\
6	Ka Keung:	[repeats location]
7	Host M2:	in mana whenua area
8	Ka Keung:	oh //okay sorry\ what what area?
9	Host M2:	/so just (b- b-)\\
10	Host M2:	um [location] in the mana whenua
11	Ka Keung:	mana wh- wh- mana //whenua\
12	Host M2:	/whenua\\ so you could go just up this walkway here
13		and that will lead you straight to [the location]
14	Ka Keung:	okay
15	Host M2:	yeah //if you can take the elevators\
16	Ka Keung:	/oh oh that go\\ up to [the location]
17	Host M2:	yeah so that goes up all the way
18	Ka Keung:	can I have one of these? [indicating map]
19	Host M2:	um yep there you go
20	Ka Keung:	excellent thank you

Ka Keung's repetition of the name of the area (describing indigenous people (Māori) who have historic and territorial rights over the land) in line 11, following an explicit request for clarification in line 8, suggests he does not understand the words the host is using. His solution, that is to look at the map and work it out for himself, is again lost on the host who is accurately providing the name of the area to which he is directing the tourist. Norms are again impacting upon the ad hoc encounter, i.e. assumptions that the use of Māori names are expected and understood as names by New Zealand English speakers. And yet it ends, just as the service encounters did and in line with the established pattern identi-

---

question as an established sociocultural pattern. In recent work Norris (2017) has identified compatible cycles and rhythms as relevant components of taken-for-granted routines, drawing on the example of the lack of success in some family skype chats where seasons, time zones, and so on, are far apart, entailing the risk that these time and distance dislocations may negatively impact on interactions. While we do not follow this argumentation line further, this has offered an interesting perspective on how much implicit routine contributes to interaction.

fied above, with a token of gratitude. As described by Firth (1996) in the context of (Business) English as a lingua franca interactions, the speakers seem to be employing a strategy of "let it pass" rather than highlighting the miscommunication.

Arguably in these examples and the observations in the previous section there is some interplay of "cultural" patterns which needs to be further explored in understanding the role of norms and shared understandings. While the nexus of practice model allows for cultural tools as mediational means, this lack of shared understandings (exemplified by what counts as retirement age or the frequency of Māori lexical items in New Zealand English) seems to indicate we have also reached a limitation with this second approach (albeit a constraint that is acknowledged by Scollon (2001) and one which is not the intended focus of the nexus of practice concept).

This returns us to the very heart of our intentions in this paper, namely the degree to which understandings need to be shared in workplace talk to result in practices which enact norms. Our data indicates that some practices seem to be reasonably widely understood, somewhat taken for granted and able to be negotiated on the spot within interaction, while others come up against sociocultural barriers.

4 Discussion: Practices are socioculturally constrained

By expanding the scope of the type of workplaces investigated in the field, and in turn considering the approaches that illuminate the shared understandings that are at play, our analysis has led to a comparison of the goals and limitations of the two approaches we have used. The approaches contrast in terms of their underlying purpose. One highlights identity and membership of a community, the other focuses on action and the intersection of practices which characterise mediated actions.

CofP	Nexus of practice
Mutual regular engagement	One-off interaction
Joint negotiated enterprise	Complementary goals
Large shared repertoire	Narrow shared repertoire/routine

The analysis raises some questions. While the transactions represented in Examples 3-15 differ at a micro discursive level and indicate negotiation between interactants, the *components* of the particular activity types (e.g. purchasing a cup of coffee) might be more widely applicable, thus allowing us to identify the patterns of obligatory and optional elements. It is also interesting to speculate on the extent to which specific discourse structures are shared or perhaps dynamically negotiated in particular contexts between interactants. Certainly our observations of Wellington service encounters suggest that while the basic structure and components may be shared, they are typically enacted slightly differently in different settings and by different participants. If this is widespread we might also ask whether individuals can modify established practices in specific contexts by repeatedly varying them.

The importance of the repetition of practice and the effect on ongoing interactions was something that Scollon (2001) began to explore in his description of the nexus of practice, noting in his own case that as his emergent coffee drinking identity became more practiced he was able to engage with the routines of coffee ordering more easily. We find it important to make a distinction between practices that are more dynamic and negotiated on an ongoing basis with the interactants (and over time become distinctive of a particular group), and routines which are observable and recognisable, a contrast that perhaps highlights where the two different analytic models we have used diverge, even if they somewhat problematically share the same terminology.

Scollon also explicitly contrasts his approach with the apprenticeship model and situated learning found in the Community of Practice. His theoretical principles (and associated corollaries) refer to discourse as a matter of social actions, where "social" indicates a "common or shared system of meaning", and he suggests that these shared meanings arise from common history (2001: 6–8). It is no stretch to see that norms, while not the focus, are still salient even in this early theorising as being relevant to the activities that the nexus of practice intends to capture. Scollon also notes the similarities with habitus (Bourdieu 1977), big-D Discourse (Gee 1990), conversational inferencing in Interactional Sociolinguistics (Gumperz 1977) and Nishida's (1958) philosophy of nothingness. The *impact* of these norms, however, is not his focus. On the one hand he critiques Bourdieu for being too static in the concept of habitus (Scollon 2001: 144), and on the other, while he recognises norms, he does not pursue their impact himself.

And this is exactly why we need to consider norms in greater depth. The data tells us that at the most basic level interactants are bringing their past experiences to bear on the activity, experiences which seemingly represent their habitus and likely something that is shared with others in the form of norms.

In Examples 1 and 2 it was clear that much was shared. For example, there was a great deal of humorous talk in the meetings that we recorded in both organisations, something which the literature indicates is not necessarily shared across all countries (Clyne 1994; Murata 2015), arguably reflecting a wider preferred New Zealand style of workplace interaction. In terms of the construction of the humour, one-liners were common, wit was treated as commendable and overall the group members did not take themselves too seriously. In Examples 13–15 where interaction stretched beyond the most basic enactment of a transaction, lack of shared understanding resulted in (sometimes unrecognised) miscommunication. Even in the mundane transactions between these two extremes, the success of the encounter in practical terms suggested that commonalities could be found, drawing on habitus, or shared knowledge, or even "strategic competence" (if we refer back to the earlier conceptualisation of competences by Canale & Swain (1980)).

Increasingly there has been recognition that CofPs are embedded within wider social structures which constrain the ways in which shared repertoires develop. Enacting community membership means drawing on resources that are compatible with norms that operate as different layers of embedded contexts (Wilson 2017; Hugman 2018). This aligns with a social realist stance that argues for constrained agency (N. Coupland 2001; Holmes, Marra & Vine 2011) and highlights the layered simultaneity of contextual constraints (Blommaert 2005).

In the first two examples the community of practice clearly mediates between the local and the societal layers; however, we can still identify in the later cases the impact of wider sociocultural constraints or ideologies. In our own social realist model (Holmes, Marra & Vine 2011) we argue for (at a minimum) recognition of constraints at the more micro interactional norms, as well as the impact of the team, the organisation/industry, and at a macro-level, society. Even in the café interactions we see the influence of these constraints, for example in the informal greeting, use of first names rather than surnames etc. which are characteristic of a wider Pākehā style that dominates New Zealand interaction. At the societal level of the model, we immediately recognised the role of the gender order (Connell 1987), and in recent work, Holmes (2018) has fleshed out the impact of the culture order at this wider level, noting the hegemonic and hierarchical positioning of cultural perspectives within New Zealand society which impact upon and constrain all social interaction.

This focus on ideologies and structures as a constraint on agency is a growing trend within (applied) sociolinguistics (see Dawson 2019 for further discussion). That does not mean that we are returning to the fixed, essentialist position that suggests that hegemonic power structures control all our actions. Nor do we espouse a constructionist position that prioritises agency. Agency is socially constrained (Ahearn 2001). These constraints comprise multiple layers of norms. Ironically this might seem to return us to the vague assumptions about norms that we critiqued at the outset.

5 Conclusion: The enactment of norms

Throughout this chapter our goal has been to take a data-driven approach to understanding norms. As a result of our analysis, we conclude that instead of focusing on what norms *are*, the insights for us as researchers come from investigating the enactment of practices in interaction. Norms operate at an abstract level. We have seen that at this level there are many factors that must be shared for communication to be successfully accomplished. Using our discourse analytic skills and exploring practices we find evidence of the negotiation of meaning between interactants as they navigate their actions. Practices are the evidence that norms are at play. Shared practices are our access to norms.

A focus on the shared understandings that underpin practices amongst heterogeneous participants allows us to add depth to our understanding of the operationalisation of norms. This provides a means to reflect on both the culturally shared and distinct ways of doing things that underpin wider practices. In doing so we separate the shared understandings needed for successful achievement of relatively straightforward transactional activities from the degree of norm-sharing required for more complex and nuanced activities. We thus emphasise the necessary and helpful distinction that can be drawn between norms and practices, arguing that a focus on shared practices offers access to the collective understandings that support much successful interaction.

6 A final thought: Is it time to revisit universals?

Philosophically we make a commitment here to the relevance of sociocultural constraints on the negotiation of meaning. However, it is hard to overlook how much is shared even when these constraints play out in different ways depending on context. For decades claims have surfaced, circulated and dissipated regarding the role of universals, whether universals in language learning, in grammar, or in cognition. Although the data we identify here does not allow us to make any strong claims, at several points there is a hint of something that might offer a potential (Western) universal – the components of the service encounter, or the activity sequence of entering a swimming pool or using public transport, in sum, the routines that are easily accessible vs shared group practices that are opaque to outsiders, but each of which is dynamic and negotiated anew between participants.

We end by making an admittedly bold claim that perhaps it is time that we give more consideration to the possibility of universals, especially in regards to norms. Identifying potential "universals" gives us something to test, and may lead us to discover more about society, about how language is used, and the role of language in social lives. Some aspects of social interaction have already been identified as shared, albeit at the more abstract level. Rituals of encounter provide a standout example. In some cultures the focus is on the demarcation and then closing of the physical and emotional distance between hosts and guests as identified by Salmond (1974) in her highly influential discussion of Māori culture.[8] At the other extreme, silence may be the appropriate way of behaving when first encountering strangers as for the Western Apache Indians of east-central Arizona (Basso 1972) and the Cuna Indians in Panama (Sherzer 1977). Regardless of the instantiation, some kind of ritual seems to be obligatory when encountering strangers for the first time.

To these ends we encourage an analytic focus on practices, providing more analysis from which we can build outwards, starting from the specific and extrapolating to the more abstract. This abstract may stop at norms or continue out to potential social universals. Investigating this ambitious goal allows us to broaden our thinking, even if our thinking returns us to the specific level, with a more thorough understanding of the complex influences on practices.

Transcription conventions

[laughs]: :	Paralinguistic features and editorial information in square brackets; colons indicate beginning and end
+	Pause of up to one second
. . . //. . . . . .\ /. . . . . . .\\. . .	Simultaneous speech
( )	Unclear utterance
. . .	Section of transcript omitted
M/F	Male/female
?	Questioning intonation
#	Utterance boundary

Names of workplace participants and workplaces are pseudonyms.

---

[8] Salmond's analyses of the impact of these rituals on meeting structure were an important guide for us in our analysis (Holmes, Marra & Vine 2011).

References

Ahearn, Laura M. 2001. Language and agency. *Annual Review of Anthropology* 30. 109–137.
Angouri, Jo, Meredith Marra & Janet Holmes (eds.), 2017. *Negotiating boundaries at work*. Edinburgh: Edinburgh University Press.
Basso, Keith H. 1972. "To give up on words": Silence in Western Apache culture. In P.P. Giglioli (ed.), *Language and Social Context*, 67–86. Harmondsworth: Penguin.
Bell, Nancy. 2015. *We are not amused: Failed humor in interaction*. Berlin: Mouton de Gruyter.
Blommaert, Jan. 2005. *Discourse: A critical introduction*. Cambridge: Cambridge University Press.
Bourdieu, Pierre. 1977. *Outline of a theory of practice* (translated by Richard Nice). Cambridge: Cambridge University Press.
Canale, Michael & Merrill Swain. 1980. Theoretical bases of communicative approaches to second language teaching and testing. *Applied Linguistics* 1 (1). 1–47.
Connell, R.W. 1987. *Gender and power: Society, the person and sexual politics*. Sydney: Allen & Unwin.
Coupland, Justine. 2000. Introduction to Part II. In Justine Coupland (ed.), *Small Talk*, 135–136. London: Longman.
Coupland, Nikolas. 2001. Introduction: Sociolinguistic theory and social theory. In Nikolas Coupland, Srikant Sarangi & Christopher N. Candlin (eds.), *Sociolinguistics and social theory*, 1–26. London: Longman.
Clyne, Michael. 1994. *Inter-cultural communication at work: Discourse structures across cultures*. Cambridge: Cambridge University Press.
Dawson, Shelley. 2019. Identities and ideologies in study abroad contexts: Negotiating nationality, gender, and sexuality. Unpublished PhD thesis. Victoria University of Wellington.
Eckert, Penelope & Sally McConnell-Ginet. 1992. Think practically and look locally: Language and gender as community-based practice. *Annual Review of Anthropology* 21 (1). 461–488.
Félix-Brasdefer, J. César. 2015. *The language of service encounters: A pragmatic-discursive approach*. Cambridge: Cambridge University Press.
Firth, Alan 1996. The discursive accomplishment of normality: On 'lingua franca' English and conversation analysis. *Journal of Pragmatics* 26 (2). 237–259.
Fletcher, Jeannie. 2014. Social communities in a knowledge enabling organizational context: Interaction and relational engagement in a community of practice and a micro-community of knowledge. *Discourse & Communication* 8 (4). 351–369.
Gee, James Paul. 1990. *Social linguistics and literacies: Ideology in discourse*. London: Falmer Press.
Goffman, Erving. 1959. *The presentation of self in everyday life*. Garden City, NJ: Doubleday.
Gumperz, John J. 1977. Sociocultural knowledge in conversational inference. In Muriel Saville-Troike (ed.), *28th Annual Round Table Monograph Series on Language and Linguistics*, 191–212. Washington DC: Georgetown University Press.
Hay, Jennifer. 1996. No laughing matter: Gender and humour support strategies. *Wellington Working Papers in Linguistics* 8. 1–24.
Holmes, Janet. 2018. Negotiating the culture order in New Zealand workplaces. *Language in Society* 47 (1). 33–56.
Holmes, Janet & Meredith Marra. 2002. Having a laugh at work: How humour contributes to workplace culture. *Journal of Pragmatics* 34. 1683–1710.

Holmes, Janet, Meredith Marra & Bernadette Vine. 2011. *Leadership, discourse, and ethnicity*. New York: Oxford University Press.

Holmes, Janet & Miriam Meyerhoff. 1999. The community of practice: Theories and methodologies in language and gender research. *Language in Society* 28 (2). 173–183

Holmes, Janet & Maria Stubbe 2015 [2003]. *Power and politeness in the workplace*. 2nd edn. New York: Routledge.

Hugman, Nick. 2018. You're a feral, man. Banter as a discourse strategy for multi-layered indexicality. Unpublished MA dissertation, Victoria University of Wellington.

Hugman, Nick. Forthcoming. Analysing team sports discourse: From interaction to identity. To appear in *Te Reo*.

King, Brian W. 2019. *Communities of practice in language research: A critical introduction*. London: Routledge.

King, Brian W. 2014. Tracing the emergence of a community of practice: Beyond presupposition in sociolinguistic research. *Language in Society* 43 (1). 61–81.

Kuiper, Koenraad & Marie Flindell. 2000. Social rituals, formulaic speech and small talk at the supermarket checkout. In Justine Coupland (ed.), *Small talk*, 183–207. London: Longman.

Lave, Jean & Etienne Wenger. 1991. *Situated learning: Legitimate peripheral participation*. Cambridge: Cambridge University Press.

Levinson, Stephen C. 1992 [1979]. Activity types and language. In Paul Drew and John Heritage (eds.), *Talk at work: Interaction in institutional settings*, 66–100. Cambridge: Cambridge University Press.

Lønsmann, Dorte, Spencer Hazel, & Hartmut Haberland. 2017. Introduction to special Issue on 'Transience: Emerging Norms of Language Use'. *Journal of Linguistic Anthropology* 27 (3). 264–70. https://doi.org/10.1111/jola.12168.

Marra, Meredith. 2008. Recording and analyzing talk across cultures. In Helen Spencer-Oatey (ed.), *Culturally speaking: Managing rapport through talk across* cultures, 2nd edn., 304–321. London: Continuum.

Marra, Meredith. 2003. *Decisions in New Zealand business meetings: A sociolinguistic analysis of power at work*. Victoria University of Wellington PhD thesis.

Mullany, Louise. 2007. *Gendered discourse in the professional workplace*. London: Palgrave Macmillan.

Murata, Kazuyo. 2015. *Relational practice in meeting discourse in New Zealand and Japan*. Tokyo: Hituzi Shobo.

Mortensen, Janus & Spencer Hazel. 2017. Lending bureaucracy voice: Negotiating English in institutional encounters. In Markku Filppula, Juhani Klemola, Anna Mauranen, & Svetlana Vetchinnikova (eds.), *Changing English: Global and local perspectives*, 255–75. Berlin: De Gruyter. https://doi.org/10.1515/9783110429657-014.

Mortensen, Kristian & Spencer Hazel. 2014. Moving into interaction: Social practices for initiating encounters at a help desk. *Journal of Pragmatics* 62. 46–67. https://doi.org/10.1016/j.pragma.2013.11.009.

Nishida, Kitaroo. 1958. *Intelligibility and the philosophy of nothingness*. Tokyo: Maruzen.

Norris, Sigrid 2017. Rhythmus und Resonanz in internationalen Videokonferenzen. In Thiemo Breyer, Michael Buchholz, Andreas Hamburger & Stefan Pfänder (eds.), *Resonanz, Rhythmus & Synchronisierung: Erscheinungsformen und Effekte*, 85–102. Bielefeld: transcript-Verlag.

Pitzl, Marie-Luise. 2018. Transient international groups (TIGs): Exploring the group and development dimension of ELF. *Journal of English as a Lingua Franca* 7 (1): 25–58. https://doi.org/10.1515/jelf-2018-0002.

Salanoa, Honiara. 2020. The communicative competence of Samoan seasonal workers under the Recognised Seasonal Employer (RSE) scheme. Unpublished PhD Thesis, Victoria University of Wellington.

Salmond, Anne. 1974. Rituals of encounter among the Maori: Sociolinguistic study of a scene. In Richard Bauman & Joel Sherzer (eds.), *Explorations in the ethnography of speaking*, 192–212. Cambridge: Cambridge University Press.

Sarangi, Srikant 2000. Activity types, discourse types and interactional hybridity: The case of genetic counselling. In Srikant Sarangi & Malcolm Coulthard (eds), *Discourse and social life*, 1–27. London: Pearson.

Sarangi, Srikant. 2005. Activity analysis in professional discourse settings: The framing of risk and responsibility in genetic counselling. *Hermès* 41. 111–120.

Schnurr, Stephanie. 2009. *Leadership discourse at work: Interactions of humour, gender and workplace culture*. Basingstoke: Palgrave Macmillan.

Scollon, Ron. 2001. *Mediated discourse: The nexus of practice*. London: Routledge.

Scollon, Ron. 2005. The rhythmic integration of action and discourse: Work, the body and the earth. In Sigrid Norris & Rodney H. Jones (eds.), *Discourse in action: Introducing mediated discourse analysis*, 20–31. London: Routledge.

Sherzer, Joel. 1977. The ethnography of speaking: A critical appraisal. In Muriel Saville-Troike (ed.), *Linguistics and anthropology*, 4–57. Washington DC: Georgetown University Press.

Stavros, Jacqueline, Lindsey Godwin & David Cooperrider. 2015. Appreciative inquiry: Organization development and the strengths revolution. In William Rothwell, Roland Sullivan, & Jacqueline Stavros (eds), *Practicing organization development: A guide to leading change and transformation*, 4th edn., 112–130. Chichester: Wiley.

Steinman, Kenneth J., Kelly Kelleher, Allard E. Dembe, Thomas M. Wickizer, & Traci Hemming. 2012. The use of a "mystery shopper" methodology to evaluate children's access to psychiatric services. *The Journal of Behavioral Health Services & Research, 39* (3). 305–313. https://doi.org/10.1007/s11414-012-9275-1

Ventola, Eija. 1987. *The structure of social interaction: A systemic approach to the semiotics of service encounters*. London: Pinter.

Ventola, Eija. 2005. Revisiting service encounter genre – some reflections. *Folia Linguistica* 39 (1–2). 19–43. https://doi.org/10.1515/flin.2005.39.1-2.19.

Vine, Bernadette (ed) 2018. *Routledge handbook of language in the workplace*. Abingdon: Routledge.

Vine, Bernadette & Meredith Marra. 2017. The Wellington Language in the Workplace Project: Creating stability through flexibility. In Meredith Marra & Paul Warren (eds), *Linguist at Work: Festschrift for Janet Holmes*, 181–201. Wellington: Victoria University Press.

Wagner, Johannes & Rod Gardner. 2004. Introduction. In Rod Gardner & Johannes Wagner (eds.), *Second language conversations*, 1–17. London: Continuum.

Wenger, Etienne. 1998. *Communities of practice*. Cambridge: Cambridge University Press.

Wilson, Nick 2011. Leadership as communicative practice: The discursive construction of leadership and team identity in a New Zealand rugby team. PhD Thesis, Victoria University of Wellington.

Wilson, Nick. 2017. Developing distributed leadership: Leadership emergence in a sporting context. In Cornelia Ilie & Stephanie Schnurr (eds.), *Challenging leadership stereotypes through discourse: Power, management and gender*, 147–170. Singapore: Springer. https://doi.org/10.1007/978-981-10-4319-2_7.

Wong Scollon, Suzie. 2009. Peak oil and climate change in a rural Alaskan community: A sketch of a nexus analysis. *Journal of Applied Linguistics* 6 (3). 357–78.

Zorica, Mihaela Banek, Tomislav Ivanjko & Sonja Spiranec. 2014. Mystery shopping in libraries – are we ready? *QQML Journal* 2. 433–442.

Nikolas Coupland
9 Normativity, language and Covid-19

1 Construing normativity

From Friday 24th July 2020, as part of the UK government's response to the Covid-19 pandemic, a new requirement was introduced for people to wear "face coverings" in shops and some other public places. The policy was backed by a UK government law, although it applied specifically to England (because health policy is implemented separately by devolved governments in Scotland, Wales and Northern Ireland, with differences of detail and timing in force). As a legal requirement for England, the policy could result in fines (up to £100) being levied on people who failed to comply. On the other hand, several exemptions existed in the new law's scope, so that people with specific health conditions, for example, did not need to cover their faces (see https://www.gov.uk/government/publications/face-coverings – this and other cited web pages were consulted on 25 July 2020). One interesting exemption was that face-coverings could be removed in banks, for purposes of "personal recognition". Some commentators suggested that this was to maintain a distinction between compliant citizens and bank robbers.

In explaining the rule change, the government was quick to suggest that legal apparatus and fines shouldn't in practice be necessary, because people would "do the right thing". They said that wearing face coverings in public should and would become "second nature", an unthinking part of expected social behaviour, just like wearing a seat belt in a car. In phrases that had already become overused in the context of the pandemic, there was widespread discussion of whether wearing face coverings would settle into being a part of "the new normal" of "life under Covid".

In the event, although a clear majority of the population complied, some people objected (and did not comply) as a matter of principle, sometimes on libertarian grounds. They argued that it was not the proper function of governments in liberal democracies to impose such requirements on the public and that people should "make their own minds up" about what was "the right thing to do". (Some of these objectors have taken a militant stance.) Opposition parties commented that the government was making policy inconsistently, particularly in view of the fact that they previously did *not* favour the wearing of face coverings. Earlier, the government said that "the science" did not clearly demonstrate the health benefits of the practice,

---
Acknowledgements: I am grateful to the editors of this volume, also to Justine Coupland, Adam Jaworski and Ben Rampton, for commenting on an earlier draft.

https://doi.org/10.1515/9781501511882-009

and even that wearing face coverings was a bad idea, because it would "instil a false sense of security". There was debate about whether and to what extent face coverings would actually reduce transmission of the virus, and whether they were likely to be of benefit more to other people, as opposed to the wearers themselves.

Some people were reported to have implemented the new policy "frivolously", for example by wearing sequined gauze-like fabrics over their faces (which could not realistically have any utility in suppressing the transfer of virus-carrying droplets), reinterpreting protective face coverings as fashion accessories. Some opinion leaders encouraged others to exploit the exemption categories in the legislation, whether or not they strictly applied. Vox pop street interviews found many people voicing support for the initiative. They also found some non-compliers who said they weren't aware that there had been a change in policy, and some who said they had no interest in following "the Covid story". Some police chiefs said that the police force would be unable to monitor the new policy, and that they expected to take action against non-compliance only if following up specific complaints.

This episode manages to expose some of the key points of theoretical interest in the study of social norms. At the most general level there is the relationship between norms and *what is normal*. What people normally do, in the specific sense of what people normally say and how they say it under specific conditions, and then how people deviate from this normality, has of course been a staple concern of sociolinguistics. The matter initially appears to be an empirical and a distributional one (akin to the question of how many people actually followed the face covering requirement). Sociolinguists have pioneered ingenious ways to observe and capture normal linguistic/discursive action across countless contextual conditions of action and interaction. The normality of normal action has been established in diverse ways, sometimes by "dropping in on" everyday linguistic practice, sometimes with an effort to hide or to minimise the technologies that might otherwise render the normal abnormal. Then, close interrogation – sound by sound, cue by cue, turn by turn – has produced impressively detailed information about how this inferably normal action achieves its normality. Alternatively, casting a much wider net across multiple data sets has provided empirical data on how normality might be defined statistically, based on relative frequencies of a host of semiotic features. (Here I will sidestep details of claims and arguments around "natural speech", "everyday practice", and so on here. My attempts to overview and critique different formulations of authentic language are available in Coupland 2001, 2010).

But normality has been considered a suspect concept too, partly because it risks erasing diversity – the diversity that sociolinguistics has, just as obviously, taken as another of its watchwords. And this is where the relationship between norms and what is normal has to be expanded to consider *what is normative*.

Normality, even in its most neutral intended sense, almost inevitably leaches out into normativity (cf. Frega 2015), in one or other of *its* senses. Wearing face coverings in shops in England may be becoming normal practice, but in what ways might it also be becoming normative practice, and what does this precisely mean? As explained, wearing face coverings was mandated by law – an explicit "rule", then, with at least potential legal sanctions for non-compliance. (See early discussions of norms versus rules in sociolinguistics by Bell 1976 and Grimshaw 1980, among others.) But, as also mentioned, the government's hope was to establish the practice as a social norm, an expectation located somehow in the public consciousness, perhaps as a sort of social duty (in this case glossed as "doing the right thing"), perhaps as a relatively unthinking mode of action. It might well have been true, more particularly, that the government hoped to pass off a legally mandated practice as one driven more by a public moral consensus, and in so doing to absolve themselves from accusations of "heavy-handed policy making". The government might well have been keen to shift the public understanding of face covering in England away from being normative in the sense of being a top-down regulative requirement to being normative in another sense: driven either by a grounded, self-regulating, moral norm of good practice, or by a vaguer communitarian norm of "what we generally do".

We should note, then, that norm-compliance itself needs to be defined contextually, according to which of several different socio-cognitive bases exist for conformist action, and certainly defined by criteria other than the simple distribution of conformist action itself. The UK government's response to the pandemic has in fact been generally characterised by ambiguous stances on legal versus moral authority, for example in relation to working from home, social gatherings and the proxemics of so-called "social distancing". Specific policies have variously been labelled (by the government themselves, and subsequently by journalists and commentators, and often inconsistently) "requirements" and "rules" on the one hand, and "advice", "recommendations" and "sensible practice" on the other. The currently default phrase in circulation is "government guidance". In other words, although no-one doubts that new rules and norms have arisen and are impacting strongly on social practices, there has been a fundamental ambiguity in the UK about how new normativities relating to the coronavirus are precisely constituted, particularly so in view of week-by-week changes. Unsurprisingly then, it has become correspondingly difficult to define what precisely constitutes compliance, or adequate compliance, in ways I explore further below.

For the present, let me try to sketch out a simple conceptual map of the components of, and criteria for, normativity that have emerged so far from my anecdotal account of a particular moment in the UK experience of Covid-19. In relation to what we can call the *scope* of a social norm, we need to ascertain its range of applicability, its *normative field*, in at least two regards: *distribution* and *focus*. In the face coverings instance, the distribution of the normative field is restricted to particular social spaces – the prescription was intended to apply in England only, and then to a specified range of commercial and other locations. The focus of the field in this case is simply the practice of wearing of a face covering, and at its most basic, the norm presents a binary choice – whether or not to conform to (or enact) the preferred option (preferred, that is, by the government). Social norms are typically far less precisely scoped than this. Their focus might be delimited in quite abstract ways, such as "be a good citizen" or "be polite". When they are scoped at this level of generality, social norms inevitably *under-specify* the practices they seek to impose or preclude, because in their local enactment, social practices will always be contextualised in complex ways. The intended distribution of a norm (which is of course a quite different matter from its actual, observable distribution, see below) might be group-specific ("children should be polite") or on the other hand universal. Many norms are scoped between these extremes, at the level of "the culture". This is on the assumption (generally misguided) that a cultural group (a construct that is often loosely and inadequately operationalised as a polity or a national space) supports and is supported by a singular, coherent pattern of cultural life with associated normative priorities. Too often, "the culture" is assumed to be the particular set of norms set and illustrated by a polity's dominant sub-group. Nevertheless, there is always *some* significant relationship between normativity and culture, and these concepts can even be taken to be mutually defining to some extent.

The scoping of a norm implies an initiating agency of some sort. In the face covering instance the *authorship* of the norm seems clear-cut. The primary authors were the UK government, and of course it falls to official authorities to define and promote acceptable and unacceptable aspects of social action, whether or not such norms are formalised as laws. But norm authorship, if it is attributable, is generally far less specific than this. Authorship will be attributable when social observers and influencers (self-certifying or otherwise) seek to formalise new norms and promote them explicitly. Norm authorship will be less directly attributable when classes of people in positions of influence adopt particular modes or styles or features of practice, enacting and performing norms that they consider preferred but may never need to formulate explicitly. The performance of preferred norms is metapragmatic in that some level of preference-awareness is associated with the practice. When particular norms advance or retreat over time and space, or when their focus "mutates" in one sense or another, authorship as a concept starts to seem too definitive, and we have to think instead about other norm-establishing and norm-maintaining processes, still agentive, such as how norms are *policed* (see below).

Even so, a large swathe of normative practices exist whose authorship is, for the most part, unquestioned, making authorship and indeed the norms themselves to that extent invisible or silent, unless and until they are breached. What we might call *silent normativity* is the condition in which groups and cultures to a certain extent "know" how to function, and a sense of "how we act" is quite pervasive. It is the condition in which Dell Hymes's *norms of interpretation* (Hymes 1974) become feasible and socially functional, because social actors commonly distinguish conduct that is normative from conduct that is counter-normative, and can read meanings associated with this distinction. The silent quality of silent norms does not, of course, preclude the possibility that they can *become* recognisable and matters of explicit reflexive comment and evaluation, and hence contestation. Silent norms have been recognised to provide the underpinnings of social interaction at its most fundamental, indeed to provide the possibility for coherent collaborative social practice of all sorts. Harder (in this volume) similarly notes the enabling versus the restrictive functioning of norms. This view of cultural coherence and functionality paints a relatively rosy picture of social normativity, although it may be tricky to keep apart its rosier and thornier aspects.

We can define *normative valency* in two senses. The first refers to whether the norm is a (positive) prescription or a (negative) proscription, a "do norm" versus a "do not do norm". (This binary will ultimately prove to be too simple, for example when norms attach to what is feasible or intelligible as social conduct, but it is still worth pursuing as a first-level clarification.) *Prescriptive normativity* is a process of formulating an idealised model of preferred social conduct, and presenting it for emulation across a targeted distribution. This sort of modelling (or scoping) is clearly, once again, a metapragmatic process, in that it entails and is intended to promote reflexive awareness of a *model* of social action that (according to the norm) should then be re-modelled in actual practice. *Proscriptive normativity* can be a very similar process, although deviation from a positive normative model potentially entails a very wide range of options. Where proscriptions are constructed as specific dispreferred models, their focus tends to be on a specific sub-set of (metapragmatically) known and socially salient actions deemed to be undesirable or deficient in some regard. (Fabricius, in this volume, discusses the UK dialect-style shibboleth of "dropping your aitches" in precisely these terms.) Normative valency also refers to the *intensity* or force of a norm, reflecting the simple fact that some norms will exert only modest degrees of pressure to act normatively, e.g. if they are deemed "pedantic", while others may be "heavy" and amount to principles for tolerable versus intolerable human conduct. Normative valencies can change over time, either gradually or in response to some specific social event recognised to be a tipping-point.

As we have seen, normativities are backed by specific *rationales* or logics. Normative action is commonly *rationalised* as a *moral imperative*, as being in some sense a "good" mode of conduct, sometimes pro-social, "to the benefit of society as a whole".[1] The face covering example is interesting, however, in showing that while covering your face in public might indeed be to the whole community's advantage, there is some dispute as to whether it reduces viral transmission "outwards" more than "inwards", and hence as to who the immediate beneficiary is. This alerts us to how normativity can alternatively be rationalised, or re-rationalised, as a *personal imperative* or a *group imperative*, if the practice in question is held to benefit some individuals or groups more than others. The authorship (or provenance) of a particular rationalisation may, once again, be hard to discern. A moral imperative might be ascribed to "everyone" and therefore be glossed as "common sense", or even ascribed to itself, glossed as "doing what is self-evidently right". The UK government came to endorse the "properness" of wearing face coverings as a relatively late policy initiative, reminding us that the rationalisation of a normative practice is indeed a discursive process, where particular people may author particular rationales under specific circumstances. The discursive re-rationalising of a norm over time and across members of a constituency actually tends to erase the distinction between norms and rules, because norms and rules are subject to precisely the same processes of reinterpretation. In the Covid-19 case it will be interesting to track how specific top-down rules are being re-rationalised as norms, with different emphases, weight and application.

The field of a normative schema may be specifiable, but this is a very different matter from its *field of compliance*, which has to do with the distribution and focus of a community's *uptake* of a given social norm. I noted that early uptake of the norm of face covering in English shops was patchy. Not everyone did it (although most did), not everyone was aware of it, and some did it in mildly transgressive ways. Norms and their authors/ regulators might often aspire to universal, consensual uptake, but compliance may be quite different from this, distributionally speaking. Also, within a field of compliance, uptake is not necessarily a simple matter of whether or not a prescribed norm is enacted, although this is what observers might most naturally try to assess. There may also be significantly variable *styles of compliance and of non-compliance*, including some styles that express *counter-rationalisations* of the norm in question. I mentioned the instance of wearing a face covering as if it were primarily a fashion accessory, but

---

[1] For example, Andrew Cuomo, Governor of New York State, gives an explicit rationalisation of wearing face coverings as an interpersonal display of "respect" for co-present others, see https://youtu.be/K3-ZcwQxhJc. I am grateful to Janus Mortensen for making this connection.

many other normative prescriptions are liable to be performatively transgressed. This is particularly the case in complex and divided societies where any authority structure, once identified as such, is liable to meet counter-currents. Heavily individualised societies carry a propensity for norm-resistance almost by definition. Normativity, then, can paradoxically be a resource for social division – a touchstone for dividing people who align on different sides of an ideological debate, or for dividing people who are differentially affected by a norm's focus or uptake.

It is often necessary to consider whether, to what extent, and how a norm is complied with, so (as mentioned above, and as studied in detail by Hazel and Lønsmann in their chapter in this book) we should theorise a notion of *norm policing*. In the face covering case it was literally the UK police force that commented on whether monitoring the new norm did or did not fall within their remit. But far more generally than this, compliance and non-compliance are monitored for uptake within a norm's targeted constituency. This, once again, is a strongly metapragmatic process lying at the heart of normativity. Once a norm has been scoped and focused, compliance is significant not only for happening or not happening, but for *being seen* to be happening or not happening. Presumably the intent behind some normative initiatives is that the norm should become *self-policing*, meaning that members of the targeted constituency are drawn into the ideology that motivated the norm's authors, very much in line with Gramsci's (1971) theorising of hegemony. Under these conditions normativity itself fades into the background, resulting in silent normativity. Self-policing then sustains the normative practice as part of a changed social or moral order, because constituency members feel shame if/when they deviate from it.[2]

Finally, we might identify *moments of normativity*, referring not so much to particular points in time when particular norms coalesce or become applicable and more to the circumstances in which and the processes through which normativity *gains and loses momentum*, at any level of scale. The essential point here is simply that normativity refers to processes of norm-making (or "normatisation") and norm-unmaking (or "denormatisation"), even though a long view of culture may tempt us to see what is normatively stable ("the norms") in a particular culture at a given point in time. Many contributors (to the present book and beyond, e.g. Bicchieri et al. 2009) have argued convincingly for this dynamic perspective on social norms, and there is the central consideration that moments of normativity and social change go hand in hand. Green (2016: 47–67) argues that changes in social norms commonly underpin social change, but it is equally

---

[2] Adam Jaworski points out that the imposition of the National Security Law in Hong Kong, for example, is justified by appeals for citizens to obey it on the basis of ethnonational loyalty.

the case that social change tends to reconfigure social norms, and sometimes requires a process of *normative (re)stabilisation* when change has stripped away previous normative frameworks. I will argue below that this sort of quest for restabilisation is what we are seeing in the UK at this stage our experience of the coronavirus pandemic. The time-frames of normatisation and denormatisation can vary enormously, from the longue durée of, say, the civilising process (Elias 1994) to abrupt local realignments in response to unexpected health crises.

Most chapters in this book deal with complex and subtle interconnections between norms and change, and of course with norms framed specifically in relation to language and social interaction. It doesn't fall to me to review these contributions in any systematic way. But in the next section I try to identify some different ways in which "language", broadly speaking, provides fertile ground for the study of normativity and social change. In doing that I will cross-refer very briefly to preceding chapters of the book that have provided elaborated discussions of the processes I summarise. To some extent I will also try to reinterpret some of the book's main contributions through the conceptualisations I have introduced above. In a third and final section I will make some suggestions about how the current pandemic might be understood as a radical context for language-salient normative change in the UK.

2 Sociolinguistic dimensions of normativity and change

The observation that languages are intrinsically normative systems, and that *language use is in a general sense normative*, is pertinent, but takes us only so far towards understanding sociolinguistic dimensions of norms and their dynamic functioning. It is clearly the case that to participate in using a language entails participation in a gamut of shared assumptions and implications, conventional ways of meaning and modes of interaction that can be called norms (cf. Mäkilähde et al. 2019), just as language learning can be construed as progressive induction into normatised sets of formal, semantic and pragmatic principles and practices. Sociolinguistic investigation on this topic, and particularly research into language socialisation (e.g. Ochs & Schieffelin 2011), has established that such principles and practices across cultures are variable, as are patterns of socialisation. The dominant emphasis has been on acculturation *into* existing sets of normative practices, where the distribution and focus of the normative field are largely taken for granted, "given" in assumptions made about, for example, speech communities or communities of practice or cultures. Compliance is, similarly, not at issue, except in the sense of "imperfect learning" in particular cases, or in the general expectation of staged and progressive acculturation over time. Agha's account of the enregisterment (or normatisation) of Received Pronunciation (RP) in the UK (Agha 2007) is an influential contribution to understanding how sociolinguistic norms may incrementally gel or accrue over time, elaborating on rather implicit accounts of the normativity of RP and high-prestige sociolects in earlier treatments.

Early sociolinguistics in fact engaged with the concept of normativity mainly in relation to dialect varieties and their variable sub-features. Labovian variationism had set out to challenge the prescriptive normativity implied in the distinction between "standard and nonstandard" ways of speaking. The earliest theorising of standardness (e.g. as "educated speech") was unhelpful, but the political critique of normativity was always fully visible. Variationism exposed the ideological convention of dressing up value-judgements about language use – styles of speech considered inferior or deficient – in obliquely labelled conceptions of "generally expected", "appropriate" or even "received" ways of speaking. This is despite the fact that variationism took a surprisingly tolerant line on use of the terms "standard" and "nonstandard" themselves, terms which now come across as normativity dressed up as normality.

As sociolinguistics became increasingly confident in its capacities as a field of critical enquiry, researchers dealing with sociolinguistic norms became more reluctant to deal with what is normal without close attention, in concert, to normative processes. Critically framed questions about "normal for who?" and "normal in whose estimation?" came into play, whether the normative focus was dialectal "standardness" or something quite different. (To take just one "different" instance, King 2018 reviews this shift into a critical perspective as it relates to the field of language policy.) In the dialect arena, studies of normative uptake – basically the distribution of so called "standard and nonstandard" sociolinguistic variables – revealed both that "standard" usage was quite rare (e.g. normative compliance, understood as the use of RP, has a quite specific and limited distribution in the UK) and that compliance was meaningfully stratified by social class. Even so, as is well known, studies established that a large segment of an urban population showed their appreciation of the wider normativity of "standard speech" by adapting their own speech contextually towards this norm.

Standardisation as an ideological process has come to be seen as a rationalisation of the modernist and centralising project of nation-building (Kristiansen & Coupland 2011), as well as a group imperative whereby privileged people reinforced their privilege by mapping ideas of prestige and properness onto their own ways of speaking. I have suggested that, in contemporary life, at least in the UK, vernacularisation has been gaining significant traction as a counter-rationalisation of preferred speech styles (Coupland 2016a). This amounts to a denormatising force operating against RP and in favour of a more mixed normative field, where various vernacular styles (meaning the large swathe of first-learned and supposedly non-normative British dia- and sociolects) have found greater social appeal and flourished in contemporary, mediatised, public life. In the terminology used above, my suggestion is that the normativity of RP in the UK has become less intense, leading to less compliance, while alternative rationalisations of preferred speech in the public domain have also emerged. These newer rationalisations are not merely "changes in fashion", but result from the development of new priorities for communicative styling, attuned to the higher levels of dynamism and diversity that characterise service-sector work, the entertainment industries, other modes of popular culture, and social media.

In her chapter in this volume, Fabricius shows how conservative RP in Britain can evoke mixed reactions from listeners. Interpreting normative RP as a "construct resource", she tracks the decline of tapped and trilled r as a statusful feature of elite RP in Britain, before analysing its use by Geoffrey Cox, a UK Attorney General in recent years. Perhaps by virtue of his use of tapped and trilled r, he was found impressive by some observers and media commentators, but judged by others to have been over-performing, over-using a recessive feature of conservative RP in a public speech. This suggests, once again, a realignment in the normative field in which RP operates, and the rise of alternative normative pressures.

The ideological shift that Fabricius's study points to – a sociolinguistic change towards less centred and more multiple normative fields around ways of speaking – has been studied extensively in other sociolinguistic traditions too. In the first decade of the new millennium, issues linked to globalisation, increasing global mobility and social complexity were extensively researched by sociolinguists (e.g. Blommaert 2007, 2016; Collins 2005; Coupland 2003, 2011). A key theoretical emphasis in this work was polycentricity, the existence of multiple norm centres, and researchers found new relevance in the Bakhtinian concept of heteroglossia (e.g. Bakhtin 1986; Blackledge & Creese 2013). It is now common to see analyses of how multiple, contrasting norms are invoked and negotiated in social interaction, in multiethnic groups or in contexts showing other sorts of social complexity. The constraining and creative implications of negotiating multiple norms have been explored in many contexts of interaction, and in relation to writing as well as speaking (e.g. Stæhr 2016).

Relatedly, one of the most significant original contributions made by the present book is to have assembled diverse case studies of social contexts, and normative fields, where norms are not only complex and potentially multiple but (in the terms I used earlier) imperfectly scoped and amenable to new forms of rationalisation. Many of the case studies address key moments of normativity, when shared normative assumptions are lacking and needing to be assembled or reassembled (re-scoped, in terms of focus and distribution) in order to cope with uncertain and/or changing demands. Harder (this volume) points out that norms, particularly constitutive norms in established cultural contexts, tend to be resistant to innovation and change, although he also considers interesting cases of when a community, as he puts it, is necessarily emergent, "getting on its feet". This pattern of emergence is characteristic of many contemporary settings when life throws together social groups (defined at any scale) whose histories are structured around different established norms, or places them in circumstances where existing norms need to be adapted to new circumstances.

One example (dealt with in the chapter by Hazel & Lønsmann) is the context of transnational migration, where the socio-political ideal of "integration" triggers initiatives to identify and promote the cultural and sociolinguistic norms of a host community. The authors show how specific host norms (of interaction, in both linguistic and wider regards – grouped around the requirement to be punctual for work) are explicitly negotiated in a Second Language classroom for refugees. Hazel and Lønsmann show how actions held to have transgressed local social norms become accountable, as infractions of a largely tacit moral order. In her chapter, Pitzl analyses a somewhat similar social context, where a group of multi-lingual European exchange students on a year abroad in Austria progressively socialise each other over the course of a single speech event into using international and multilingual conventions for toasting (mutual salutations while drinking, e.g. "chin chin", "na zdrowie" and "cheers").

In Kraft and Mortensen's analysis, what is normatively known by participants, and which norms are "properly" available for creative deployment in interaction is less clear. They track the use of national stereotypes in playful (and some not-so-playful) interactional frames in workplace meetings at a Norwegian construction site. National stereotypes, they argue, are normative structures that their participants are, on the whole, quite familiar with, and this provides them with resources for both constructing and interpreting rich patterns of indexical creativity in their talk. So the authors are able to document a second-order reworking of existing norms (national stereotypes), as new discursive norms emerge in the group meetings for how rather gross stereotypes can be made locally meaningful among multi-national participants.

Another main contribution of the volume is to advance our understanding of the link between normative processes and reflexivity, an area of theory that is reviewed in detail by Piippo (this volume; see also Coupland 2016b and chapters in Part 1 of that collection, perhaps particularly Jaffe 2016). Piippo then illustrates how a model of "easy-to-understand" language, a style of Finnish featuring simplification, slow delivery and scaffolding through gestural emphases, came to be adopted as a "teaching register" consciously developed and adopted by teachers working in "adult basic literacy training" courses in Finland. The register exists as a normative focus for these teachers, who are able to discuss its qualities as well as to perform it as part of their commitment to second-language-only teaching strategy.

In their chapter, Marra, Holmes and Vine set out to contrast different sorts of service and workplace encounters on the basis of how predictable they prove to be, and hence how readily negotiable they may be to participants, based on their discourse structure. Simple, transactional service encounters are clearly based in shared repertoires that function as conversational routines, perhaps as matters of cultural habitus, while less routinised service encounters (at an information desk at a museum) appear to be less clearly normative in structure. One of their conclusions is that the normative ordering of workplace encounters varies radically. While there may be norms that "universally" apply to such encounters, other aspects are not subject to clearly shared normative constraints, so that conversational coherence needs to be achieved in situ.

So the chapters richly demonstrate how social normativity is fundamentally associated with, and often focused on, language. The analytic aim of some chapters is to identify normative units – codes, styles, registers, genres – that, in the general case, have been historically scoped in different ways according to different priorities, or that, under fluid circumstances of contact, are scoped in more obviously dynamic, emergent ways. Emphasising the reflexive dimension of norms, as most chapter do, forces us to attend to language from another point of view too, because (as I argued above) the reflexive authorship and rationalisation of normative prescriptions and proscriptions are themselves forms of discursive action, metapragmatically entertained. So are compliance and non-compliance, if we see them as actions taken in the awareness of pre-existing models. In the face coverings case that I considered earlier, for example, once we become aware that the action is governed by a normative prescription, then "to wear" and "to not wear" are (equally) subject to evaluative scrutiny, by ourselves and others. Each form of (in)action is subject to either praise or sanction, according to how it does or does not match up to a prefigured model. While wearing a mask has been fully normatised for, say, surgeons and nurses performing operations, for members of the public, in the current moment of normativity, it is a highly reflexive element of social practice. Norm policing may sometimes be a purely cognitive operation (in an individual's evaluation of their own conduct, or in one person's intersubjective evaluation of another's conduct), but it will very often involve overt metacommentary on normative and counter-normative social practice. For example, comments like "What do you think you're doing?", or "You know as well as I do that that's unreasonable" are a staple of relational discourse, and it is likely that specific norms of interpersonal conduct come to be appreciated as such *only through* metadiscourse.

Normative metadiscourse shows up in the lexico-grammar of languages, in English most obviously in the modality system for distinguishing 'should' or 'may' from 'must', and so on. But in future research, there is a good case for developing a more systematic approach to how norms are discursively articulated. After all, it often goes unnoticed that languages have some very economical ways of referring to normative practices, sometimes lexically coded. I'm thinking of the class of English adjectives that refer to the normative associations of specific social roles, in words such as 'scholarly', 'professional' and 'presidential'. There is precisely the same degree of ambiguity in these words that exists in the distinction between normal and normative. "Presidential behaviour", for example, may simply refer to "what presidents (demonstrably) do", but quite readily extends into "what presidents *ought* to do", so that "acting unpresidentially" can be an accusation or even a rationale for impeachment, and so on (cf. Sclafani 2017). But in far more diffuse and complex ways too, boundaries around what is possible, desirable, permissible, etc. around any given role are subject to repeated (re)negotiation, and not least in the discursive servicing of that role in social interaction.

Several contributors to this book have also pointed out that language and discourse assume particular significance in the context of *normative change*. Social change can make it necessary to negotiate new forms of normative consensus, or at least a set of provisional conventions to allow social interaction to proceed. Most examples of this discussed in the literature and in this book arise mainly from global mobility of different sorts, and the need to reconcile or renegotiate different existing normative orders, possibly as a bridging process into a new normative culture. The main emphasis, that is, tends to be on resocialisation, or "cultural continuity through discontinuity", in a classical narrative of threat and resolution. Normative change, however, as we are all finding out, can be abrupt and destabilising, with little by way of resolution in sight. It can sweep away norms, unconvincingly seek to impose others, and promote radical uncertainty about social relations and social identities. Normative change is always fertile ground for studying *sociolinguistic change* as I have tried to define it (Coupland 2016a) – changes in relationships between language and society rather than changes in language and language use themselves, including changes in how social life is discursively enacted and represented. In the final section I offer some brief and personal reflections on how the coronavirus pandemic is currently being experienced in the UK, in sociolinguistic and other regards, as a crisis of normativity.

3 Coronavirus, aggravated anomie and "the new abnormal?"

As I write, the number of reported deaths globally from Covid-19 stands at over 668,000, almost 46,000 of these in the UK. Confirmed cases worldwide stand at over 17 million. Today's headlines include that the UK government have voiced its fears that a "second wave" of the infection is "rolling across Europe", and that people with coronavirus symptoms will have to "isolate for longer under toughened guidance" (*The* [London] *Times*, 30th July 2020). Suggestions about what life "post-Covid" will be like in "the new normal" seem to be, at best, speculatively futurological (cf. Jaworski & Fitzgerald 2003), when the present is so uncertain.

In the last five months public discourse in the UK has accommodated a range of new phraseology implying constraint. Shops and cafes that have re-opened declare themselves "Covid-secure", meaning that they restrict access to limited numbers of customers, provide hand sanitising gel and "maintain social distance". The phrase "social distance" has been accepted by almost everyone, and few have critiqued how the normative prescription of maintaining *physical* distance from other people who are not members of the same household has complicated so many different bases of sociality, over and above reducing direct social contact and social intimacy of a measurable sort (cf. Adami 2020). Many people are trying to comply with the original governmental prescription, to stay two metres away from others, or the recently amended criterion of "one metre plus", staying one metre distant if other "mitigations" are in place (mitigations that include the use of face coverings, as discussed earlier in the chapter).

The UK was largely "in full lockdown" for around three months, albeit with different specific constraints operative in different parts of the country, and is now said to be "emerging from lockdown", except that "key workers" have been working throughout, including care workers in care homes (where rates of infection and death are widely recognised to have been disastrous). Technical terms for apparatus needed to minimise cross-infection have become commonplace points of reference (e.g. "PPE", personal protective equipment), and epidemiological concepts (e.g. "the R number") similarly. The concept of "quarantine" has returned to being primarily associated with infectious or potentially infectious humans, when its main pre-Covid sense related to the enforced sequestration of animals being transported internationally. It now refers mainly to an institutionalised, normative two-week period (currently under review) of "self-isolation" required of either people with Covid-19 symptoms or of people returning to the UK from specified other countries (with listings changing week by week). Other new, semi-technical terms have come to the fore, including "shielding" (now used as an intransitive verb, so that very vulnerable people can be called "shielders"), referring to more extreme forms of self-isolation required of people at greatest risk of death because of specific health conditions, also including (at least initially) people over the age of 70. The pandemic as a topic not only dominates news broadcasts, policy debates and much of day-to-day conversation, it has triggered new linguistic repertoires. "Stay safe" is, for example, now a frequent email sign-off and a regular caption on government notices, and accounts of travelling have become both more newsworthy and more morally loaded. "We haven't been anywhere for months" can be heard as a grumble about "being in lockdown", but perhaps also as a declaration of self-policed conformity, and hence a claim to moral probity, that is, virtue-signalling.

The normative climate enveloping the UK is shifting and difficult to characterise. The stability that is generally implied in the concept of normativity and its sub-components (normative field, focus, uptake, etc.) is generally lacking. We can observe that the initial authorship of the most transformative norms (or candidate norms) has been official and top-down, although an ongoing series of government policy announcements, usually specifying normative constraints on social conduct, have needed to be rationalised and mobilised by others. These include some people in "key" social roles (teachers, medical professionals, shop managers, etc.), but in fact by everyone. The normative field is continually being defined and refined, aspirationally (because compliance is patchy in many regards, and well outside of the specific issue of covering your face in shops), at all levels in authority hierarchies, so that very few people are exempt from the burdens of norm interpretation, alongside the society-wide burden of expected normative compliance. That is, we are all having to rationalise new normativities, decide on what constitutes compliance and whether it is actually feasible in specific contexts, as well as deciding whether or not and how to comply in specific respects. While it is a theoretical truism to say that the intensity or valency of normative pressures can be variable, it is clearly true that Covid normativity in the UK remains generally intense, even in the current phase of (supposedly) "moving out of lockdown". The normative constituency is far from uniform. Younger people perceive less risk and threat, but many older people are navigating norms against a background of fear – including fear of death, not merely fear of being "uncitizenly". There is pervasive uncertainty, about what "safe" actually means, if anything, and about what the future holds, but also about what constitutes rational action in circumstances where there are competing demands (e.g. whether or not to visit an elderly relative who lives alone, in contravention of lockdown and distancing requirements).

I have emphasised normative constraint, and hence implied there is a climate where proscriptive ("do not do") norms predominate over prescriptive ("do") norms. It is interesting, then, that the UK government's series of policy announcements have been framed with positive valency, sometimes in multi-part slogans. The most durable composite slogan so far, promoting the lockdown, was "Stay home, protect the NHS [the UK National Health Service], save lives". The slogan was officially withdrawn on May 14th, as official policy changed (see https://www.gov.uk/government/publications/coronavirus-covid-19-information-leaflet/). "Stay home" is of course prescriptive in its lexico-grammar, but its social implications lay in *avoidance* practices such as "do not leave the house except for very specific essential purposes...". "Protect the NHS" materially meant *not* going to hospital emergency clinics and general practice clinics (so as not to overload these services, again with a small number of specified exceptions) and *not* buying medical-grade face masks (because this would threaten the necessary supply to hospitals, etc.). "Save lives" was a very clear instance of under-specification in the authoring of a norm, as was the quite vapid phrase "Be alert", the slogan-element that replaced "Stay home". The implications of these particular slogans were never to my knowledge clarified, although "Save lives" inevitably contributed to the social perception that there was, and is, an acute death risk and that mitigation actions (i.e. actions of avoidance and abstinence) were urgently required. But as the infeasibility of specific mitigations became obvious (the prescription to stay two metres away from others, in other words the *pro*scription of physical closeness, e.g. in school corridors or in shop doorways, could not be achieved, just as it is not being achieved now by some people who rationalise "coming out of lockdown" as a permissible return to non-distanced activities), the practicalities of "staying safe" and "saving lives" have necessarily had to be re-rationalised by individuals, without "safe" courses of action being credibly identified in many cases.

For some time, death has been directly thematised in daily government announcements of numbers of known Covid-related deaths per day and per week, also in dissemination of data relating to so-called "excess deaths" (the number of current deaths over and above the expected rate for the time of year). Human stories of dying and death-avoidance permeate media outlets, including stories of survival with drastic health consequences after intensive care. So there is a damaging mix of powerful perceived threat and uncertain mitigation, which we might characterise as a particularly morbid condition of *aggravated anomie*. Anomie is commonly understood to refer to normlessness, although the current moment of normativity in the UK is not at all lacking in normative pre- and proscriptions. On the contrary, social life is saturated by oppressive, rigid, aspirational normativities that, in many cases, people can neither fully accommodate nor simply ignore. To this extent the contemporary condition of coronavirus-related anomie is closer to Durkheim's original (1897/1979) analysis of how people's failure to negotiate rigid social norms, and an individual's either insufficient or excessive integration with society, leads to suicide.

We are still discovering and trying to rationalise what may or may not prove to be new normative practices "under Covid" (a now-familiar metaphor that accurately reflects the oppressiveness of social life bearing the effects of the pandemic). Rampton (2020) observes that, although there are already many projects under way, it will take years of systematic ethnographic and other socially-oriented research to reach a comprehensive overview. An excellent overview of issues is available in Adami (2020). As mentioned above, I see no reason to expect that a consolidated field of normative compliance will be in evidence in the near future, because the "waves" model of the coronavirus's spread is matched in unpredictable waves of norm authorship, norm rationalisation and norm interpretation in people's efforts to make sense of top-down policy demands.

It is easy to point to interactional routines that have become impossible or redundant under Covid – those accompanying (or enacting) supporting a football team, paying by cash, dating, face-to-face collaboration in some categories of workplaces, and many others. Social interaction, even with non-familiars, of course persists, much of it mediated through online platforms. But when physical co-presence actually happens, it does so with new degrees of uncertainty over not only proxemics but interpersonal rights and obligations. Do we thank people for stepping out of our path if it is a prescribed avoidance action, and censure or snub people who try to hand us leaflets or packaged groceries? With familiars, isn't a more serious agenda necessarily implied now in "how are you"-type questions? Is it insensitive to ask "how's work?" when there is a much-increased probability that people will soon lose their jobs in the economic crisis that is widely predicted for the UK? Interactional mini-rituals of this sort may or may not settle into new normative patterns over time, as countless normative fields of sociolinguistic practice, now destabilised, are partially re-ordered. But there are already signs that the pandemic is leading to realignments of the social order in more structural respects too. These shifts need to be confirmed or denied in detailed research, and some of that research will need to be sociolinguistic, because the discursive representation of social groups and intergroup relations is at issue, as well as the negotiation of actual relationships between groups and their members. Let me briefly mention three relevant aspects, in closing, in my final three paragraphs.

I mentioned the new propensity to publish cross-national comparisons – of how, statistically speaking, the coronavirus has impacted on health and death in different countries, and how those countries have "managed" the virus. As this shows, not only has the coronavirus acutely restricted and problematised international contact and mobility, it has also led to new conceptualisations of national capability and adequacy, and league tables of countries ranked according to how well they have succeeded in suppressing transmission, and hence "how safe" they are. In itself, this league table perspective is damaging to international relations (visible, for example, in current diplomatic antagonisms around which countries do and do not "deserve" to have quarantine-free access to the UK). Accounts of the UK's "poor performance" in combating the virus can easily be fed into longer-term accounts of Brexit and the UK's "loss of global influence" as it leaves the European Union and negotiates its new antagonisms with China and Russia, and to some extent with the United States. We might anticipate that the UK experience of coronavirus will in due course become part of the historical grand narrative of Britain's growing isolation in global exchanges, trade and politics. Sloganised representations of how the UK, after Brexit, would become a "newly outward-looking country" and have "more respect and authority on the global stage" now seem strikingly at odds with current realities. Disputes over "how well" or "how badly" the different "national governments" of the UK have fared (where the term "nation" has never been convincingly applied to the central and devolved administrations in England, Scotland, Wales and Northern Ireland) are exacerbating internal divisions and, not least, providing a new footing on which to lobby for Scottish independence.

As a second aspect, in the UK the virus is known to have affected people of different ethnic backgrounds with different degrees of severity. Although generalisations are complicated by contextual factors such as geography, history of deprivation, specific ethnicity and age, the UK Office of National Statistics concludes that, up to the end of June 2020 (and using the Office's own stark category labels), Black people were 1.9 times as likely to die from Covid-19 as White people, with Bangladeshis and Pakistanis 1.8 times as likely to die, and Indians 1.5 times as likely to die (see https://www.bbc.co.uk/news/uk-52219070). One politically pressing implication of this relates to the fact that Black and Minority Ethnic (BAME) people are "over-represented" as workers in health and care services in the UK, which has clearly been a major factor in the relative rates of dying. There is the further implication that people who were believed (post hoc) to be particularly vulnerable to the virus featured disproportionally in front-line health and caring roles. No official steps have apparently been taken to redress this problem in the UK's future moves to cope with the virus. So debates around the virus have assumed a worryingly ethnicised dimension, and have focused new inter-racial tensions regarding obligations and entitlements. The issue plays directly into racially sensitive policy debates about the ethics of social care provision in the UK (e.g. the earlier assumption that carers were "unskilled workers"), about new criteria (post Brexit) for migration into the UK (with little prospect, at present, that BAME care workers will meet entry criteria), and hence about the future of the social care sector as a whole. Covid-19 policies and their effects have complicated and probably damaged egalitarian and racially inclusive principles and how they are inscribed in social life in the UK.

As a final example, normative responses to the pandemic have regularly thematised age. A central aspect of this has once again been in connection with the criterion of "vulnerability": the risk of severe illness and death from Covid-19 increases with age. The charity Age UK records how, at the start of the lockdown, the UK issued advice to a specific group of people who needed to "shield" (take extreme measures to isolate themselves). The group was defined as "People aged 70 and over, people with long term conditions, pregnant women, and those considered extremely vulnerable" (see https://www.ageuk.org.uk/information-advice/coronavirus/). The risks confronted by older people are severe, and the UK government's original lockdown policy reflected this. Viewed as a discursive scoping of norms, however, it focused its explicit proscriptions on a composite social group that equivalenced "people aged 70 and over" with "those considered extremely vulnerable", and we know that older people in the UK are a highly diverse social group as regards health, wealth and many other factors. The UK government clearly took the view that their obligation to protect people aged over 70 overrode their obligations under UK equality legislation, which (among many other protections) precludes "less favourable treatment on account of age". What constitutes "favourable treatment" in relation to "staying at home" and so on is of course debatable. The point, however, is arguably less a legal one than a normative one in a more general sense. A normative discourse that represents older people as an "extremely vulnerable" group on the basis of age-in-years alone sets back long-running efforts to resist societal ageism by several notches. Covid-19 age discourse is already exacerbating inter-generational conflicts over resources and social entitlement, in a climate where huge numbers of people, mainly young and middle-aged, are expected to be unemployed and impoverished as the UK struggles, in economic recession, to repay its Covid-related borrowings. "The young grow poor and the old die" would be a particularly unpromising sloganised legacy from the UK's experience to date of the coronavirus.

References

Adami, Elisabetta and others on behalf of the PanMeMic Collective. 2020. PanMeMic manifesto: Making meaning in the Covid-19 pandemic and the future of social interaction. *Working Papers in Urban Language and Literacies* 273. (Available at https://www.academia.edu/43734918/WP273.)
Agha, Asif. 2007. *Language and social relations*. Cambridge: Cambridge University Press.
Blackledge, Adrian & Angela Creese (eds.). 2013. *Heteroglossia as practice and pedagogy*. Dordrecht: Springer.

Bakhtin, Mikhail M. 1986. *Speech genres and other late essay*. (Eds.) Caryl Emerson & Michael Holquist. (Trans.) Vern W. McGee. Austin: University of Texas Press.

Bell, Roger. 1976. *Sociolinguistics: Goals, approaches and problems*. New York: St. Martin's Press.

Bicchieri, Cristina, Richard Jeffrey & Brian Skyrms (eds.). 2009. *The dynamic view of norms*. Cambridge: Cambridge University Press.

Blommaert, Jan. 2007. Sociolinguistics and discourse analysis: Orders of indexicality and polycentricity. *Journal of Multicultural Discourses* 2 (2). 115–130.

Blommaert, Jan. 2016. From mobility to complexity in sociolinguistic theory and method. In Nikolas Coupland (ed.), *Sociolinguistics: Theoretical debates*, 242–259. Cambridge: Cambridge University Press.

Collins, James. 2005. Polycentricity and interactional regimes in "global neighborhoods". *Ethnography* 6 (2). 205–235.

Coupland, Nikolas. 2001. Stylization, authenticity and TV news review. *Discourse Studies* 3 (4). 413–442.

Coupland, Nikolas. 2003. Introduction: Sociolinguistics and globalisation. *Journal of Sociolinguistics* 7(4). 465–472.

Coupland, Nikolas. 2010. The authentic speaker and the speech community. In Carmen Llamas & Dominic Watt (eds.), *Language and identities*, 99–112. Edinburgh: Edinburgh University Press.

Coupland, Nikolas (ed.). 2011. *The handbook of language and globalisation*. Oxford: Blackwell.

Coupland, Nikolas. 2016a. Labov, vernacularity and sociolinguistic change. *Journal of Sociolinguistics* 20 (4). 409–430.

Coupland, Nikolas (ed.). 2016b. *Sociolinguistics: Theoretical debates*. Cambridge: Cambridge University Press.

Durkheim, Émile. 1979 [1897]. *Suicide: A study in sociology*. (Trans. J. A. Spaulding.) New York: The Free Press.

Elias, Norbert. 1994. *The civilizing process*. Oxford: Blackwell.

Frega, Roberto. 2015. The normative structure of the ordinary. *European Journal of Pragmatism and American Philosophy* 7, 1 (online, no pp.) https://doi.org/10.4000/ejpap.370

Gramsci, Antonio. 1971. *Selections from the Prison Notebooks of Antonio Gramsci*. New York: International Publishers.

Green, Duncan. 2016. *How change happens*. Oxford: Oxford University Press.

Grimshaw, Allen D. 1980. Social interactional and sociolinguistic rules. *Social Forces* 58 (3). 789–810.

Hymes, Dell H. 1974. *Foundations in sociolinguistics: An ethnographic approach*. Philadelphia, PA: University of Pennsylvania Press.

Jaffe, Alexandra. 2016. Indexicality, stance and fields in sociolinguistics. In Nikolas Coupland (ed.), *Sociolinguistics: Theoretical debates*, 86–112. Cambridge: Cambridge University Press.

Jaworski, Adam & Richard Fitzgerald. 2003. "This poll has not happened yet": Temporal play in election predictions. *Discourse & Communication* 2 (1). 5–27.

King, Kendall A. 2018. Language policy at a crossroads? *Journal of Sociolinguistics* 23 (1). 54–64.

Kristiansen, Tore & Nikolas Coupland (eds.). 2011. *Standard languages and language standards in a changing Europe*. Oslo: Novus Press.

Mäkilähde, Aleksi, Ville Leppänen & Esa Itkonen (eds.). 2019. *Normativity in language and linguistics*. Amsterdam: John Benjamins.

Ochs, Elinor & Bambi B. Schieffelin. 2011. The theory of language socialization. In Alessandro Duranti, Elinor Ochs and Bambi B. Schieffelin (eds.), *The handbook of language socialization*, 1–21. Malden: Wiley Blackwell.

Rampton, Ben. 2020. Teaching students to research Covid communication. *PanMeMic* Pandemic Meaning Making of Interaction and Communication, featured 02/07/2020. https://panmemic.hypotheses.org/. Also available as *Working Papers in Urban Language and Literacies* 271.

Sclafani, Jennifer. 2017. *Talking Donald Trump: A sociolinguistic study of style, metadiscourse and political identity*. London: Routledge.

Stæhr, Andreas. 2016. Language and normativity on Facebook. In Karel Arnaut, Max Spotti, Martha Karrebæk and Jan Blommaert (eds.), *Engaging superdiversity: Recombining spaces, times and language practices*, 339–361. Bristol: Multilingual Matters.

Index

accommodation 25, 131–132, 133, 136, 149, 151
accounts 45, 50, 51, 53–57, 59, 62
African American Vernacular English (AAVE) 100
ageism 229
agency 6, 203, 214
American English 29, 97
Amharic 74
anomie 24, 226
Arabic 50, 59, 73, 80, 81, 82
asymmetry in interaction 5, 12, 47, 62, 78–79, 89–91, 111–112

background expectancies 7, 43
backstage vs frontstage contexts 190–192
British English 97, 158, 162
Bulgarian 74

Catalan 135, 139
Chinese 74, 160
code-switching 4, 128, 132, 134, 139, 141
collective intentionality 24
communication accommodation theory (CAT) 131
community of practice (CoP/CofP) 15, 151–152, 186–190, 195, 209, 201–203, 218
community-level facts 26, 28–30
constitutive norms *See* operational norms
construct resource 14, 37, 40, 100, 157–159, 162–163, 165, 171, 178, 179–181, 220
construct-RP 157, 165–167, 181
contextualization cue 4, 115
convergence 43, 131–132, 136, 139, 140–141, 149, 151–152
conversation analysis 2, 78–79, 132, 135
conversational routine 11, 50, 51–53, 61, 222
corpus linguistics 132
covert norms 161
creativity 13, 14, 113–114, 120, 125–129, 132–133, 139. *See also* multilingual creativity; norm-following creativity; norm-transcending creativity

cultural norms 43, 48, 185, 221. *See also* sociocultural norms
Czech 148, 149

Danish 11, 31, 43–44, 48–50, 57, 59, 61–63, 97, 134–135, 140, 141, 147, 148, 149, 160
Dari 74, 82
deontic stance and deontic status 47, 62
descriptive norms 3–4, 21, 34, 99, 101
discourse analysis 132, 175, 185–186, 189–190, 204
discursive norms 13, 93, 98, 109, 120, 221. *See also* interactional norms
discursive practices 8, 9, 11–12, 15, 71, 100, 104, 111, 120
divergence 43, 131–132, 136, 141, 145, 161
doxa 29, 36
Dutch 135, 139–141, 147, 148, 149

easy to understand Finnish *See* Finnish; Selkokieli and Selkosuomi
echoing 132, 139, 149
ELFA (Corpus of English as a Lingua Franca in Academic Settings) 142–143
embodied action 45, 83–85, 87
emergent communities 22, 34–39, 47. *See also* transient communities
emerging norm 120, 125, 139, 144
emic understanding 189, 196, 198
English 128, 131, 134, 135, 140–141, 149, 160, 168, 173, 223
English as a lingua franca (ELF) 13, 125–129, 201
enregisterment 7, 72, 76–77, 89, 90, 101, 157, 164–167, 178, 180, 219
epistemic primacy and epistemic rights 43, 47, 57, 62
ethnography of speaking 2
ethnomethodology 2, 5, 7, 11, 44–46
evaluative norms 10, 21, 23–25, 31, 36, 39
exclusion 12, 44, 46

field of compliance 16, 216, 217, 225, 227. *See also* norm compliance
Finnish 70, 74–77, 80–84, 86, 89–91, 221. *See also* Selkokieli and Selkosuomi
Finnish /r/ 84
French 1, 148, 160

German 134, 135, 141–142, 144–145, 147, 148, 149, 152
gestures 84–88, 92

habitus and habituation 10, 25–28, 29, 39, 195–196, 202–203, 222
Hungarian 151

iconicity 88
identity politics 17, 38–39, 40
ideologies of language *See* language ideologies
inclusion 12, 37–39
indexical creativity 221
indexical field 101, 111, 117, 158, 164, 178, 8
indexicality 8, 35, 88, 157, 158, 164, 175, 180
indexicalization 8, 98, 101, 106, 111, 119–120
indicators 160, 163
individual multilingual repertoires (IMRs) 130, 142
individual-level facts 26, 28–30
institutionalized norms 58–59, 224
interactional norms 4, 5, 13, 98, 117, 119–120, 203. *See also* discursive norms
interactional sociolinguistics 2, 4–5, 132, 185, 202
interpretive norms 158–159
Italian 148, 151

joint enterprise 187, 190
joning 100

Kurmanji 74

Labovian stereotypes 160, 162–164
language attitudes 31–34
language change *See* language variation and change
language choice 4, 13, 64, 128, 140
language contact 130–131

language ideologies 32–33, 69, 71–72, 81–82, 163, 219
language policy 63, 81–82, 219
language socialization 46–49, 57, 61, 64, 73–74, 76, 77, 79, 88, 218. *See also* socialization
language variation and change 4, 14, 26–27, 29, 30, 40, 127, 129, 158, 161–162, 164–165, 180–181
Latin 99, 148, 149
let-it-pass strategy 201
linguistic anthropology 2, 5
linguistic change *See* language variation and change
linguistic norms 3, 6, 22, 31, 33, 46, 98, 125–126, 180

Malayam 74
Māori 200, 201
markers 160, 163
meaning-making mechanisms and resources 4, 15, 72, 79–80, 87, 88, 106, 157
meaning-making practices 70, 74, 83, 92–93
metalinguistic comments 12, 17, 37, 71, 76, 82, 87, 96, 108, 128, 162–163, 180, 223
metapragmatic behavior *See* metasemiotic conduct
metapragmatic comments and metapragmatic discourse *See* metalinguistic comments
metapragmatic processes 12, 214–215, 217, 222
metapragmatic valuation 7
metasemiotic conduct 72, 74, 77, 83, 87, 89, 90
micro-diachronic approach 13, 125, 132–133, 137–138, 151
mirroring 132, 139, 141
mock disalignment 109
mock othering 114
modern Copenhagen 31–32
moments of co-presence 195
moments of normativity 16, 217, 220–221
monolingual ideology *See* monolingualism
monolingual norm *See* monolingualism
monolingualism 71, 81, 97
moral order 11–12, 44–46, 217, 221

multilingual cheering 139–142, 145, 147–149, 152, 221
multilingual creativity 128, 131–133, 139–141, 144–145, 147, 151–152. *See also* creativity; norm-following creativity; norm-transcending creativity
multilingual norm 131, 145–151
multilingual practices 139, 142, 144, 152
multilingual resource pool (MRP) 130–131, 135, 142, 149, 151
multilingualism 63, 71, 73–74, 80, 92, 127, 128–131, 140–142
multimodality 12, 79–83, 87–88, 91–93
mutual engagement 186, 190, 201
mystery-shopper method 15, 191

national category *See* national stereotypes
national stereotypes 12–13, 35–36, 98, 104–106, 107–109, 111–112, 114, 116–121, 221. *See also* stereotypes
native-RP 165–167, 181
New Zealand English 97, 200, 201
nexus of practice 15, 195–196, 201–202
non-standard varieties 3, 79, 163, 166, 219
norm authorship 15, 214–216, 225–227
norm compliance 16, 47, 212–213, 216, 217, 218–219, 220, 222, 225, 227. *See also* field of compliance; style of compliance and non-compliance
norm development 125, 127, 131–133, 136–137, 139, 142, 145, 147, 152. *See also* norm formation
norm distribution 15, 214–216, 218, 221
norm emergence 127, 151
norm focus 15, 214–217, 218–219, 221, 222
norm formation 98–99. *See also* norm development
norm of expectation 159, 161
norm policing 3, 64, 214, 217, 222
norm rationales and norm rationalization 15, 216, 219–220, 222, 225, 226, 227
norm talk 44, 57, 63
norm-following creativity 126–129. *See also* creativity; multilingual creativity; norm-transcending creativity

norm-transcending creativity 13, 126–129, 132, 139, 151. *See also* creativity; multilingual creativity; norm-following creativity
norma 99
normality 75, 112, 212–213, 219
normalized model of behavior 75, 83
normative change 16, 218, 223
normative field 15–16, 214, 218, 220, 225, 227
normative frameworks 47, 98, 100, 120–121, 218. *See also* normative systems
normative multiplicity 162
normative order 9, 11, 25, 35, 44, 47, 223
normative packages 120
normative systems 30, 34, 126–127, 128–129, 218. *See also* normative frameworks
normative valency 15, 215, 225
normativity 15, 21–22, 36, 39, 71–73, 75, 91, 93, 125, 211–226
normatization 7–8, 16, 217–218
norms
– as emergent 35, 37, 98, 102, 109, 114, 120–121, 127, 139, 151, 152
– as enabling 9, 11, 16, 34–35, 215
– as ideological 71
– as negotiable 6, 10, 23, 25–28, 35, 44, 48, 98, 131
– as processes vs products 7–8, 12, 29, 88–89, 93, 185
– as reflexive models 6–8, 12, 70, 71–72, 74, 75, 77, 91–92, 98–99, 106, 120, 222
– as shared understandings 15, 185–186, 191, 195–196, 201, 204
– breaching of 44, 45–46, 62, 71, 91, 99–100, 115, 119, 215
– critical approaches to 5, 9–10
– definitions of 6–7, 21, 44–45, 70–72, 97–98, 99–100, 125–126, 157, 159–163, 185, 186, 212–218
– deviance from (*see* norms: breaching of)
– in classroom settings 37–38, 43–44, 45, 46–47, 48, 57, 60, 61–62, 64, 75, 76, 79, 82, 88, 92–93
– in variationist sociolinguistics 3–4, 5, 14, 159–162, 180, 219

– in interactional sociolinguistics 185
– micro vs macro approaches to 69–70
– sedimentation of 6–7, 115–116, 152
– violation of (*see* norms: breaching of)
– vs rules 1, 3, 24–25, 44, 126, 161, 213, 216
– vs shared practices 204–205
– vs stereotypes 99–102
norms of correctness 160
norms of covert prestige 160
norms of interaction 2, 4, 8, 127, 221
norms of interpretation 2, 4, 5, 8, 9, 112, 215
Norwegian 114, 134, 135, 147, 148, 149

operational norms 10, 22, 23–25, 29, 31, 34, 35, 36, 38
other-repetition 131–132 139, 141, 149
othering 13, 98, 104, 109, 112, 116–120
overt norms 161

parallel conversation 139
penal code, the 24–25
perception norms 14, 162–163, 180
Polish 134, 135, 140–141, 147, 148, 149
polycentricity 220
polylingual norm 97
positioning 12, 57, 62
post-vocalic /r/ (in English) 30, 160
pragmatic presupposition 101
pragmatics 97, 132
pre-established norms 112, 120–121, 127
prescriptive norms 3–4, 15, 99, 101, 214, 215–217, 219, 222, 224–227, 229
prestige norms 30, 32, 39
prevocalic /r/ (in English) 14, 37, 158, 165, 168–175, 178–179
production norms 14, 158–159, 168–169, 171, 179–180
proscriptive norms *See* prescriptive norms

Received Pronunciation (RP) 165–167, 179, 219–220
reflexive models *See* norms
reflexivity 6–7, 12, 69–73, 112, 221–222
register 7, 12, 69, 72, 76–79, 87, 88–93, 100, 164, 167, 180, 222. *See also* semiotic register

register shibboleth 164–165, 178, 215
ritual insult 100, 118

scaling 11, 12, 13, 60, 203
scheme of interpretation 7, 11, 44
Selkokieli and Selkosuomi 70, 76–79
semiotic register 75, 79–83. *See also* register
semiotic repertoire 76, 83
semiotic sedimentation 129
service encounters 15, 192–195, 196–201, 202, 204, 222
shared repertoire 15, 186–190, 201, 203, 222
shibboleth *See* register shibboleth
silent normativity 215, 217
similects 131
social change 8, 26–28, 35, 40, 217–218, 223
social media 16, 158–159, 175–178, 220
social norms 1–3, 6, 24–27, 43–46, 64, 70, 99, 212–218
social realism 203
socialization 36, 43–44, 46–49, 57, 61, 73–74, 87, 218. *See also* language socialization
sociocultural norms 196, 198. *See also* cultural norms
sociolect 165–167, 179, 219–220
sociolinguistic change 14, 167, 220, 223
sociolinguistic norms 3–4, 7–8, 14, 125, 133, 157–158, 161, 180, 185, 219, 221
sociolinguistic variable 159–161, 219
Somali 74
Sorani 74
Spanish 134, 135, 139, 140–141, 147, 148, 160
speech community 2–3, 5, 29, 34, 159–160, 164, 165, 185–186, 218
standard varieties and standardization 3, 5, 10, 21, 33–34, 70, 76, 78–79, 86, 89–91, 99, 165–166, 185, 219
status function 24
stereotypes 33–34, 38, 89–91, 99–102, 120, 136, 187. *See also* Labovian stereotypes; national stereotypes
style 7, 14, 97, 101, 158, 167, 176, 179–180, 189, 219–220, 222

style of compliance and non-compliance 216
style of interaction 186, 189, 203
style-shifting 159–160
styling 108–109, 179, 220
Swedish 114

T_0 134, 135
teaching register *See* register; teaching register norms
teaching register norms 12, 69, 72, 81–83, 87, 88–93, 222
Tigrinya 74
transient communities 9–10, 11, 98, 99, 125, 129, 131–133, 139, 141, 152, 190
transient international groups (TIGs) 13, 125, 129, 131–133, 135, 139, 141, 152
transient multilingual communities (TMCs) *See* transient communities

transient social configurations *See* transient communities
translanguaging 80–82, 128, 140–141
translation 75, 81–82
translingual norm *See* multilingual norm

variationist sociolinguistics 2–5, 14, 159–160, 162–166, 180–181, 219
verbal routine *See* conversational routine
vernacular and vernacularization 5, 31, 164–167, 219–220
VOICE (Vienna-Oxford International Corpus of English) 134, 142–143

workplace norms 49, 58–61, 185–186, 201

www.ingramcontent.com/pod-product-compliance
Lightning Source LLC
Chambersburg PA
CBHW071738150426
43191CB00010B/1625